The Shaman's Doorway

*Once every people in the world believed that
trees were divine, and could take a human or
grotesque shape and dance among the shadows;
and that deer, and ravens and foxes, and
wolves and bears, and clouds and pools, almost
all things under the sun and moon, and the
sun and moon, were not less divine and
changeable. They saw in the rainbow the
still bent bow of a god thrown down in his
negligence; they heard in the thunder the sound
of his beaten water-jar, or the tumult of his
chariot wheels; and when a sudden flight of wild
ducks, or of crows, passed over their heads,
they thought they were gazing at the dead
hastening to their rest; while they dreamed of
so great a mystery in little things that they
believed the waving of a hand, or of a sacred
bough, enough to trouble far-off hearts, or
hood the moon with darkness.*

W. B. Yeats

The Shaman's Doorway

Opening Imagination
to Power and Myth

Stephen Larsen

Foreword by Joan Halifax

Station Hill Press

Published by Station Hill Press, Barrytown, New York 12507.

Produced by the Institute for Publishing Arts, Barrytown, New York 12507, a not-for-profit, tax-exempt organization.

Cover design by Susan Quasha.

Grateful acknowledgment is also made for permission to use the following material:

VANGUARD RECORDS for permission to reproduce Vanguard's the "Country Joe & The Fish" album VSD 79266. The photographer is Joel Brodesky, the producer of the record is Sam Charters. Courtesy of Vanguard Records.

MARVEL COMICS GROUP for permission to reprint *Dr. Strange Vanquishes Yandroth* © 1967 and *Dr. Strange* Copyright © 1973 by Vista Publications Inc., Marvel Comics Group. 625 Madison Avenue., N.Y., N.Y. All rights reserved.

MCGRAW-HILL BOOK COMPANY for permission to reprint material from *Shamanism: The Beginnings of Art* by Andreas Lommel, translated by Michael Bullock. Copyright © 1967 by Evelyn, Adams & Mackay Ltd. Used with permission of McGraw-Hill Book Company.

TOPKAPI SARAY MUSEUM Müdürlügü, Istanbul for permission to reproduce photo of Shaman dancing with spirits from the *Faith Album of Usiad Mehmed Siyah Kalem.*

HILDA NEIHARDT PETRI of the John G. Neihardt Trust for permission to quote from *Black Elk Speaks* by John Neihardt.

THE HAMLYN PUBLISHING GROUP LIMITED for permission to reproduce material from *New Larousse Encyclopedia of Mythology* Copyright © 1969 by the Hamlyn Publishing Group Ltd. Courtesy of Hamlyn Publishing Group Ltd.

CARL LEVETT for permission to quote from *Crossings: A Transpersonal Approach.*

DOUBLEDAY AND COMPANY INC. for permission to quote from "Navajo Song," *Technicians of the Sacred* ed. by Jerome Rothenberg. Copyright © 1969 by Doubleday & Company Inc. Courtesy of Doubleday & Company.

ROSARIUM PHILOSOPHORUM Frankfurt, 1550 (illustrations are all drawings by Robin Larsen copied from 11 woodcuts of the *Rosarium Philosophorum*, 1550 which appeared in vo. 16 of *The Collected Work of C. G. Jung*).

RIJKUNIVERSITEIT BIBLIOTHEEK, Leien for permission to reproduce "The Crowned Hermaprodite," from the manuscript, "De Alchimia," attributed to Thomas Aquinas, Codex Vossianus Chymicus 29, Fol. 91. Courtesy of Rijkuniversiteit Bibliotheek, Manuscript Department, Leiden University Library, Leiden, Holland.

GYLDENDAL PUBLISHERS for permission to include pages from *Intellectual Culture of the Hudson Bay* by Knud Rasmussen.

Library of Congress Cataloging-in-Publication Data

Larsen, Stephen.
    The shaman's doorway : opening imagination to power and myth / Stephen Larsen.
      p. cm.
    Reprint. Originally published: New York : Harper & Row, c1976. With new foreword and preface.
    Bibliography: p.
    Includes index.
    ISBN 0-88268-072-2 (pbk.)
    1. Myth. 2. Mythology. 3. Consciousness. 4. Imagination — Religious aspects. 5. Shaman. I. Title.
    BL304.L37 1988
    291.1'3—dc19

Manufactured in the United States of America.

Contents

Foreword v
Preface to the Second Edition vii
Preface xi
Introduction 1

1 **The Mythic Imagination** 16

Five Stages of Mythic Engagement 33
Mythic Identity—Oracles and Schizophrenics 45
The Unearthly Calling: The Shaman's Vocation 59

2 **The Enactment of Vision** 82

The Mother of the Sea Creatures 82
Iroquois and Senoi Dream Enactments 88
Black Elk's Vision 103

3 **Priests, Scientists, Yogis** 118

Belief and Orthodoxy 119
Science and Myth 126
Yoga—Suspended Engagement 139

4 **Myths of Relationship and Integration** 159

Whole Earth, Whole Body 161
Dialogue: The Two Snakes of Aquarius 169
The Sorcerer's Apprenticeship 182
The Myth of the Crippled Tyrant 205
The Mythic Androgyne 216

Epilogue 231
Source Notes 235
Bibliography 245
Index 255

To my mother and father
parents to the body
and loving guides to the spirit

Foreword

This study of shamanism, psyche, and society takes us on a journey through history and myth, bringing us directly to the challenge and quandary of contemporary society. It was written and first published in the mid-seventies when the impact of Don Juan's teachings [or Carlos Castaneda's acute insight] was breaking apart not only anthropology circles but also the mindset of many young westerners who yearned to take the fire ignited in the sixties into their lives in the seventies.

Although legal research and popular experimentation with hallucinogens was diminishing, many people in the United States and Europe yearned to move away from the trend of psychic and social repression characteristic of that time in order to discover through other means the deeper substrate of history and mythology resident in the psyche of all humans no matter what culture, what tradition. The bitter and wild flavor of the shaman's initiatory journey was on the tongue of many people in our own culture who had not heard of these seers and healers.

Between Carlos Castaneda, mythologists Joseph Campbell and Mircea Eliade, and a few intrepid anthropologists whose teachings and books became patterans along the way for explorers on the relatively uncharted territory of shamanism, this ancient tradition has found itself in the focus not only of anthropology and mythology, but also such diverse disciplines as psychology, ecology, and ethnopharmacology.

To this end, Steve Larsen's study on shamanism and mysticism makes an important contribution to the contemporary literature dealing with these "master's of ecstacy." In this beautifully written text, Larsen enters the lair of the shaman and the schizophrenic. He calls forth a number of the most vivid mythic themes that weave through shamanic cultures. This material is always displayed against the background of present-day society. We are reminded that these patterns, these songs and seeings, are part of our own lives today. The shamanic influence can connect us not only with our past, but also show us how to enter the future in a sane and compassionate manner. It is well over a decade since *The Shaman's Doorway* was written, but like shamanism itself, the content of this volume is timeless.

Joan Halifax

Ojai, 1988

Preface to the Second Edition

When *The Shaman's Doorway* was first published thirteen years ago it proposed a bold set of assumptions derived from the challenge of its subject. My goal was to invite modern men and women to join me in an ancient quest, a re-awakening to the spiritual universe which has always lain just beyond the borders of disbelief and secular materialism—beyond, it would seem, the boundaries of our present world-view. I had no way of knowing if anyone would respond to my self-appointed mission. Was I on the path of the true visionary, I wondered, or rather on that of the mad prophet beckoning the unwary into the unknown? At the time, despite the work of Eliade and others, shamanism was still a somewhat recondite field known mainly to anthropologists. How could it have relevance to the lives of people now?

Since then (and this is also the shaman's joy) I have seen confirmation of my personal vision and its transpersonal relevance; the book seems able to speak to the minds and hearts of many people. From a variety of places and professions I have received feedback more important to me than reviews or book sales, indicating that *The Shaman's Doorway* has touched people's lives. Moreover, within a few years a small but very special group of people were indeed becoming a new species of shaman. Is it, I have wondered, that the archetypal subsoil of the North American continent invites the personal vision quest? Not necessarily fully cognizant of what they are doing, on the very mounds and middens of Native American communities, today's young people are enacting time-honored rituals, heeding their dreams, undertaking vision quests, participating in shamanic workshops at growth centers, trying to encounter their personal demons. I see now that this contemporary fascination with shamanic process extends far beyond North America. European, Australian, and Japanese people seem equally to be drawn to reviving their visionary path. Shamanism is close to the roots of humankind, not just one ethnicity or tradition.

In 1979 Joan Halifax, originally a scholar of enthnomedicine, published an extraordinary collection of visionary narratives: *Shamanic Voices*. It was evident how the voices of yesterday spoke clearly and deeply to the hearts of today. Two years later she published the visually rich: *Shaman: The Wounded Healer*. Also in 1982 anthropologist Michael Harner, who had studied shamanism among the Jivaro of South America, published *The Way of the Shaman* and began to conduct experiential shamanism workshops. During the next few years the number of vision quests, personal improvement seminars, and spiritual healing courses had increased enormously. Over the course of a decade, this ancient personal-magical-mythical field of endeavor has been blossoming again. The old rhizome has new shoots and flowers.

Though a few individuals through their work and writing are clearly pioneers and initiators of this movement, I do not wish to imply that contemporary shamanism emerged simply as a consequence of their efforts, charismatic as some may be. Rather it is evident that people of integrity everywhere are turning to the inner quest as a vehicle for transformation. We who feel ourselves to be pioneers are simply spokespersons for a vast movement toward personal growth and wholeness—a process which Dr. Carl Jung called "individuation" and defined as the masterpiece of human psychological development. Paradoxical as it may seem, the collective spiritual path of our time seems to be an impulse toward personal refinement and individuality. Each of us seems destined through pain and limitation, as well as joy and success, with many confrontations both inner and outer, to grow personally toward some increasingly archetypal version of our own unique selves.

It is in my own work as a psychotherapist that I have found the most relevance of shamanism for modern people. Life dismembers us, sooner or later, and there would seem to be vast differences in how individual human beings respond to that ultimate challenge. The primordial shamanic tradition has presented a viable pathway for threading that dark labyrinth. It says that in this life we are to live as if death watches over our shoulder. I think it does. The shaman engages in conscious confrontation with death before his/her literal time has come. This is because the inner (spiritual) meaning of death is transformation.

Joseph Campbell, for me an important teacher and friend, showed forth this principle in his own life right up to the time of his recent death. Say yes to life, even though you know it will devour you. Because amongst the obstacles and, to be sure, the cruelties of life are signs that we are on a primarily spiritual adventure (even though it seems to be taking place in what we regard as an unmistakably physical world). The shamanic path—the key to the immortal, adamantine body—lets the beauties and mysteries of life do something more than offset its agonies. Wonder must overcome terror in the balance of things. And the task of the shaman is to embody and transmit this message; to bring meaning and healing into life; and to create a growing sense of accord with the informing root of all being.

The modern shamanic path consists in a creative and affirmative relationship to life. It will be impossible to have true believers or card-carrying shamans because we are to be found among all arts and professions: therapists, artists, clergy, writers, poets, musicians, filmmakers. The creative shaman is the person who dedicates him/herself not only to visionary experience, as I hypothesized in this book a dozen years ago, but to the revelation and sharing of the experience. Thus our lives are made richer day by day, year by year, by an influx of creative works into them: the gifts of wonder.

Stephen Larsen

July 1988

Preface

The creation of a book, like any ritual, can be a self-transforming experience. Especially when handling mythological materials one gets the feeling of their aliveness, and their life altering potential. As this book is a collection of such materials, assembled from many different places and times and woven into a personal tapestry, I feel a far more than scholarly indebtedness to a living continuity of pattern makers, from the antlered sorcerers of the paleolithic caves to the street corner shamans of today. Everywhere, and throughout history, human consciousness has been penetrating, recreating and enriching the mysterious universe in which we live. To encounter the scope of this quest and to share in it has been, for me, to find a meaningful place in a cosmos otherwise terrifyingly complex and ambiguous.

I am particularly indebted to the following guides, universe-watchers, shaman-brothers, for their insights and assistance in preparing this book: to Joseph Campbell, for his ground-breaking and meticulous scholarship, his loving and compassionate reading of my early manuscripts; to Stanislav Grof and the staff of Maryland Psychiatric Research Center for providing an opportunity for in-depth research on the visionary levels of consciousness; to Joel Bernstein for his unselfish sharing of a powerful personal experience of Shamanism; most of all to my wife Robin, whose supportiveness on many levels has been vital: as a mythological scholar, intuiter of symbols, friend, and lover. Thanks are due also to Edward Whitmont for his personal guidance and wisdom; to Peter Furst for his scholarship, his personal interest, and the permission to use photographs of Huichol Shamans; to Mrs. Clara Stewart Flagg for permission to quote from Kilton Stewart's "Dream Theory in Malaya"; to Mrs. Hilda Neihardt Petri for permission to quote from "Black Elk's Vision"; to the McGraw-Hill Book Company to quote from Andreas Lommell's *Shamanism*; to Doubleday Anchor Books for permission to quote from Jerome Rothenberg's *Technicians of the Sacred*; to Carl Levett for permission to quote from *Crossings*.

In addition, this book could not have been completed without the nimble fingers of Sue Martin and Sandy Beck, nor the thoroughly humane and careful editorship of Clayton Carlson, Elisabeth Jakab and Beverly Lancaster.

Stephen Larsen

December 1975

Introduction

We are living in an age which, on the surface of things, is dominated by a dynasty of scientific materialism potent as never before. And yet witches stalk the streets of San Francisco and the devotees of Krishna prance and jingle on Times Square. Within the safe enclosure of technical mastery fountains of ancient mystery have once again erupted, peopling the landscape with familiar yet fantastic forms: gurus, shamans, wandering bards, exorcists. Against the bleak and secularized backdrop of our outer landscape comes, unbidden, a new cast of actors, costumed, beaded, and bearded, ready to act a play for which as yet we lack the script. Dancing they come, to an irresistible music, prying loose the gates of dream, unwilling to live without a myth.

But what is our myth? What is the script of this mystery play we call life, which shows no signs—despite our best efforts—of growing less mysterious with the passage of time? Our collective history is a library of mythic scripts, dramas in which our ancestors found themselves ever and again captured in a world of timeless fantasy: virgin births and resurrections, miracles and epiphanies, crusades and inquisitions. Mankind has not only dreamed its myths but, never fully waking, has acted out nocturnal fantasies far into what we thought to be the light of day. "Whence the force of these unsubstantial themes . . . " asks the eminent mythologist Joseph Campbell, in the prologue to his epic work *The Masks of God,*

by which they are empowered to galvanize populations, creating of them civilizations, each with a beauty and self-compelling destiny of its own? And why should it be that whenever men have looked for something solid on which to found their lives, they have chosen,

not the facts in which the world abounds, but the myths of an immemorial imagination—preferring even to make life a hell for themselves and their neighbors, in the name of some violent god, to
accepting gracefully the bounty the world affords?[1]

It is our most significant and recurring dreams that appear
to merit the title *myth*, and our history is surely a dream-jour-
nal, the chaotic-seeming surface of which is tied together by
these perennial themes emerging in countless disguises, recognized or unrecognized, throughout the millennia.

Mythic symbols and themes have in fact been so entwined
with human doings that we are led almost to question whether
the mundane reality our present beliefs picture is the same
that has always been there. The great Celtic myth cycles,
for example, show a bright world so close to this one that it
was taken for granted there were apertures in every hollow
hill, and points of power from which magical energy could
be admitted from that world to this. The men of Homer's
time, it seemed, could easily envision the strivings of airborne
immortals taking place above and in counterpoint to their
own terrestrial struggles as they fought outside of Ilium.

The great hieratic city-states of the ancient Near East were
built to be exact copies of the cosmic mythic order, with their
gates open to the four directions and the world mountain-
ziggurat in the center, where the celestial world might contact the doings of men. And European history right through
the Enlightenment has been dominated by priestly orders
and kings whose consent to govern is divinely bestowed.

But our present relationship to myth seems different in
some basic way. Our age is full of paradoxes, psychomytho-
logical conundrums meant, perhaps, to boggle the mind and
then lead it beyond itself. At last the supreme pontiff of the
Western Hemisphere has received the criticism he so well de-
serves for his archaic stand on birth control, his mantle of
mythic authority finally stripped away; yet in the next moment people are flocking to the feet of a fifteen-year-old "perfect master." Bishops preach about the moribund condition

of the Deity, but simultaneously an exotic cargo of practices, from yoga to Sufism, is unloaded on our cultural docks, imported to satisfy the spiritual hunger of a ravenous domestic consumer market. Old-time mysteries are revived: the Tarot of the gypsies, Chinese oracle books. And the bright archetypes of astrology, easily weathering a century of scorn, flit through minds and conversations.

Such preoccupations, no less than our traditional ones, must be described as "mythological," for surely their logic is not derived from the common-sense data of the world around us. But scientific method was supposed to have "demythologized" us, and Sigmund Freud sounded the death knell to the future of such illusions. Myth has been described as the adolescent wish-fulfillment fantasies of the species; we are now supposed to have "come of age"—why then these persistent regressions? Is modern man, true to his genealogy, just a late-blooming schizophrenic, less consistent but no less delusional than his ancestors?

Science has in fact rendered "mythological" all assertions about the nature of the universe which are not verifiable by experiment. From the animistic beliefs of primitives to the highest metaphysics of philosophers and theologians, all models of the universe or the workings of reality which cannot be explicitly validated in the experimental paradigm of science become unverifiable theory—*myth* for short. And the most prevalent modern meaning for myth is, in fact, attractive fiction, tempting but unprovable.

But against the background of history the eye-opening years of our rational, scientific enlightenment seem a brief moment in the morning of consciousness. We have culturally yawned and stretched a little, but the shadowy myth-susceptible dreamer is still there just below the surface of our new-found awareness. My specific approach in this book will be to explore contemporary consciousness from the viewpoint of our dream-susceptible history. The worst folly in our present time and state, it seems to me, is to deny how newly awakened we are, and how sweet regression is.

The reader will find that I am more concerned with mankind's dreams and illusions than with his grasp of factual
reality. Yet the two, it seems, are inseparable, inversely proportional aspects of human consciousness. I shall suggest
herein that a balanced awareness needs both. Our life together
on this planet must become the theater of wakefulness, involving a consciousness of each other as objective entities, not bit-
players in each others dream dramas. History documents all
too well the nightmare adventures of somnambulistic man.
Subsumed in myth, the dimensions of consciousness, free will,
and compassion are left out, and one is easily capable of becoming the nightmare in another's waking dream.

Yet the psychologists tell us we must not do without dreams.
Dream-deprived human beings universally become restless,
bored, impatient, distractible—the very picture, in fact, of
modern man: deprived perhaps only because he has become
certain he must remain mythless and never dream again.

I envision that our emerging mode of consciousness must
wear a Janus face. One pair of eyes, freeing itself from myth,
looks into the three-dimensional landscape we inhabit together. The task of this face is to see things, not as we wish
or fear them to be, but as they are. The other face remains
turned within, still enraptured with the primeval forms of a
mythic consciousness we may never outgrow. This pair of eyes
recognizes that myth is the bubbling lifespring of our consciousness, that comes from inner reservoirs no man has fully
fathomed. It is the source-font of our highest creativity as well
as of our worst delusions, and the secret is all in how it is
tended.

That a major and unique mythological-psychological-histor-
ical event is under way in our present time is unmistakable.
Serious historians have announced the end of an age, and
our budding mythologies cry the beginning of a new—Aquarian—age, full of marvels and heralded by portents. What is
certain is that our old mythological dynasties, the great orthodox traditions that have guided and shaped men's lives on
this planet for thousands of years, have begun to release their

hold on our collective imagination. Throughout most of our history the mythologizing tendency in man has been anchored both to a literalized projection on the outer landscape and to traditional cultural forms. The first anchor has already torn loose, and we are dragging the second, blown by the winds of change.

My perspective in this book will be that it is not our capacity for the mythological or religious mode of consciousness that is dying in this current time, but a specialized style of relationship to it, characterized by traditional and orthodox forms, in which the universe is seen as the literal projection of one's belief system. The withdrawal of these mythically inspired cosmologies actually began for Western civilization several centuries ago, as science began objectively to describe the physical universe.* The intolerability of this withdrawal is captured beautifully by Brecht in his play "Galileo." At the end of the play the old cardinal, Galileo's antagonist, says to him,

OLD CARDINAL: So you have degraded the earth despite the fact that you live by her and receive everything from her. I won't have it! I won't have it! I won't be a nobody on an inconsequential star briefly twirling hither and thither. I tread the earth, and the earth is firm beneath my feet, and there is no motion to the earth, and the earth is the center of all things, and I am the center of the earth, and the eye of the creator is upon me. About me revolve, affixed to their crystal shells, the lesser lights of the stars and the great light of the sun, created to give light upon me that God might see me— Man, God's greatest effort, the center of creation. "In the image of God created He him." Immortal . . . (His strength fails him and he catches the MONK for support.)

MONK: You mustn't overtax your strength, Your Eminence.[2]

From crystal spheres, a literal Garden of Eden, the "center of creation" to—as John Lilly says it—"a mud ball rotating around a type G star"[3] hasn't been an easy transition for the

---

*Joseph Campbell links the beginning of the withdrawl of the mythic cosmology to end of the fifteenth century—Galileo, Giordano Bruno, the voyage of Columbus.[4]

mythologizing animal. And yet here we are, forced to an inevitable conclusion: withdrawn from geography, astronomy, sociology, myth has not yet vanished, just returned to its source realm within, the realm traditionally studied by psychology.

The force that has been so perennially active throughout human history, informing man's perception of the world and subtly shaping his every dealing with it, is being and must be withdrawn from the theater of history and relocated in the psyche. To the attentive observer of human nature it is apparent that a tendency in man with roots reaching back to his very origins is not going to wither away overnight. We have merely pruned the branch, without affecting the root systems deep within, and the ancient stem is bound to put out new shoots. While we have demythologized outer reality, the mythic imagination in man is very much alive. Mircea Eliade, the religious historian, writes apropos of this,

. . . the myth of the Lost Paradise . . . or the Image of the perfect man, the mystery of Woman and Love, etc.: All these are to be found (but how desecrated, degraded and artificialized!) among many other things in the semiconscious flux of the most down-to-earth existence—in its waking dreams, its fits of melancholy, in the free play of images when consciousness is "taking time off" (in the street, the underground railway or elsewhere), and in all kinds of distractions and amusements. There it lies hidden, the whole treasury of myths, "laicised" and "modernised." . . . In order to survive the Images take on "familiar shapes.[5]

The insights of the psychoanalysts began to bring the actuality of this situation home to us seventy years ago, but we are still only dimly aware of its full implications. Literature too, around the turn of the century, began to suggest the presence of the mythological in the everyday. From Dostoevski's "underground man" to Joyce's *Ulysses* we began to become aware of the image of the hero, not only as depicted in the ancient myths but as it functions now, in the consciousness of everyman.

More recently another kind of experimentation with the

psyche showed us the ubiquity of the mythological in the psychological. The psychedelic drugs, in the space of a mere decade, seem to have introduced a veritable cornucopia of mythic forms into the collective mindscape. Now the realm of myth and faerie truly became accessible to everyman. Art and music to announce the epiphany appeared overnight. Book and record covers, the posters on the walls beckoning us to visit Tolkien's Middle Earth, all proclaimed the reappearance of the living landscape within. Hip messiahs and gurus, bards, magicians, all appeared in a twinkling to function as guides for the journey. For as Andrew Weil has pointed out, in the phase immediately following the psychedelic "opening" to the mythic realm the most natural tendency is to take up a spiritual or mystical practice, whether astrology, the *I Ching*, yoga, or perhaps witchcraft.[6] Psychedelics have shown us that the realm of myth is present in the here and now, and what is required is simply to alter one's state of consciousness, attuning it to this other dimension just a hair's breadth away.

We are dealing now with a collective condition in man which is qualitatively new. Myth, withdrawn from its projection on the common outer environment and no longer bound to culturally propagated forms, is to be recognized as *part of consciousness*. Hence it becomes, perhaps for the first time in history, the responsibility of the individual.*

Now it appears that when the mythic imagination is cultivated it is the creative source realm of the highest and best in human endeavor, the inspiration of the finest flowerings of our culture. But when neglected, deprived of conscious cultivation, it is equally capable of becoming a choked and tangled garden of weeds. Instead of giving birth to the useful and the beautiful, the profound and the sublime, the same creative force can produce titans, monsters, and grotesques—as did the Earth Mother in the Greek legend, left to herself in a

---

*Highly developed individuals throughout the ages have become aware of this fact and have responded to myth on psychological and metaphorical levels. But for everyman myth was inextricably tied to his own local social conditioning.

demiurgic frenzy of creation. Mystery then remains caught at the most primitive levels of inflection: the sleazy phantasmagoria of the *National Enquirer*, the "Twilight Zone" of TV.

This book is intended as a simple instruction manual for owning and operating a mythic imagination in the present time. Its underlying premise is that a new technology of consciousness is required for dealing with our present—and radically novel—way of being-in-the-world. We are meeting conditions of living that are totally radical with a psyche at least a portion of which is thoroughly conservative, rooted in the archaic past. Already our collective response to a demythologized, industrialized, technological environment is an escalating cycle of alienation, dissociation, confusion. Yet we cannot return to the days of our ancestors—to literal, orthodox mythology. What is required is a form of consciousness that recognizes the enduring needs of that shadowy myth-susceptible dreamer still waiting just below the surface of awareness: our deeper, older self.

Freud used an iceberg metaphor to describe the psyche; nine-tenths of the self—the older self—floats below the surface of consciousness, and one-tenth is visible above. Jung was fond of a perhaps more organic metaphor: he saw the psyche as an ancient tree, the living blossoms and flowers of which must trace their origins—and their secret sustenance —to gnarled archaic roots, long enduring, deep within the earth. This is, perhaps, the image that has subliminally guided me as I developed the major themes of this book. I believe the flower of our radically transforming consciousness, if it is to survive, must retain and renew its connections with the ancient root system within.

Reaching back through human history in search of images, prototypes, models for such a quest as it seems we must undertake, I came again and again upon the mysterious figure of the *shaman*. Still active in remote communities and in the writings of Carlos Castaneda, his owllike face can also be seen peering at us from the 30,000 year old cave crypts of the paleolithic era.

Le sorciére. (ink copy) Cave of Les Trois Fréres, France. Paleolithic period: 30,000 to 10,000 B.C. Graffito and painting on rock wall, width 29½".

The earliest human communities of which we know seem already to have required the services of a mediator between the bright world of myth and ordinary reality. The shaman fills this role. He is the prototype of the artist, the priest, the dramatist, the physician, all rolled into one. Gradually a realization began to dawn: the shaman is man's basic creative response to the presence of the mythic dimension.

Men's earliest consciousness seems to have envisioned the presence of other worlds next to this one. The all-too-mysterious events of this world were somehow more comprehensible as the doings of spirits, of gods and demons. If men were to attain their needs and wants they must somehow reach through the apertures between the worlds to contact that more causal level.

But in this field, perhaps before any other, it was realized that specialists were needed, men (and women) who seemed to have abilities beyond others to dream, to imagine, to enter states of trance. Thus the vocation of the shaman developed, out of human needs and a common belief in the presence of a supernatural dimension. On behalf of others, or the community as a whole, the shaman would enter an altered state of consciousness, giving access to the world of spirits, or ancestors. There he would enact a ritual of discovery, propitiation, cure, or salvation. Through solving the problem on the symbolic plane, it was believed that the physical problem—illness, lack of game, bad weather—would also be resolved. The shaman became the first "technician of the sacred."*

Eventually a kind of geography and sociology emerged out of the shaman's otherworldly doings. The experiences, encounters with supernatural beings, ascents and descents to the various spirit realms, yielded the first human mythologies. The tribe also came to participate, through ritual, in the shaman's trance adventure. It became generally known, for example, what must be done in order to "release" the soul of a sick man believed to have been captured by malevolent spirits, or how to release the game that the Mother of the Animals was withholding from the hunters.

Concerning the relationship between the mythic world and the human world, various limits, taboos, observances were established that further strengthened the idea of an interdependence, or symbiosis, between the two. Just as the human community depended upon the good will of the spiritual dimension, so too the spirits required certain behaviors of the community. Out of this interaction developed the religious life as well as, most likely, a moral consciousness.

As these originally visionary discoveries hardened into more permanent structures of belief and value, orthodoxies and dogmas developed, and the shaman's role was gradually transformed into that of the priest. This is a very different order of being. Unlike the shaman, he does not personally and ecstatically enter the supernatural dimension to renew contact between the mythic and the human worlds. His function is rather to celebrate an encounter with the sacred or a revelation of the divine that happened in the long ago.

*Mircea Eliade suggests this very apt term for the shaman. See his *Shamanism* (cited in full in chap. 1, n. 37).

The priest is the steward of traditional mythological forms. In his ritual celebration he periodically reawakens the awareness of the sacred in members of the community.

As societies became more organized, so did religious orthodoxies. Their objective was no longer merely to establish contact with the supernatural, but simultaneously to support the structure of the human community. There was a fusion of religion and politics, church and state. In almost all orderly, stable societies there has been a preference for the priestly way. The shaman is a much too dangerous character to have around. He is often a solitary, half-mad creature through whom a god—or demon—may begin speaking unexpectedly. Or he may suddenly keel over in a trance, leaving his body lifeless and glassy-eyed, only to return from the invisible realm of myth with some outrageous demand, not at all in keeping with orderly social processes. The shaman's primary allegiance is to the supernatural dimension, not to the society.

Here we see that there may indeed be a conflict between immediate visionary experience and the social order. Most of the experiences on which our present religious traditions have been based happened in the long ago, and from the safe vantage point of a current perspective may be interpreted in any number of ways. It seems to be a common human belief that the miraculous and wonderful could easily have happened in the distant past but could not happen today at all. And churches have developed a great variety of unpleasant ways of dealing with visionaries and heretics (the two are often identical) who interrupt the more orderly processes of religion.

Here we return to our original theme. While the orthodox, priestly orders have led us to a stable society and common-sense religious forms, our contemporary situation seems to show us unmistakably that we have outgrown this whole system. The myths that have guided and shaped our destinies in the Western Hemisphere for the past two thousand years emerged from the doings of a particular group of Semitic nomads wandering around the Mediterranean Near East. Congregations are still called flocks, and the pastor "the shepherd." New Testament metaphors emerging from Galilee involved fishing. The presence of deserts, of hostile neighboring tribes, of sinful municipalities, runs throughout our central mythologies. There is, in fact, not a single traditional mythology that has not grown up in a cultural cradle, thus perforce being shaped by specific local social and physical conditions. It is no wonder, then, that as we have outgrown these conditions we have simultaneously experienced our religious traditions as dying.

Yet there is another dimension to this situation. Through the disguise of the local cultural wrappings, in almost any of the major religious forms, there stand out, unmistakably, great shining constancies of the human spirit. The grand themes of mythology are eternal and transcultural. They speak directly to the perennial mysteries that surround our existence: birth and death, the heroic in man, human love, and human suffering. It is on this level that neither myth nor religion can be discarded. They give a depth and meaning to life, an eternal and time-transcending quality to otherwise all-too-meaningless individual experience.

We have, then, two dimensions of mythology which must be distinguished: the culture-bound aspect, which has a primarily socializing function, which I shall define as *orientation*, and the psychological aspect that lends depth and richness to human existence, whatever its setting, which I shall call *guidance.*

Whenever religious traditions have grown stale and outworn, there has come a time of psychological unease: dissatisfaction, criticism, alienation. In the last major such time for Western civilization—which we might date beginning about two thousand years ago—there was a fantastic proliferation into the collective mindscape of messiahs, movements, cults. At such times there is, it seems, a grand mythological competition to see which, of a great many erupting spiritual movements, will or can survive. Rome had to contend not only with the varieties of its own polytheism, but with Zoroastrianism, Manichaeism, and a number of Gnostic cults, as well as early Christianity. A great many charismatic figures leaped onto the mythic stage: Simon Magus, for example, with whom Peter engaged in magical-spiritual duels. Occult traditions, fortune-tellers, diviners did a thriving business; for whenever human existence feels itself uncertain it looks again for guidance to that invisible world in which, it seems, we have never ceased to believe.

The analogy to our present time is clear. At the end of two thousand years we are again left with a "heap of broken images" as T. S. Eliot calls them; or as Joseph Campbell has described it, "the terminal moraine" left by our great mythological traditions. At such times the visionary quest must again become dominant over the traditional religious forms. Man needs a living mythology that springs out of the present conditions of his living, his joys and sorrows, fears and expectations. Guidance, the psychological aspect of myth, must continually be renewed within the experiencing of every-man, as he uses myth to measure his experience and finds that experience in turn must be the measure of myth. As Jerome Bruner says, "When the myths no longer fit the internal plights of those who require them, the transition to newly created myths may take the form of a chaotic voyage to the interior; the certitudes of externalization are replaced by the anguish of the internal voyage."[7]

The internal voyage, the plunge within, is the way of the shaman as opposed to that of the priest. The shaman is the prototype of the spiritual, the psychological, adventurer. I believe that at the present time our priestly, *orienting* relationship to myth is on the wane and the shamanistic, *guiding* aspect once again emergent. We are unhappy with our orthodoxies and ask for experience, even if it means, as Bruner says it, "the anguish of the internal voyage."

The four chapters of this book each take up a different pattern of themes related to the development of a visionary quest, a new "technology of the sacred." Chapter 1, "The

Mythic Imagination," takes up the problem of meaning in relation to myth and presents a model for the evolution of the mythic imagination on both cultural and psychological levels. It then moves to a consideration of "mythic identity" in the patterns of schizophrenia and possession, and concludes with a comparison to the "unearthly calling" of the shaman vocation.

Chapter 2 studies the variety of ways in which men have shared their visionary experiences. Starting with a shamanistic enactment, a visit to the Mother of the Sea Creatures, we move to two preliterate societies in which the enactment and interpretation of dreams have functioned as a daily ritual: the American Iroquois and the Malaysian Senoi. The chapter concludes with a discussion of one of the most remarkable visionary documents of our time, the Great Vision of Black Elk, an Oglala Sioux. This Chapter suggests the necessity and vitality of enactive rituals whereby vision may be shared and made real for the entire community.

Chapter 3 returns to the theme of "technicians of the sacred" with a consideration of three of the "stages of mythic engagement": the orthodox practices of the priestly orders are contrasted to the objective secular technology of the scientist. The Eastern yogic technologies of inward control are then compared to scientific methods. The summarizing theme is that all three technologies are further elaborations of practices once belonging to the shaman. As specializations they have gone beyond the shaman's generalized practice, yet there is a hint that the best of these separate technologies might be reintegrated in the service of a more contemporary shamanism, a fifth stage of mythic engagement.

The last chapter considers emerging mythogenic patterns: myths of integration and renewal. Our modern world, really, is permeated by myth, and what is needed is not so much a completely novel mythology as one that takes account of the themes latent in our current predicaments, both outer and inner. The ecological crisis, for example, seems an extension of how we tend to treat our bodies in this technological society. Sociological and psychological problems express each other, by analogy. The unifying theme of the chapter is that of *dialogue*, which appears symbolically in the myth of the Aquarian Age. Dialogue seems like an indispensable ingredient in our relationship with ourselves, each other, the planet. The myth of the Crippled Tyrant is the shadow predicament of our time. The tyrant is the walled-off, unredeemed old man who resists the changing element in life. The final theme is the return of the feminine motif, so long repressed, which leads to a consciousness able to open itself in a more receptive way to the flow of life's energies, and to reaffirm our human existence with all its limitations.

As consciousness changes, so too does myth. And as we work with mythic patterns, we find too that they are the precise catalysts which initiate changes in consciousness. The ultimate dialogue must be between consciousness, the undiluted perception of self and world, and those patterns to which consciousness has proven most susceptible: the archetypes that underlie the shapeshifting bright world of myth.

1

The Mythic Imagination

What to others a trifle appears
Fills me full of smiles or tears
For double the vision my eyes do see
And a double vision is always with me
With my inward Eye 'tis an old Man grey
With my outward a thistle across my way.

William Blake

For those of us whose vision is ineluctably drawn toward contemplating the mystery dimension of life, myth does not require explanation, but attention. Myth is the ever changing mask that the mind of the beholder fits over a reality he has never truly seen.

For those of us whose attention is drawn to the final and imperative unveiling of the real, vision must ever be cleared of its myths, so that in time there will be no more mystery.

Of these two basic approaches in relation to the dimensions of myth and the imagination, the first leads to that of the poet and mystic, whose impulse is to celebrate the mystery of existence in its many masks of meaning, whereas the second leads to the perspective of the scientist, whose basic aim is ever to seek ways past and beyond man's illusion-susceptible tendencies. To have dialogue between the two perspectives seems impossible, yet necessary.

In researching studies aimed at demonstrating the "meanings" of myth, one invariably encounters partisans of one group or the other. It has always baffled and piqued minds engaged in the pursuit of rationality that most men should continually prefer representations of reality which are fantastic and obviously fictional to a factual view of things. The field of mythology has attempted in various ways to explain this embarrassing trait that continues to haunt the "rational animal." In exploring the classical literature of thought and opinion on myth I find four different approaches, each of which seeks in its own way to show it as a distortion of the real. The first is *euhemerism*. Originating with a Greek philosopher of the fourth century B.C., Euhemerus the Messenian, this approach portrays myth as a successively distorted reporting of an originally real event. Euhemerists are unwilling to see the fantastical happenings of myth as real, even in the long ago; nor are they willing to credit someone with the temerity or imagination to fabricate myths from scratch, as it were. Such modern thinkers as Robert Graves, on the one hand, and Mary Renault on the other might be classed as euhemerists.

The second group might be called the *natural-explanatory* school of thought, which sees myth as the earnest attempt of well-meaning but ignorant primitives to explain the mysterious causes of what we know as "natural" events. No less an authority than Sir James Frazer, author of the encyclopedic twelve-volume *Golden Bough*, subscribed to this view. In his own words, "The tendency to discover the causes of things appears to be innate in the constitution of our minds and indispensable to our continued existence,"[1] and again,

By myths I understand mistaken explanations of phenomena, whether of human life or of external nature. Such explanations originate in that instinctive curiosity concerning the causes of things which at a more advanced stage of knowledge seeks satisfaction in philosophy and science, but being founded on ignorance and misapprehension are always false, for were they true, they would cease to be myths.[2]

According to this school of thinking, because the primitive cannot comprehend how the sun gets across the sky or why the moon changes shape and disappears, he hypothesizes golden chariots or envisions the moon as dying and resurrecting.

The third view might be called the *wish fulfillment* approach and could be summarized by Roland Barthes' definition, "Mythology is in accord with the world not as it is, but as it wants to be."[3] This was the approach that appealed most to Freud. As Freud says of all "religious" ideas, "These . . . are illusions, fulfillments of the oldest, strongest and most insistent wishes of mankind; the secret of their strength is the strength of those wishes."[4]

The fourth view, of *social emanation,* assumes that the structure of the mythology is simply an echo of the social structure of the community. This is the view of a majority of modern anthropologists, especially of the influential "structural-functionalist" school.

Now it is obvious that none of these approaches could claim exclusive validity without simultaneously contradicting the others. It is also obvious, if one is willing to follow the persuasive arguments put forth, that none could be entirely without merit. Surely some of the world's myths are distortions of actual events; surely some (but certainly not all) emerge from curiosity about natural events. Some fairy tales seem to be largely wish fulfillment; and surely there are unmistakable connections between myth and social structure.

The real problems seem to me to arise when any one or another of these approaches is put forward as *the* comprehensive explanatory system of the whole range of mythology. Then we are obliged to point out that many myths have nothing to do with explanations of natural events, either in intention or content; that the cognitive processes of reducing some myths to wish-fulfillment explanations are less believable than the myths themselves; and we are forced to question why social structures ever and again need to justify themselves through fantasies. Clearly each of these explanatory systems has something important to say. But equally clearly, each has its own conceptual axe to grind and tries consistently to reduce an incredible variety and wealth of material to a cognitive explanatory mode.

It seems to me that all these systems have one thing in common: they are unwilling to accept the status of myth in and of itself, as something that carries its own meaning rather than deriving it from somewhere else.

I find that I cannot help but see in these literalistic intellectual approaches an echo of some of the seventeenth- and eighteenth-century Christian interpretations, which saw Greek mythology as the distorted second- or third-hand version of (factual) Old Testament happenings. Writes one such interpreter in the seventeenth century: "Jupiter is none other than Ham, Bacchus is Nimrod, and Saturn is Noah."[5] Is it so awfully far from this to Frazer's attribution to all primitives of the nineteenth-century scientist's intellectual curiosity?

But in all these approaches, the aim of which is to reduce the bright, vivid, playful world of mythology to some kind of principle, there is a weightiness, a heaviness of vision that negates and alienates the character of myth itself. As the religious historian Carl Kerenyi says,

We have lost our immediate feeling for the great realities of the spirit—and to this world all true mythology belongs—lost it precisely because of our all-too-willing, helpful, and efficient science. It explained the drink in the cup to us so well that we knew all about it beforehand, far better than the good old drinkers. . . . We have to ask ourselves: is an immediate experience and enjoyment of mythology still in any sense possible?[6]

In the subsequent chapters of this book we explore a variety of materials, "realities of the spirit," with a mythological content: folktales, legends, dreams and fantasies, psychedelic experiences. I prefer here to use another approach to myth, the aim of which is not to *explain* and analyze but rather to celebrate and *experience* its meaning. To guide us to this approach, let us follow for a while the thinking of a distinguished contemporary mythologist.

Joseph Campbell gives four functions of myth, which provide a broad and more meaningful scope for our understand- of it, without reducing it to some "nothing-but" type of explanation. These functions, he says, are generally found in an operative, living mythology.

The first is what I have called the mystical function: to waken and maintain in the individual a sense of awe and gratitude in relation to the mystery dimension of the universe, not so that he lives in fear of it, but so that he recognizes that he participates in it, since the mystery of being is the mystery of his own deep being as well. . . .

The second function of a living mythology is to offer an image of the universe that will be in accord with the knowledge of the time, the sciences and the fields of action of the folk to whom the mythology is addressed.

The third function of a living mythology is to validate, support, and imprint the norms of a given specific moral order, that namely of the society in which the individual is to live. . . .

And the fourth is to guide him, stage by stage, in health, strength, and harmony of spirit, through the whole forseeable course of a useful life.[7]

Professor Campbell here gives us a sense of how myth *functions* rather than presuming to define what it *is*. His four functions also take us beyond the bounds of any one reductive explanatory system. Surely something as pervasive and long-lived as myth serves more than a single purpose. And really all our descriptions and explanations are heuristic devices, designed to render comprehensible to our analytical minds what is really a unified, living totality. We must learn to ask ourselves when and where our causal, logical explanations are appropriate.

Now as we look more closely at the functional aspects of myth, we see that the second and third of Campbell's functions correspond to a *sociological* level of adaptation, and the first and fourth rather to *psychological* needs. Perhaps we can use this distinction better to understand a dual aspect in the functioning of myth.

The sociological level corresponds to what Professor Campbell introduces as "a second womb." The human child, like the marsupial, is born a bit too soon. It needs a protective, nurturing context in which to develop further. Myth fulfills this requirement for human development. It contains and structures the growth of the child into a functional member of the society he lives in. It also presents him with a picture of the universe essentially in harmony with his social environment. (This is the aspect the structural anthropologists have fixed on as being the sole function of myth.) This general function, which I shall refer to as *orientation* corresponds roughly to Campbell's second and third functions: "to validate, imprint and support the norms of a specific moral order" and "to offer an image of the universe that will be in accord with the knowledge . . . and fields of action" of that social order.

On the psychological level, though, the focus is not on social integration but rather on the structure and dynamics of the psyche. Campbell's stages one and four would refer to different aspects of this domain. The first he describes as "mystical." It is this aspect of myth that reminds man that he participates in the mystery dimension of the universe, so that he recognizes its wonders as the same as "the mystery of his own deep being as well." To the scientist this may seem like a dispensable service. But to the child, poet, and mystic in each of us it is not, especially when we consider that the response to this "mystery dimension" of reality seems to be one of man's basic ways of being which we shall never outgrow. I shall explore this idea in more depth further on.

Campbell's fourth function of myth "is to guide (everyman), stage by stage . . . through the whole forseeable course of a useful life." This function of myth would help the individual through those difficult existential choices and crises we all encounter, and provide him with a pattern for dealing with the mysterious universe within: his dreams, inexplicable moods and emotions welling up from inside, fantasies and imaginings, and such unforeseen and awesome plunges within ourselves as schizophrenia. The imprints of mythology then function as guiding symbols, signposts of the inner landscape, cue cards for the mythic drama one may unexpectedly find oneself enacting.

Jerome Bruner, the developmental psychologist, points out

another psychological aspect of myth. He tells us that it may also act as the guiding pattern for our divided inner selves: the multiple and often conflicting personality aspects of which we all are composed. Says Bruner, " . . . the mythologically instructed community provides its members with a library of scripts upon which the individual may judge the internal drama of his multiple identities. . . . Personality imitates myth," and "myth becomes the tutor, the shaper of identities."[8]

It is to these psychological aspects of myth that I apply the term *guidance*. Far from wishing to define and subdivide further than has already been done, I see the functions of *orientation* and *guidance* rather as operational definitions, categories that may be consciously applied by the mind of the beholder, not to divide and analyze but to allow myth to show us that she is not one thing but, like The Goddess, of multiple aspects.

Myth, in its living, holistic actuality is neither orientation nor guidance alone. Rather, it may function in either of these ways, or both simultaneously, in the psyche of the experiencer. However, in a specific context one or the other aspect may emerge as the more important. Generally orientation, our experience of our local social order (and through it, the backdrop of the universe standing behind), tends to become anchored to fixed patterns. At the extreme, these patterns harden into orthodoxy, and we mistake the universe we have mythically and socially collaborated in creating for the truly unknowable one that has always been there. It is the orientational aspect of myth that must pass with the passing of historical and social conditions. But my concern in this book is with the psychological level of myth, the level at which human beings have not only generated myths but proven susceptible to them, fascinated by them, overpowered by them, time and again through the centuries.

The developmental psychologists have described in detail how the young child's starting frame of reference spontaneously includes many mythological elements. Before it acquires the abstract, conceptual thinking that characterizes the human adult, its thinking is primarily imagistic and syncretic. The child assumes that the universe is all alive (animism) and magically responsive to his wishes (egocentricity). He is unable to distinguish between objective and subjective experience (*participation mystique* as Levy-Bruhl calls it[9]), and imagines that his parents are at once extensions of himself and great powers in the universe, omniscient and omnipotent.

This way of looking at things seems also to form the background of most mythological and religious frames of reference. Human consciousness in its naïve state spontaneously contains all the basic ingredients of the mythological way of conceiving of the universe. In our conceptual and abstracting socialization process the objective is to supplant this primitive, magical thinking by rational processes.

Jean Piaget's developmental psychology, for example, evaluates the child's developmental progress by how far egocentric, magical thinking has been replaced by abstract conceptual thought. The goal is to develop the "fully operational" thinking of the educated adult in our society, possessed of flexible and "reversible" abstract categories, an "objective" sense of self, of time and space and causality.[10]

But now as the mythical mode of consciousness is replaced by a more socialized form, we may well ask what happens to that prior mode.

In a primitive or ritually oriented society we see a very different type of process. Rather than being suppressed or subordinated, the primary, mythic type of consciousness is engaged and brought into relationship simultaneously with the mythology and the social system of the group. Mythic meaning and social meaning are thus brought together rather than separated, and the archaic type of thinking is fused with mythic images and social realities. This constitutes orientation into what has been referred to as the "mythologically instructed community."

In such demythologized societies as our own, however, while abstract categorical thinking is nurtured, the primary, mythical type of thinking is neglected. And much like those unfortunate children who, neglected by their parents, are locked away in a darkened room out of sight, the mythic imagination seems to stay "autistic," remaining in a primitive, self-preoccupied state. Unrelated to, it lacks the capacity to relate intelligently to consciousness. It only emerges when consciousness is taking time off, in fantasy and dreams.

Both Freud and Jung became very interested in the autistic, undirected type of thinking that belongs to fantasies, and both men felt it was the key to unconscious motivations and conflicts.* While directed socialized thinking is geared to the demands of the outer environment and requires effort and attention, undirected thinking emerges when attention is relaxed. And rather than requiring effort, it seems to dissipate tension already accumulated in the directed style of thinking. It is responsive to the dynamics of the inner rather than the outer environment. Hence its images are representative of what goes on in the unconscious regions of the self—"autosymbolic," as its functioning has been called.

Freud called this kind of thinking "primary process" and believed there was a continuum between daydreams, night dreams, and the thinking of children and primitive people. "These," he says, "we consider to be the older primary processes, the residues of a phase of development in which they were the only kind of mental process."[11] He felt, however, that when this kind of thinking appeared to any degree in an adult it was a sign of regression and pathology, of a kind of wish fulfillment which, abandoning its dependence upon real objects, sought rather a magical satisfaction. Eventually he came in his thinking to prefer this wish-fulfillment interpretation for almost any product of the imagination, whether dream, fantasy, myth, or work of art.

Jung, on the other hand, became increasingly fascinated by the similarity of symbolic forms in all products of the

*In researching the literature of psychology I have come across the following terms, all of which seem to refer to nondirected thinking in one or another of its aspects: autistic, autosymbolic, daydreaming, eidetic, fantasy, iconic, imagistic, magical, mythological, paleological, paralogical, physiognomic, preconceptual, prelogical, primary process, primitive, syncretic.

imagination, and took the position that "primary-process thinking" was an ordinary and natural mode of consciousness. He says,

The unconscious bases of dreams and fantasies are only apparently infantile reminiscences. In reality we are concerned with primitive or archaic thought-forms, based on instinct, which naturally emerge more clearly in childhood than they do later. But they are not in themselves infantile, much less pathological. To characterize them, we ought therefore not to use expressions borrowed from pathology. So also the myth, which is likewise based on unconscious fantasy processes, is, in meaning, substance, and form, far from being infantile or the expression of an autoerotic or autistic attitude, even though it produces a world-picture which is scarcely consistent with our rational and objective view of things. The instinctive, archaic basis of the mind is a matter of plain objective fact and is no more dependent upon individual experience or personal choice than is the inherited structure and functioning of the brain or any other organ. Just as the body has its evolutionary history and shows clear traces of the various evolutionary stages, so too does the psyche.[12]

There is, then, a crucial difference between Freud and Jung in how they have regarded this archaic, autistic, prelogical type of thinking which would nevertheless seem to be one of the fundamental psychological modes of man. Freud sees it as bound to the pleasure principle and largely expressive of wishes unattainable in reality. The presence of primary-process thinking in the human adult indicates both regression and repression, and is a clue to the presence of neurotic conflicts. Jung sees this type of thinking as a natural and instinctive—albeit archaic—mode of the psyche, in and of itself neither infantile nor pathological.

The perspective I maintain in this book is more like that of Jung than of Freud. The faculty in man that generates and is susceptible to images, his "image-ination," appears in many more contexts than infancy and pathology. It appears not only in art and "visual thinking," but in creative processes of all kinds. (One recalls Kekule's discovery of the benzine ring through the image of a snake swallowing its tail.) It is capable of being neglected, or developing a very high degree of refinement. The imagination may be educated or cultivated almost endlessly. And the elements or symbols in which it deals may be highly complex; be they visual, musical, or conceptual, they vary all the way from the concrete to the very abstract.

It is the substrata, the earliest and deepest levels of the imagination, that seem to be mythological. Later accretions of experience and complicated, abstract symbol systems may be layered over these deeper levels. But when you are sleepy, or emotionally aroused, or slightly drugged, or ecstatic, they emerge, and then your computative abilities go down, your intelligence quotient drops. You become a more primitive and a more mythological creature.

Children in our culture are not mythologically indoctrinated for the most part. But their fantasies, games, and stories abound in the raw stuff of myth. One only has to look into a comic book to find the talking animals, the fantastic heroes, the magical adventures. There are the invulnerable men of steel with their Kryptonite Achilles' heels. And numerous caped wonders—bearing the signs of their totem animal—Hawkman, Spiderman, Batman, zoom through the air, fighting evil. There are Incredible Hulks with irresistible power, tricksters, evil magicians, and their modern counterparts, the mad scientists. And then there is the whole grisly, macabre cast of the underworld, prying open tombs, creeping through swamps and basements, hiding under your bed.

Adults, for the most part, are rather scornful of their children's preoccupations and wish they would "grow up." Yet they, too, read the funny papers and the *National Enquirer*. The same mythic cast appears, just slightly disguised, in adult entertainment: the repetitive heroic exploits of Wyatt Earp or whoever, the family comedy of "The Munsters," the oh-so incomprehensible mysteries of "The Twilight Zone."

But the mythic imagination operates not only on these primitive levels. It has been refined, by men and women more conscious of its creative potential, into the grandeur of Greek drama, the inexhaustible riches of art, poetry, religious iconography. Related to by consciousness in an equal dialogue, creativity flowers and bestows a meaning and a beauty that make life truly worth living.

It is this meaning dimension that seems to emerge as a genuine key to our understanding of myth. "Myth . . . seeks to bestow a meaning that is valid in whatever time it appears," writes Mircea Eliade. And Mark Schorer, writing on the necessity of myth, says, "A myth is a large controlling image that gives philosophical *meaning* to the facts of ordinary life; that is, which has organizing value for experience. Without such images, experience is chaotic, fragmentary and merely phenomenal."[13]

In the mystery that surrounds us all we have learned to find consistencies, recurrences of patterns we find meaningful. These have been in reality made up from single instances, individual human experiences where something was touched, a response released, that carried meaning. If such an experience is potent enough, our attention is engaged and we stay with the experience, interpreting and differentiating what originally was our *felt* meaning. In this way we *assign* meanings, cognitively, to experienced meaning. We make our mistake when we confuse the assigned with the felt meanings. They are not the same thing.

Eugene Gendlin takes up this issue very nicely in his book *Experiencing and the Creation of Meaning*. He says that "any datum of experiencing—any aspect of it, no matter how finely specified—can be symbolized and interpreted *further and further*, so that it can guide us to many, many more symbolizations. We can endlessly 'differentiate' it further, we can synthesize endless numbers of meanings in it."[14] But, Gendlin argues, we should not imagine that by differentiating the original moment of feeling in this way we have defined or explained *it*. This attitude comes from the one-sidedness in our approach to experience. We have been socialized into accepting the verbal descriptions or explanations for our experiencing, rather than attending to the moment of felt meaning in and of itself. It is true that each new differentiation of an original experience may yield new meanings (which, too, are valuable in and of themselves), but this may not be taken to explain the moment itself. That moment, says Gendlin, is "preconceptual." "We must investigate prelogical, 'preconceptual' experience as it *functions together with* logical symbols, but not substitute one for the other."[15]

In that preconceptual moment a type of meaning we might call *primary meaning* emerges. It may be attached to a symbol or image, but is not necessarily defined by that symbol; the symbol has merely functioned to evoke, or has itself been evoked by, the meaning. When we begin to differentiate or further explain the symbol, we are already referring to an order of *secondary meaning*. This resides in and is carried by verbal definitions and logic. It is to the order of primary meaning that I suggest we must refer the symbols of myth and dream, if we would even begin to grasp their import.

W. H. Auden, the poet and essayist, distinguishes two basic modes of the imagination which he terms "primary" and "secondary." The Secondary Imagination is concerned with things and events, but "the concern of the Primary Imagination, its only concern," he writes, "is with sacred beings and sacred events. The sacred is that to which it is obliged to respond."[16] The faculty in man, then, which is susceptible to and also generates myths is more than merely an archaic stage of cognitive development or a primitive curiosity about how things work; it is rather an alternative mode of consciousness, with an a-priori, instinctive impulse toward this different, sacred mode of comprehension.

There is a continuum, it seems, between the most primitive forms of mythic consciousness and the highest forms of mysticism. The meaning that motivates primitive magic and ritual is another aspect of the truth sought by the mystic: that the universe is—beneath the illusion of separateness—interconnected. Consciousness awakens to wonder and mystery, and puts aside planning, scheming, reasoning. I think of the passage of Yeats that stands at the beginning of this volume. He describes this attitude as "the ancient religion":

Once every people in the world believed that trees were divine, and could take a human or grotesque shape and dance among the shadows; and that deer and ravens and foxes, and wolves and bears, and clouds and pools, almost all things under the sun and moon, and the sun and moon, were not less divine and changeable. They saw in the rainbow the still bent bow of a god thrown down in his negligence; they heard in the thunder the sound of his beaten water-jar, or the tumult of his chariot wheels; and when a sudden flight of wild ducks, or of crows, passed over their heads, they thought they were gazing at the dead hastening to their rest; while they dreamed of so great a mystery in little things that they believed the waving of a hand, or of a sacred bough, enough to trouble far-off hearts, or hood the moon with darkness.[17]

It is this faculty of perception informed by primary meaning that I shall define as the *mythic imagination*. The mythic imagination prefers representations and forms, not because they accurately reflect and describe reality, but because they touch the realm of inner, primary meaning. The Taos Pueblo Indian who believes that his prayers cause the sun to rise every morning never considers that simplest of all empirical tests, invariably suggested by white men: "Well, try not doing it one morning and see if it still comes up." The ritual, and his beliefs and emotions invested in it, have an experiential, mythical meaning that far transcends his curiosity.

Primary meaning may be thought of as a unitive quality present in one form or another throughout all religious and mystical experience, whether primitive or modern. In the absence of this feeling dimension, surely the empty forms of myth and religion come more to resemble those absurd theories about reality and patent fictions of which so many theorists have complained. But when these forms are experienced in the presence of primary meaning, they indeed appear full of meaning, lit up from within as it were. And then they become a gateway which lures man from his waking, three-dimensional consciousness to a contemplation of what has been called the *mysterium tremendum et fascinans*, the universe seen in its sacred aspect. It is this experience that Professor Rudolf Otto termed *numinous*.[18]

In the presence of the numinous, consciousness changes tracks and begins to operate in a different way. It is no longer concerned with labeling, categorizing, or manipulating the universe that surrounds it; rather it is speechlessly content to behold, in reverence and awe, the cosmic mystery of which it too is a part. In Professor Otto's classic work, *Das Helige* ("The Holy"), he separates the *experience* of the sacred from any of its specific, particular inflections. The sacred experience is a universal capacity in man, which however may emerge only under certain conditions, outer and inner. When it emerges, its function is to attune the consciousness to a sacred experiencing of the cosmos rather than the ordinary profane mode.

The universe, in this state of consciousness, may be experienced as a living, intensely meaningful, yet at the same time mysterious entity. As Jacob Boehme says, "I saw and knew the being of all things . . . I saw and knew the whole working essence . . . and likewise how the fruitful bearing womb of eternity brought forth."[19] And Angela of Foligno describes it, "I did comprehend the whole world . . . and the abyss and ocean and all things. In these things I beheld naught save divine power."[20] Compare these accounts to the following Navajo Indian song of sacred awareness:

> In beauty I walk
> With beauty before me I walk
> With beauty behind me I walk
> With beauty above me I walk
> With beauty above and about me I walk
> It is finished in beauty
> It is finished in beauty[21]

Joseph Campbell quotes the awakening of the Hindu saint Ramakrishna: "One day, it was suddenly revealed to me that everything is pure spirit. The utensils of worship, the altar, the door frame—all pure spirit. Then like a madman I began to shower flowers in all directions. Whatever I saw I worshipped."[22]

Surely there is a continuity present in all of these various experiences, occurring to very different people in widely separate times and under different skies. Religious or mystical ecstasy is a condition of the psyche, a universal, separate mode of consciousness that envisions reality as sacred. As Ramakrishna says, "Whatever I saw I worshipped."

Primitive man's attraction to the mythic is not just a result of his cognitive inferiority, nor his susceptibility to wish-fulfilling delusions, but of his preference at times for a different mode of consciousness which lends to his experience this sacred quality. Campbell takes up this issue in regard to the masked dramas:

> In the primitive world, where the clues to the origin of mythology must be sought, gods and demons are not conceived of in the way of hard and fast, positive realities. The phenomenon of the primitive mask, for example is a case in point. The mask is revered as an apparition of the mythical being that it represents, yet everyone knows that a man made the mask and that a man is wearing it. . . . In other words there has been a shift of view from the logic of the normal secular sphere, where things are understood to be distinct from each other, to a theatrical or play sphere, where they are accepted for what they are *experienced* as being, and the logic is that of "make-believe"—"as if."[23]

The meaning of myth, then, is to be *experienced*; and that moment of primary meaning is to be sought, or rather to be courted, in the open, playful—yet all too serious—atmosphere of the masked drama or the religious festival. This meaning cannot be compelled nor defined. It does not show itself to the critical scientist, nor to the bemused anthropologist stuck in logical, analytical modes of secondary meaning. It simply presents itself to the receptive consciousness, and we can only truly know it in that moment of experiential impact. This, then, is the moment of meaning that takes us beyond ourselves.

Here we may see the important relationship between myth

and the varieties of religious experience throughout the ages. Myth is not fully understood unless one enters into an altered state of consciousness; yet at the same time the myth itself, related to in this "as-if" way, may provide the trigger or the catapult for ecstatic experience. A beautifully vivid passage from Joseph Campbell captures this atmosphere of mythic consciousness.

The spirit of the festival, the holiday, the holy day of the religious ceremonial, requires that the normal attitude toward the cares of the world should have been temporarily set aside in favor of a particular mood of dressing up. The world is hung with banners. Or in the permanent religious sanctuaries—the temples and cathedrals —where an atmosphere of holiness hangs in the air, the logic of cold, hard fact must not be allowed to intrude and spoil the spell. The gentile, the "spoilsport," the positivist who cannot or will not play, must be kept aloof. Hence the guardian figures that stand at either side of the entrances to holy places: lions, bulls, or fearsome warriors with uplifted weapons. They are there to keep out the "spoilsports" the advocates of Aristotelian logic, for whom A can never be B; for whom the actor is never to be lost in the part; for whom the mask, the image, the consecrated host or tree or animal cannot become God, but only a reference. Such heavy thinkers are to remain without. For the whole purpose of entering a sanctuary or participating in a festival is that one should be overtaken by the state known in India as "the other mind" (Sanskrit, *anya-manas*: absent mindedness, possession by a spirit), where one is "beside oneself," spellbound: set apart from one's logic of self-possession and overpowered by the force of a logic of indissociation, where A is B, and C also is B.[24]

This then is man's relation to primary, mythic meaning: he may not compel, direct, nor properly explain it. At best, as he has done throughout the ages, he may decorate the world with banners and play this ancient game of belief—and then, per-haps, if he is to be blessed, it will emerge to fill his experience from within—and for a moment his consciousness may show him the presence of eternity in time and space.

Five Stages of Mythic Engagement

The concept of "primary meaning" may provide a framework for understanding mythic experience, but it does not communicate anything of the awe, the numinosity, and the power that religious experience has carried for man throughout the centuries. All the various forms of it may be seen as a coming to terms with this compelling power, and when it has become inflected into a specific system of mythological images, men will fight to the death over what God is to be called, and whether he is one, or few, or many. For along with the potency of religious experiencing comes an irresistible urge to represent, describe, and systematize what at first may have been only a blinding light or an indescribable sense of joy, awe, or reverence. And once the vision has been thus crystallized it is regarded as the ultimate nature of the universe, the manifest Word of God.

We always assume ourselves to be rational creatures, and we are not content until we have explained, or have had explained, the most powerful of our feelings. Jung cites the case of one Brother Nicholas of Flue, who has now been canonized as a saint. Brother Klaus had a numinous experience of so profound a nature that his own face was changed by it. Jung quotes Woelflin's account:

All who came to him (Brother Klaus) were filled with terror at the first glance. As to the cause of this, he himself used to say that he had seen a piercing light resembling a human face. At the sight of it he feared that his heart would burst into little pieces. Therefore, overcome with terror, he instantly turned his face away and fell to the ground. And that was the reason why his face was now terrible to others.[25]

This experience was so profound that for years Brother Klaus struggled to get it into a form which he could understand, or to which he could relate. He read devotional booklets by mystics and worked for many years on a *mandala* (in this case a circular wall-painting), called the "pilgrim's wheel," which may perhaps have helped, as a tangible static representation to stabilize what had been all too alive in the original experience. Jung calls this process "elaboration of the symbol." Firsthand mystical experience is sometimes so powerful that one must render it, translate it, shape it, into a form comprehensible to consciousness. And we know that even the intrepid shaman does not venture into the realm of primary meaning without a myth in mind. He goes to rescue a soul that is kept in a bottle by a supernatural being, or to visit the Mother of the Sea Creatures. The myth is the vehicle for a supernatural transaction that brings healing or resolution.

Thus the forms of mythology and religion have a dual purpose. They reawaken man to an experience of the divine, and yet also safeguard him from having to deal with it in its formless aspect: pure power and meaning. As Jung says of traditional religious symbolism,

That people should succumb to these images is entirely normal, in fact it is what these images are for. They are created out of the primal stuff of revelation and reflect the ever-unique experience of divinity. That is why they always give man a premonition of the divine while at the same time safeguarding him from immediate experience of it. Thanks to the labours of the human spirit over the centuries, these images have become embedded in a comprehensive system of thought that ascribes an order to the world, and are at the same time represented by a mighty, far spread, and venerable institution called the Church.[26]

These considerations pave the way for our discussion of the stages of mythic engagement. In what ways has man traditionally handled his powerful encounters with this compelling level of meaning, and what patterns are available to him now?

I have worked out five typical patterns of relationship between man and his primary, mythic imagination:

1. Mythic Identity
2. Mythic Orthodoxy
3. Objective Phase
4. Suspended Engagement
5. Mythic Engagement and Renewal

The use of the term "stage" implies a developmental relationship between what might otherwise have been called simply "patterns." This was intentional. As will be seen, the stages apply to both individuals and cultures as a means of formulating their relationship to the mythic imagination in a developmental way. But I hope to make clear that these stages are most useful when considered as tentative, heuristic ways of thinking about our subject matter rather than implying any ultimate categories of experience.

On the next page I briefly describe the typical ranges of experience and behavior belonging to each stage, and then move on to some further ideas about their implications and the relations between them.

Stage 1. Mythic Identity (possession)
    The mythic imagination is activated with little or no relationship to the actual properties of "outer reality." *Examples*: Individual: psychosis, possession, certain forms of religious ecstasy, certain forms of psychedelic experience, shamanism. Collective: mass hysteria, collective rituals involving spirit possession (*bimbes*), etc., charismatic leadership.

Stage 2. Mythic Orthodoxy (religion)
    The mythic imagination and "outer reality" are held to a fixed relationship. Revelation hardens into dogma. A given mythic hypothesis is accepted, and alternative points of view are unwelcome. *Examples*: Individual: fixed personal beliefs about the ultimate nature of reality, delusions. Collective: orthodox religion, mythology, ritual.

Stage 3. Objective Phase (science)
    Man imagines that he can eliminate the mythic imagination from his involvement with outer reality, and is partly successful. There is a determination to accept no mythic hypothesis without empirical verification. The relationship to the "reality principle" is systematized. *Examples*: the thoroughgoing scientist, the inveterate skeptic, modern man.

Stage 4. Suspended Engagement (meditation)
    The "meaning" aspect of the mythic imagination is activated in an attempt to achieve "contentless experience." There is a deter-

mination to accept no mythic hypothesis. Commitment is withheld from any experience short of a major breakthrough in
consciousness (*samadhi, satori*). *Examples*: Zen and yoga meditation, some aspects of psychedelic experience.
Stage 5. Mythic Engagement (dialogue, transformation, and renewal)

The creative capacity of the mythic imagination is activated and
engaged. Its guiding function is utilized for self-discovery and
creative transformations of the personality. Assertions about the
ultimate nature of outer reality are not made; rather learned
truths are recognized as psychological. The ability to return to
the world of "common sense" and normal experiencing is re-
tained. *Examples*: the mythological hero quest, the creative
artist, some aspects of psychotherapy, some aspects of psychedelic
experience, the creative shaman.

These stages might be thought of most simply as descriptions
of man's responsive postures toward direct contact with the
mythic imagination. Man is deeply and compulsively concerned with myth and the dimension of the sacred. But he also
has a world of practical everyday realities to attend to. Though
there is a potential for mythic experiencing present in each of
us, it is most often masked by the exigencies of reality orientation. And reality orientation is best accomplished with eyes attuned to practicality, not enraptured with mythic forms.

In the first stage, mythic identity, consciousness is caught
up, fascinated as it were, in the field of primary meaning. What
stands out for the perceiving eye is what it finds meaningful,
and what it finds meaningful is in-formed from within. In this
first stage there is no differentiation between felt experience
and the object of perception. Reality is living mystery. In such
mystical rapture the mind loses its immediate grasp of reality.
The saint forgets to eat, and his mind is, as Saint Augustine
says, "stripped of the world." The oracle or medium becomes
possessed and speaks and acts without personal responsibility.
The schizophrenic listens to his inner voices and does not look
before he crosses the street. The myths informing consciousness are identical with the perception of reality.

But fortunately for the world and its necessities, such total mythic seizures happen to few, and when they do they are often brief. The total fascination with the *mysterium tremendum* leads to more stable forms of contemplation that leave the mind free for other things. Man seeks to stabilize his relationship to the mythic. This leads to what Jung called "symbolic elaboration." One cannot neglect the revelatory power and meaning of such experiences—nor, it seems, sustain their immediacy. The forms of the vision, the words that can be found to describe it, even the conditions that led to the experience may become its symbols, objects of reverence and awe for the experiencer and for those with whom he shares his vision. Prophecy leads to priesthood, and revelation solidifies into doctrine and ritual. The immediacy of an original experience is tamed, subdued, and controlled. The fixed forms of mythic meaning are brought into a supportive relationship to everyday life. Orthodox religion replaces primary revelation. This constitutes the second stage of mythic engagement: a stage of stability, of crystallization, a vision of the sacred which is safer, more possible to live with than the often numinous, terrifying immediacy of mythic seizure.

But our history shows us the deficiencies of the human mind fettered to orthodoxy. Shall I name a few? Intolerance, conservatism, rigidity, blindness to any possibility outside the system, persecution of heretics, and so forth.

I have mentioned earlier the positive, nurturing aspects of a traditional mythology, and introduced Campbell's "second womb" metaphor. Mythology fulfills the function of a psychological womb that brings the developing psyche to maturity. But when that psyche ought to have reached maturity—to have "grown up," as we would say—then the womb becomes a straitjacket, a cumbrous armor, a helmet over the head that restricts clarity of vision. And stumbling around in the dark, armored, weapons in hand, throughout our long dark history we have most generally tended to be hostile to whomever we meet—often our neighbors, equally hostile, equally armored. Many of us would like to finish with orthodoxy.

Orthodoxy is, in its regressive aspect, a kind of fixation on a specific body of mythic forms. Reality is unavailable except through the mediation of those forms, and the larger universe becomes reduced and fixed in its possibilities. Psychologists have recognized that belief systems are simplifying solutions to the otherwise overwhelming complexities of reality. If I can, for example, attribute the varieties of human suffering to sin or "bad karma," I may be spared the pain of empathy or the incredible responsibility of changing things. The myth continues to protect one from the awesome nakedness of experience. Freedom is, as both Erich Fromm and Eric Hoffer have suggested, anxiety-inducing, and most human beings seem to prefer a catechism to rule their experience rather than face the anguish of ambiguity.

The third stage is our present one of Western civilization. And since its basic stance is toward objectivity and away from all myth, its function might better be called "disengagement" than "engagement." Looking back on his turgid aeon in the psychic womb, it is no wonder that modern man has characterized history as a nightmare from which he has been struggling to awaken. And like those dreams whose potent images and subtle feelings linger on into wakefulness, giving their tone to the experiences of the day, our history is still with us. Of what did we dream? Was it not kings and slaves, heroes and maidens, gods and demons? Surely our history has been a "big dream," for its dramatis personae are archetypal and the doings of our ancestors of a piece with the myths in which they believed.

But we are at a critical juncture in the morning of our consciousness. We may either, as we have been doing these one or two past century-minutes, repress the dream with a shudder and try to go about our intentional business of the day. Or we may, like the wisest of our ancestors, or the Senoi of Malaysia, spend a few moments with our dream-history, nightmare though it be, in hopes of understanding its message. But our cultural response has been to deny and repress. To the still dream-susceptible waking mind, myths seem like a terrifying regression back into sleep. Our modern usage for the term myth holds it equivalent to "attractive fiction," a falsehood which is especially dangerous because we continue to be susceptible to it. We are fearful that somehow, waking, we still dream.

Myths are the *shadow* of the scientist; they are the unproven but tempting hypothesis, the generalization that ties so many things together and seems so "right." The relationship of myth and science might be described as inversely proportional. Where myth is prevalent, science is disadvantaged and vice versa. Chemistry was never developed while alchemy had captured human imagination, pursued with the zeal of a spiritual quest projected into matter. And how could the Periodic Table of the Elements be discovered by a mind preoccupied with the discovery of the Philosopher's Stone? Are we not dealing with the most fundamental sort of split in man's modes of consciousness, that of the sacred and the profane? We are forever getting them mixed up. Alchemy developed the crucible, the retort, and the laboratory and used them for centuries; but the alchemist was all the while engaged in a mythic quest, the psychospiritual aspects of which have been so well documented by Jung.

And how could we map the stars objectively, or calculate the distances of interstellar space, while the incomparably more meaningful archetypes of astrology were entangled with our conceptions of them? Is Jupiter god and archetype, or is he rather a huge rotating ball of methane and ammonia? Science and myth show us radically different pictures of the universe, and we are presently so aware of the catastrophes that result when we confuse them that we keep them strictly segregated. At least for now, myth is riding in the back of the bus. In a later chapter I explore more fully some aspects of this still uneasy relationship.

The fourth stage of engagement, like the third, might better be called "disengagement."* The East has developed a techno-

*Yet I feel the overall designation of "stages of engagement" is justified; we need to disengage only where we are most helplessly, obsessively involved or engaged to start with.

logy of the sacred as efficient as our profane one. As science is
the technique parexcellence for disengaging the profane from
the sacred—and thus achieving an objectivity of perspective—
so Eastern spiritual disciplines also seek for an objectivity of
perspective through disengagement. But where the technique
of science places the emphasis on the profane, that of yoga
emphasizes the sacred.

In the major Eastern spiritual disciplines man's ordinary experiential relationship with the universe is conceived of as illusory. One Hindu term for this, *maya*, sees the universe as an
endless dancing, ever changing yet ever the same, the beautiful
illusion. *Samskara*, emphasizes more the irresistibly seductive
quality of this illusion so many of us take for real. The illusion
is believed to operate in the processes of conscious experience;
and so the techniques of liberation from this condition involve
withholding consciousness from ordinary confluence with
reality. There is an interesting analogy between science and
meditation: each is determined to withhold a certain type of
mythologizing from the experience of reality. For the yogi, the
mind interminably presents reality through its own inner representations. Such personal and subjective myths are to be transcended in favor of a total breakthrough of experiencing,
moksha, enlightenment. And the scientist, too, is certain that
the surface of things is an illusion, and determines to go beyond
those "appearances." The yogi wishes to transcend illusion in
order to experience the real, the scientist wishes to transcend
illusion in order to know and perhaps finally manipulate the
real.

But we cannot ignore the differences between scientist and
yogi. The yogi prefers to dismiss the reality of the visible world
around him. His operating myth is that nothing is real short of
complete enlightenment. And traveling to India we can see on
all sides the tangible, horrible effect of this philosophy of disengagement on this our mutual, real illusion that never changes.
Lepers, starving children, and corpses alike are left to their
own devices, i.e., the results of their various *karmas*. And if,
as many mystically attuned Westerners report of the spiritual

atmosphere, "the vibrations are very high" and a sacred consciousness is indeed prevalent, why, on the profane level, seen three-dimensionally by our profane vision, are conditions so terrible? Perhaps a few high-flying, supercharged yogis have pierced the veil, but for the man in the street life is uniformly awful, and he, like everyman in our culture, is seldom ecstatic but must rely on orthodox images and rituals for his consolation, his glimpse of an eternity beyond the daily round of suffering.

The scientist, on the other hand, is eminently concerned with conditions in the three-dimensional world. He has discovered the methods and implements of making indifferent nature more humanly livable. He is concerned with banishing a mythic-religious viewpoint which insists that evil spirits are the source of man's many diseases, in favor of an outlook able to discover the actuality of secular microbes. We have, thanks to the scientist, a remarkable technology. But led by the pure scientist, we are also in the process of raping the globe, the Great Mother whose planetary body we live upon. And surely our tract housing is the ugliest form—if most comfortable—of community living that man has ever designed. The scientist has identified with practicality to the neglect of the forms that nourish the soul.

The following diagram may help to illustrate these four stages a bit more clearly and indicate the possible relations between them.

Each stage is an attempt to cope with the simultaneous presence of the primary and secondary levels of meaning. Mythic identity we might think of as man's basic developmental state, both individually and in the history of the race. Value is determined from within, attention is centripetal, turned toward primary mythic meaning. The vocabulary—the symbols and images—used by the conscious mind are organized and patterned by the mythic, archetypal dynamics of the psyche.

Following a clockwise movement in the diagram, the immersion in mythic forms leads to a stabilized relationship to them.

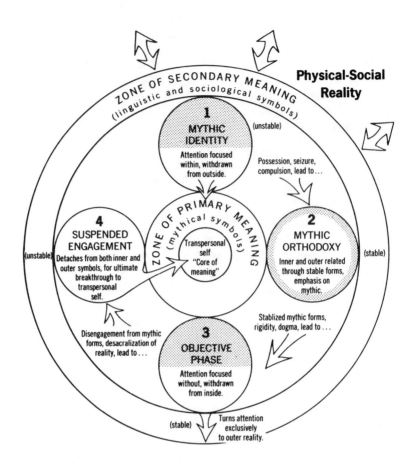

Fig. 1. The Four Stages of MYTHIC ENGAGEMENT

The symbolic vocabularly of the psyche is mythic, but determined by an outer, socially grounded system of conventions. Relationship to both inner and outer dimensions is mediated by this fixed vocabulary of mythic symbols.

Continuing to follow the clockwise movement (historical sequence), we come to a point where, either individually or collectively, the traditional system of orthodox symbols is experienced as insufficient, inappropriate, outdated, or whatever. In the mind no longer satisfied by the conventional symbolism a loss of meaning is felt, and a search is instigated for renewal of the sense of meaning. This may turn inward (back to stage 1), culminating in a novel mystical revelation and the beginnings of a reformist movement, or a new religious form. Or it may turn outward, as in our present historical situation, leading to a debunking of all mythology and focusing on the "objective" processes of the real.

The mastery of outer reality then progresses to an unprecedented degree, but there is a corresponding sense of loss of inner meaning, a desacralization of experience. This initiates an involuntary movement of compensation, either back into orthodoxy (regression) or forward into the psychological variety of spiritual disciplines, which have the advantage of focusing on the mythic within, rather than reconfusing myth with reality (and sacrificing the gains of objectivity).

The clockwise movement around the figure may be thought of as historical progression, but there are other relationships suggested by the diagram. Stages that are opposite each other tend to be oppositional in character. Myths are the "shadow" (neglected, unconscious function) of the scientist, and reality orientation the "shadow" of the mystic. The opposite viewpoint is specifically excluded from consciousness and hence, as we shall see, comes to operate in an unconscious, left-handed way, often undermining the intentions of the dominant function. Stage 4 disciplines, for example, emphasize the psychological, while stage 2 systems emphasize the literal aspects of primary meaning. And in the more conscious forms of stage 4 disengagement, such as Zen, experience must bypass all fixed categories, doctrines, dogmas, whereas orthodox forms often specifically prohibit the seeking of direct religious experience.

We have here our recurrent and major styles, traditions of relationship between secular and sacred modes of consciousness. Our present historical vantage point gives us a perspective hitherto inaccessible. We can see both the advantages and the deficiencies of our earlier modes, and we can and must weigh our present one.

We know that mythic seizure, while ecstatic, is also tricky and leads into identity with the forms of numinous experiencing. We know that orthodoxies, when no longer nurturing, are straitjackets. And we have our scientific methodological feet under us well enough, it would seem, to be able to stand up and see how we feel. What are the deficiencies of *homo scientificus* as a major world outlook? Do we like the purely mechanistic vision of the universe that stretches before us? Or do we still long for the kind of vision that gives us a place in a living cosmos we can find more meaningful? And how come these yogis are doing such a booming business on our doorstep, just when we thought we had kicked the peddlers of such illusions out the door, once and for all?

There are many of us who feel that none of these modes is an acceptable way of relating to our present world of inner and outer realities, of revolutionary possibilities and archaic impulses. We need an approach to living, here and now, that affirms and acknowledges our being in physical matter and yet reawakens the life of the spirit.

Stage 5 in my developmental sequence of the mythic imagination is not yet complete. And that is really what the rest of this book is about. In the remainder of this chapter I work with a broad range of materials illustrating the relation between human consciousness and myth. My object is not only to point out certain patterns in their traditional relationship, but ever to look through these, transparently as it were, for hints, premonitions, of what may be evolving within us now.

There is a vitality in our delusions, the kernel of a method in our madness. In the next section we journey through madness, possession, and later into the terrifying onset of the shamanic vocation. In each case we shall see a human response, a kind of dialogue with an inner world of terror or ecstasy, a firsthand contact with the shapeshifting universe of the psyche. Whether we consider what we find to be simply a fun-house mirror of ordinary biological urges (as do the psychoanalysts), or contact with another world filled with living beings of its own (as have our ancestors since time untold), I leave to your own judgment. What is certain is that our dreams and visions, the dramatis personae of our imaginations do act *as if* they were independent entities with a life of their own. And yet, paradoxically, often as not they show up as hidden, undiscovered parts of ourselves. We begin with mythic identity, the most intimate and basic of our relationships to myth. The shaman's doorway leads us now into the psyche (stage 1), and perhaps we shall come back out through it again at the end of the book (stage 5).

Mythic Identity—Oracles and Schizophrenics

Anyone who has had a true vision from God will detect a false one almost immediately. . . . It is the most impossible of all impossibilities that this can be the work of the imagination. . . .

Saint Theresa

Unless I have the incorruptible conviction: This is the solution, I do nothing. Not even if the whole party tried to drive me to action. I will not act; I will wait, no matter what happens. But if The Voice speaks, then I know the time has come to act.

Adolf Hitler

Men shiver with apprehension when one among their number is seized by that inner reality beyond and within the world of our mutual common-sense interests. It is our long-term collective experience with madmen and prophets, psychopaths and evangelists, that has bred this response. We are all, I think, subliminally aware of the uncanny force that has been released by single men who have touched the truly potent levels within. The messages that have come from them have polarized populations, started wars, and made their influence felt through centuries.

And we know the psychological level of that shiver as well . . . the immediate, experiential response that Otto and Jung termed "numinous." On some inner, primary level we are all susceptible to the mythic, the supernatural. We are the offspring of generations of believers, men and women who have lived and died for a myth. And on this same level those strange, electric souls, human beings we call charismatic, reach behind the logic and common sense of our waking world to touch the place in us where the myth is more real than the evidence of our senses. If you have ever locked eyes with a schizophrenic you may have had a shivery, uncanny sensation; it is the half-formulated feeling-thought that this being in front of you inhabits a different world, that it is as real as your own, and that you may have just stepped into it.

When a breakthrough of mythic meaning seizes an individual in our midst there are a few alternatives. If his message speaks the language of the local collective religious system, he may be appointed official seer, oracle, or saint. If the message is unorthodox, but still speaks to enough people, a new religious movement may be started, in which his role is that of prophet, evangelist, or radical reformer. The movement may be successful or the reverse: he may be crucified. In either case he could be anathematized or canonized by a subsequent generation. Lastly, if the message is outside orthodox religious forms and speaks to almost no one (or is simply incomprehensible), he may be either ignored or locked up.

Hence the politics of mental illness. As a number of reformers have recently reminded us,* a major aspect of any mental disorder is how the local society defines it. One culture's

*R. D. Laing, Thomas Szasz, for example.

prophet is another's madman, and so on. But is there not more to it than this?

The great religious movements in our history have always brought with them messages of transpersonal importance. There has been something in each of them that spoke through the limitations of our separate identities to our common situation. The truly effective transpersonal message must somehow touch and speak to the collective archetypal predicament. In its subsequent elaborations, such an original message is stabilized and reinforced by a doctrine, a morality, an approach to living. In this way our great religious traditions have invited participation, structuring the mystical experience into the business of daily life for everyman.

But some messages simply do not make it, they are not for everyone; rather it seems as if their import might better have been kept personal instead of being broadcast. In the late fifties and early sixties a strange little man used to stand with his podium and flag on the corner of 116th Street and Broadway in Manhattan, across the street from Columbia University. He would preach loudly and emphatically to whoever would listen, and even sometimes when there was no one there to hear. He was unquestionably sincere and hardworking in his evangelism. He was on that corner almost every day, rain or shine, even in winter. The only problem was that the man was almost incomprehensible. Finally, from listening to him several times and reading his literature, I began to get the gist of his message: he was a messiah, at least potentially. He called himself an "Umke," (a word with private associations no doubt) who was one of four "Umkes" abroad in the world. When the four finally got together they would rule the world. A new dynasty for mankind would ensue.

During the many years I watched this man I do not think he made many converts. People usually walked away muttering or smiling. Sometimes students came to tease, whereupon the "Umke" man would become furious and even more incoherent and would march to another corner. Perhaps it just appealed to Columbia students to have a chance to bait a messiah. But

more meaningfully, I think they were testing. And they found
what they wanted. A few inches below the surface of this
would-be-world-transforming messiah was a snarl of personal
problems: inadequacy, temper, irascibility. The Umke-man's
religion was a personal one and had no room in it for anyone
else (except maybe those three other Umkes).

In any religious experience or mythic belief we must learn
to look for that personal formula. What does this particular
belief mean for this particular individual? How does it function
in the context of the rest of his life? Is what appears to be a
transpersonal message good for everyone, or maybe only meant
for him? This is indeed the danger of personal mythic seizure.
The breakthrough of very potent energy from what Jung
called the *archetypal* level of the psyche is inevitably intercontaminated with the personal psychological configurations of
the individual.

The wisdom in our great orthodox traditions is that they
bind the individual pattern to a more general formula. The
successful transpersonal pattern must be generally applicable
to an incredible range of human temperaments and predicaments. The myth must be able to touch something in everyone.
Madman and saint both speak of God, but the question is,
how? Baba Ram Dass* tells of going to visit his younger brother
in a mental hospital. The brother believes himself to be Christ,
and has been institutionalized for this delusion. Ram Dass
comes to visit, wearing Hindu holy-man clothes, beads, and
flowing beard. The brother, in ordinary attire and suddenly
feeling very conventional by comparison, asks, "How come
I'm in here and you're not?" The answer—which Ram Dass
agrees is a most complex and difficult one—must be looked
for more in terms of the personal dimension of his belief than
of its transpersonal message.

In the context of a personal life the mythological or transpersonal elements are invariably shaped by the unique personal

*This is Richard Alpert's name in religion, given by his *guru*. See *Be Here
Now* (New York: Crown Publishing, 1971) or *The Only Dance There Is*
(Garden City, New York: Doubleday Anchor, 1974).

configurations of that individual. His idea of God is coterminous with his private vision of perfection, and his conception of the Devil must always resemble his own deepest personal fears and loathing. In any breakthrough of the numinous level of meaning, whether we call it a religious illumination or a mythic seizure, there will be this admixture of personal and transpersonal. And we might imagine a continuum, from highly personal visions at the one end to those of a more generally applicable, transpersonal cast at the other. The more entangled with personal problems, the more subjective and purely private someone's mythology must be, hence the more likely to lead to institutionalization rather than messiahship.

Heinz Werner, the developmental psychologist, hypothesizes that perception and imagination are rooted in a common faculty in the nervous system and were originally identical.[27] He cites evidence obtained from the study of eidetic imagery and perception in support of this hypothesis. And surely there is plenty of psychological evidence that our perception is mediated by a process of internal imagery, generated from within yet neatly fitted to incoming sensory data in such a way that we seem to be experiencing the object directly. These inner images are bound to our concepts and learning history, and organize and shape the tumultous data of incoming sensory stimulation to both our motivations and expectations. This is commonly called "set" in perceptual theory.

But when the mythic imagination is involved, perception and experiencing also take up archetypal imagery, along with the problems of the personality and outer events, in a truly bizzare admixture. Perhaps we can best follow this complicated process through a living example.

Dorothy is a woman in her mid-forties. She has been committed to a mental hospital for several years, diagnosed as a "paranoid schizophrenic."[28] Her private reality is of a substance with myth: she lives in a world populated by the famous of both history and mythology. They are her grandfathers, great-grandfathers, and uncles. They include "John the Baptiste," "Uncle Satin" (Satan), "The Diviner, first Catholic Pope on

earth," and "Grandfather Cain" and "Grandfather Abel" (pro-
nounced ah-bell), founder of the "House of Abel," to which
she is related.

Uncle Satin rules "Chosen," China, and was first priest to
"the god of the fields and grain." He it was who built the Great
Wall and brought peace and plenty to the land of Chosen.
Dorothy's family came to this country, she tells us, to settle
in the "fountain of youth" region; they were "homeopathics,"
and were seeking "the 'right water,' that had the power to mend
bones . . . " So far, so good. Dorothy tells us she is related
to the great family of "Royals." And all these people, famous
in both history and mythology, are her relatives. "Royals" are
defined as people "who live by God's laws."

But now enter the heavies. Dorothy is persecuted—no, tormented—by another class of being in this paradisal, mythic
landscape. These sinister creatures she calls "the British and
Dutch Confucia." They are described as having large pointed
ears, incipient horns (not always visible), and are cloven-
hoofed, or as she says on one occasion, "ape-hoofed." The
Confucia, in contrast to the Royals, do not live by God's laws,
they are unscrupulous, they commit rape and "steal blood."

Dorothy has been a particular object of these wicked creatures' attentions and we hear "they were at my person night
after night." Finally her father "caught their old Dutch agent
(chief of the Confucia) by the collar and threw him down the
stairs." But their persecution has not stopped there. Questioned
by her psychiatrist as to why she has been confined to a state
mental hospital, she responds, "The British and Dutch are
doing that." The Confucia are in fact responsible for most of
the trouble in the world, wherever it happens. "They break into
nations, cause civil strife, and steal." They love to contaminate
the blood of Royals with their own, and now they are intermixed throughout the human race, and you can hardly tell
them apart—"except," Dorothy tells us, "by the evil in their
hearts."

There would seem to be three levels of ingredient going into
the makeup of Dorothy's curious world. First, the input of

sensory data. Dorothy can walk down hallways, eat her meals, respond to questions, talk to people. But on a secondary level a mythological or archetypal dynamism is evidently at work, bending the materials of her perception, memory, and knowledge of history into mythic forms: "fountain of youth," "gods of the fields and grain," and the strange, animal-human Confucia, who immediately recall to us the fauns and satyrs of mythology. The third level is personal. Though the ingredients, the "bricks" as Joseph Campbell calls them, are clearly universal archetypes, the particular form they take is unique and personal in scope. "Uncle Satin," for example, does not behave as Satan is supposed to (we might expect him to be the chief of the "Confucia"). Rather, he is a Royal, "who lives by God's laws." The action of this archetypal company in their mythological landscape follows no known or recognizable pattern. For an understanding of their dynamics we must look into Dorothy's personal psychology. And here we must restrict ourselves to a few guesses, since there is little additional information on this case. She is greatly concerned about matters of family, and her own sense of self-importance is connected with this issue. She dramatizes her relatives as the great and famous persons of her strange world. In this she is not unlike many of us except insofar as she is completely unable to distinguish the mythic from the outer situation. Dorothy's fundamental split seems to be concerned with sexuality; she is persecuted and tormented by creatures mythologically (and explicitly) associated with sexual activities. The satyrs are associated with Pan, Dionysus, and the orgiastic, frenzied aspects of sex. I might also mention that the Greek myths tell us of women who have rejected Dionysus and have been smitten with madness: an ancient mythic truth that slept for centuries till Freud rediscovered it.

The mythic vision that has replaced the world of consensual reality for Dorothy is highly intercontaminated with her personal problems. Rarely do we see myth in pure form in the delusions of psychotics. Rather we find particular, idiosyncratic renderings of mythic themes, somehow simultaneously expressing both mythic and personal meaning. Whenever individual consciousness descends into the mythic, and whenever the mythic invades consciousness, there is always this element of the personal present. We see this in guided fantasy sessions and in the majority of psychedelic experiences as well. While the hidden archetypal level of meaning often seeks to express itself through the only available symbolic units— usually one's more conscious memory images—so too are the a-priori mythological forms bent and shaped by the configurations of personal psychology, especially by nonconscious areas of conflict, repression, or fear.

In the taped psychiatric interview with Dorothy (available in the McGraw-Hill series, "*The Disorganized Personality*"), her whole manner of speaking, the tone of her voice, carry much better than I can describe her self-assurance and certitude about the "rightness" of her perception of the world. She talks like a Sunday-school teacher explaining biblical events to a class of children. For Dorothy, her crazy, topsy-turvy, mythical-personal vision has become an orthodox, literal dogma. What ought to function as a symbolic metaphor for her own psychological state is read as the literal workings of reality. Hence the possibilities for therapy to be found in working through the symbolism of her mythic delusion, in the way I have described as "as-if," are lost—projected concretely on the world outside.

For this reason psychiatrists generally regard paranoid schizophrenia as the most difficult to cure of all of the schizoid disorders. In contrast to the more withdrawn type of schizophrenic in which the person retreats to an inner world of his or her own making,* the paranoid projects his psycho-mythology on the world outside, entirely losing the ability to differentiate projection from actuality.

When more than one person shares the same belief system— unique though it may be—we are already moving in the direction of religion rather than pathology. The world abounds in

*See *I Never Promised You a Rose Garden* by Hannah Green for a readable account of this inner type of mythologizing.[29]

all kinds of very peculiar belief systems which are mistaken for literal reality: that the earthly paradise is here, but within the earth, the doors of access being in the walls of high mountains; that the last judgment is literally just about to come upon us, with tombs opening and stars falling; that various Hindu teenagers are the world messiah, and so on. Some belief systems have institutionalized the phenomenon of mythic identity and include it among religious and ceremonial practices. But what is most striking is that in these cases the madness often follows patterns which are perfectly familiar to the mythology and symbolism of the belief system. Possession by demons is such a phenomenon.

Possession might be thought of as one of the purest forms of mythic identity. The directiveness, the responsibility, that comes from what is generally called "the ego" is suspended, and what seems to be an alien force seizes consciousness. Looking into the variety of forms taken by this phenomenon around the world, we find that in almost all cases the possessing agency acts "as-if" it were an entity, even a personality. The entity is usually recognizable as a personification appearing in local mythology. If the possessed person is a Christian, the possessing entity acts "as-if" it were the very Devil or one of his minions. If the possessed is an Eskimo, the entity acts "as-if" it were one of the deities or spirits familiar to the shamanistic pantheon.

In rural areas around the Japan Sea there has been until very recently a widespread belief in possession by "fox spirits." While possession is a universal event, and possession by animal spirits happens in other parts of the world (for example, lycanthropy or werewolfism in Europe), the specific details of this form of possession are unique to Japan. The usual symptoms of fox possession are

a torrent of nonsensical talk, voices speaking in one's ear, the face elongated to resemble a pointed snout, a huge and indiscriminate appetite and nocturnal feelings of suffocation. . . . The patient's personality is apparently entirely displaced by that of the fox, who speaks through her mouth in a dry, cracked voice, often in a language of a coarse obscenity which horrifies the poor woman when she returns to her normal state of mind.[30]

What we might call schizophrenia is there recognized as possession, and the therapy is not chlorpromazine but exorcism, either by a professional exorcist or a Buddhist or Shinto priest. In a more gentle way than our Christian exorcists, they engage in a *mondō*, a dialogue with the possessing entity. And as all three, exorcist, possessed, and fox spirit, believe the local mythology, it often seems to be successful.

Trance and possession are common events throughout the nontechnological societies of this planet. Across much of Asia, Africa, and South America, trance is entered and possession sought in all manner of religious ceremonies, and special ceremonies used for problem-solving and the curing of illness. In most of these cultures trance is entered voluntarily so that that possession may take place. Almost universally, entering the trance is simultaneous with the suspension of the conscious part of the personality. This is done so that what is believed to be a supernatural agency, which has no physical means of expression, may enter and inhabit the body for the special purposes for which the communication has been sought.

At the times when he or she is "possessed," a person is not held responsible for his actions whatever they may be, for it is believed that he is no longer in control; rather his physical being is the vehicle of the spirit or deity. A classic example of a spiritual tradition of which possession is an extremely important part is found in the *Voudon* religion of Haiti which, like the quite similar complex of Afro-Brazilian cults, is an admixture of African and native Indian elements.

In Voudon the possessing entities are called *loa*, which means more than "spirits," coming rather closer to "gods." The loa are not regarded as distant cosmic principles, but rather as living and accessible entities, concerned with and involved in the fate of men.[31] And regularly, it is believed, the loa perform that act of spiritual intimacy which the Christian believes happened only once in history, the descent of the god into a human body for the purposes of communion with men, a sharing of their common plight. The possession is always regarded as a sacred event.

In their major characteristics, the loa are familiar archetypes from the mythology of the world. They resemble rather closely Aphrodite, or Hades, or the ubiquitous Hermes-trickster figures. But their specific disguises belong to the insular mythology of Haiti. Ghede, for example, Lord of the Dead, is strikingly costumed in black coattails and top hat, wearing wraparound sunglasses with one lens knocked out. The loa are believed to be originally ancestral forces which, with increasing distance from their personal, historical lives, become more the representatives of cosmic principle. As Maya Deren suggests, "the ancestor becomes archetype."[32]

The priest or *houngan,* as he is called, is occupied with serving the loa and often functions as their vehicle or *serviteur.* The loa are in fact really believed to be sustained by the worship and attentions of men.* When a loa "mounts" a serviteur, as they say, those in attendance are quick to notice the characteristics of personal style that distinguish a particular loa. This may include a facial expression, tone of voice, gait, peculiar mannerism. When the loa is recognized, he is usually costumed appropriately and the music is changed to suit his taste. The god is celebrated as present in their midst.

Ghede usually behaves in a shamelessly erotic fashion, which is taken for granted as one of his recognized attributes. "Only Ghede can swallow his own drink—a crude rum steeped in twenty-one of the hottest spices known."[33] And this drink is given to a manifestation of Ghede—partly, as Maya Deren suggests, as proof against a possibly insincere serviteur who might wish to take erotic advantage by pretending to be mounted by Ghede and in turn try to mount some of the more attractive parishioners. It is unlikely, she adds, that someone not in trance could stand this rigorous test.

---

*There is a sophisticated psychological insight here. As in Tibetan Buddhism, the "gods" are recognized as ultimately manifestations of human thought forms.

Possession by the supernatural in Voudon and its related traditions, then, is cultivated and ritualized. It is not the same as the random and chaotic phenomena that appear in our mental hospitals. The mythic seizure, sought in its terrifying immediacy as in shamanism, is still bound to the forms of an orthodox mythological tradition. The relativity always accompanies contacts of the personal with the numinous, and produces those intensely private mythologies which are incomprehensible to others and are labeled as madness, is here constrained by the forms of the traditional mythology. The serviteur, like the shaman, is mad in the service of the community. As with the shaman, his plunge into contact with the supernatural is protected by his communally indoctrinated beliefs as to what he may expect and what his role is.

For those who have never witnessed a genuine possession it is difficult to convey the "otherness" of this event. Even those predisposed to dismiss such things as autohypnosis or charlatanism occasionally find it mind-boggling. The following description was recorded by an observer from a *National Geographic* team traveling through Tibet in the 1930s. The ceremony discribed is a rather commonplace one in which the spirit of Chechin, one of the chief guardian deities of Tibet, enters a human oracle called the *Sungma* for ritual communication—usually as to questions of a political or religious nature.

Soon the Sungma began to accompany the Lamas in their mumbling prayers, while the incense went the round, and the silent audience awaited the spirit of *Chechin*. Suddenly sonorous blasts and large trumpets and deafening clash of cymbals burst forth, and the Sungma moved uneasily in his seat.

A deep, gargling sound escaped him, and his hands clasped his throat. The attending lama, a brother of Balung, now lifted the huge (fifty-pound, iron) hat upon the Sungma's head and tied it firmly under the chin. By this time the performer was fully possessed by the spirit. The gargling sound is believed to be a sure sign of the presence of *Chechin*, who the classic relates, died by suffocating himself with a kattak, a silk scarf.

Balung (the Sungma) sat dreaming for a while; then all at once his body began to sway and his legs to shake. Frantically he threw himself backward while the lamas held him and tried to balance him. He spat and groaned; blood oozed from his mouth and nostrils; his face became purple—inflated to such an extent that the leather chin strap burst.

He took a sword handed to him, a strong Mongolian steel blade. In the twinkling of an eye he twisted it with his naked hands into several loops and knots!

The lamas continued their praying; the Sungma swayed and shook, groaned and sputtered blood. The audience became frightened and surged back.

The Sungma tossed the 50-pound hat above his head; adjusted it again, meanwhile puffing like a steam engine. The perspiration running down his face mingled with the blood which oozed from his nose and mouth.

The attending lamas wiped his face, and tried to comfort him. A lama now stood in front of him with a round silver platter on which reposed an offering, a triangular pyramid of *tsamba*, or barley flour dough. This the lama held to the Sungma's face, so that his forehead touched it. The lamas changed the tune and tempo of their chant.

Still shaking, the possessed Sungma took a handful of rice and threw it violently into the crowd. At this point the abbot of the monastery approached, bowing and kowtowing, only to be beaten severely on the back with the flat of a sword wielded by the Sungma. Fear spread among the crowd; the abbot fled; the Sungma continued to shake from head to foot with uncontrollable convulsions![34]

There would certainly seem to be something *other* than the personality of the Sungma present here; and neither the oracle nor the lama might have predicted the behavior of the "deity." The "deity," in fact, acts like a madman, as such behaviors would surely be interpreted outside the mythological context. It is mentioned that "Sungma Balung chu dje must not eat chickens, eggs, or pork, or take snuff; for Chechin, it is said, has a violent dislike for these things. Because Balung chu dje is inordinately fond of snuff, Chechin made him in one of his shaking fits smash his beautiful agate snuff bottle."[35] The spirit possessing the Sungma or the shaman may not at all be counted on to have his own interests in mind; frequently the contrary is the case. Hence the dread and terror of such intimate supernatural confrontations.

To underline this *otherness*, as a concluding point in this discussion of possession, I relate the following grisly incident. Balung's predecessor was a man named Sumpo chu dje. Like Balung, he was the oracle, the instrument of Chechin. He was originally a lama, but wished to give up his monastic life in order to marry.

Chechin did not approve of the idea of his chu dje taking a wife, and while in possession of the man's body threatened to kill him if he did so. The Mongol Sungma however, followed the dictates of his heart and married. One day while possessed by Chechin the unfortunate man disemboweled himself, and in his dying agony hung his entrails on the lamaistic images on his private altar. Later Chechin appeared in the present Balung chu dje.[36]

Thus the fate of those who "oppose the gods" in this form of relationship—there was no dialogue, no give and take here between Sumpo, the conscious ego, Sumpo the human being, and his supernatural tenant—or, if you prefer, the split-off, autonomous "content" of the personal or collective psyche that manifested as Chechin. The decision and the power are unilateral, absolute.

While the madness, the mythic identity, is bound and employed in the service of the community, it is not at all integrated within the psyche of the human medium. There is no intrapsychic development, no personal growth fostered in this kind of confrontation. The oracle is mad in the service of the community, but mad nonetheless.

In the context of the modern psyche, Jung would call such a phenomenon "possession by the archetype." The ego is subordinated to an autonomous psychic power of greater potency than itself. Our next section, on the vocation of the shaman, shows us a similar confrontation between the mythic and the personal, but one which allows more room for dialogue, for personal growth, as well as the serving of the communal good.

In these states—of schizophrenia, of possession, of mystical ecstasy—we begin to become aware of the presence of a common underlying dimension of human consciousness in which man may be totally overwhelmed by myth. But what of everyday life? Of what relevance to most of us is mythic identity?

To this the only answer I know is to tune within. I have caught myself at the most unexpected moments, and in ordinary circumstances, drifting in and out of heroic postures, martyrdoms, fantasies of Dionysian frenzy. The great value of myth is that it shows us these otherwise transient states in bold outline. And from the extreme examples found in madness and possession we may intuit a little bit about the hidden forces that seem to rule our lives, driving us with compulsive power or luring us with visions of ecstasy. It is only when we step back a little from the compulsions that pull and push us so, that we become aware how much we are swayed and how little control we have of our own behavior and destinies when caught up in identification with the dynamics of mythic imagination.

The Unearthly Calling: The Shaman's Vocation

The shaman is the archetypal technician of the sacred, and his profession is precisely the relationship between the mythic imagination and ordinary consciousness we have been discussing. There seem to be two different ways in which one may be called to this magical profession. In the first the shaman is selected either because of hereditary reasons (his ancestors were shamans) or because he asks for initiation. The second way is that of the spontaneous "vocation" (call or election), and such a shaman is believed to have been selected by the spirits. The shaman of the spontaneous call is almost invariably thought of as superior, at least among the peoples of Siberia and those of Arctic North America. The spontaneously called shamans are designated "greater shamans" and those who inherit the office "lesser shamans." The "lesser" is in a sense designated by the social community, but the "greater" by a supernatural order of power.[37]

The shaman who has been elected by the spirits shows a recognizable symptomatology: he often becomes extremely nervous and withdrawn, and begins to act strangely. He may also experience epileptoid seizures—regarded by primitive peoples almost the world over as the sign of a supernatural manifestation. The Siberian term for the psychological condition is *amurakh*: nervous, solitary, easily frightened, and with a proclivity for imitation and obscenities.

The symptoms of this preliminary phase have led many investigators to suggest that in the tradition of shamanism primitive cultures have merely found a convenient way to accomodate their psychologically ill individuals. And there may indeed be a measure of truth in this. However, it would seem simplistic and inaccurate to equate the shaman literally with any of our established diagnostic categories, whether hysteria, schizophrenia, or epilepsy, all of which have been suggested by various theorists.

While agreeing that there may be superficial similarities between certain psychopathological disorders and shamanism, Mircea Eliade suggests this is because both emerge from a common ground in the deep structure of the psyche and not because the shaman is simply a dressed-up schizophrenic or hysteric. He says,

> That such maladies nearly always appear in relation to the vocation of medicine men is not at all surprising. Like the sick man, the religious man is projected onto a vital plane that shows him the fundamental data of human existence, that is, solitude, danger, hostility of the surrounding world. But the primitive magician, the medicine man, or the shaman is not only a sick man; he is, above all, a sick man who has been cured, who has succeeded in curing himself. Often when the shaman's or medicine man's vocation is revealed through an illness or epileptoid attack, the initiation of the candidate is equivalent to a cure.[38]

The Tungus of Siberia call this initial period "the first indwelling of the spirits," and behavior that would be incomprehensible in a socialized human being, when ascribed to the presence of supernatural forces is more easily explained. In the presence of such manifestations the afflicted individual is given special consideration, and established shamans are called in to work with him.

If we contrast this with the cultural vacuum in which the schizophrenic, hysteric, or multiple personality must face his unbidden malady in our culture, then we see that the primitive culture provides a context, lacking in our own, for both acceptance and cure of such a disorder. Certainly a major part of any "mental illness" belongs to the definition of that state by the social order, as writers such as Thomas Szasz and R. D. Laing have pointed out. And in a shamanistic culture an individual suffering from what Eysenck would call "an excessively labile nervous system" would be called *amurakh*, and his condition seen not as the preliminary to a degenerative or pathological state, but as an invitation to shamanize. And the act of beginning to shamanize, or the initiation as shaman, constitutes the cure. As one shaman's account says,

No shamans were known among my nearest forefathers. My father and mother enjoyed perfect health. I am now forty years old. I am married but I have no children. Up to the age of twenty I was quite well. Then I felt ill, my whole body ailed me, I had bad headaches. Shamans tried to cure me, but it was all of no avail. When I began shamanizing myself, I got better and better. It is now ten years that I have been a shaman, but at first I used to practice for myself only, and it is three years ago only that I took to curing other people. A shaman's practice is very, very fatiguing.[39]

But the initiation of the shaman may in itself be an extremely severe ordeal, imposed either from without or within, or in many cases both. The initiation from without is usually imposed by senior shamans, and is, as British rock climbers term their most difficult climbs, "exceptionally severe." The initiate might be plunged into icy water, slashed all over with knives of quartz, left out on the ice to fast for thirty days alone; or as was done to one young Eskimo woman, hung up on some tent poles for five days in midwinter, and after being taken down, shot in the chest with a stone instead of a real bullet, "that she might attain to intimacy with the supernatural by visions of death."[40]

As I have already suggested of the rituals of initiation, these tortures certainly serve the purpose of binding the attention of the initiate to the proceedings. But in shamanism it is evident that another important purpose is served: the physical outer initiation imitates the symbolic events of the psychological, inner one.

The stages of this inner psychological initiation appear in the mythology, not only of the shamans, but of every major religious or mythological system: the old, self-concerned man must die and a new one be born. The shamans have a particularly vivid and grisly version of this symbolism, however. The Tungus say, "Before a man becomes a shaman he is sick for a long time. His understanding becomes confused. The shamanistic ancestors of his clan come, hack him to bits, tear him apart, cut his flesh in pieces, drink his blood."[41] The Yakuts, another Siberian tribe, describe it thus:

They cut off the head and place it on the uppermost plank in the *yurta*, from where it watches the chopping up of its body. They hook an iron hook into the body and tear up and distribute all the joints; they clean the bones, by scratching off the flesh and removing all the fluid. They take the two eyes out of the sockets and put them on one side. The flesh removed from the bones is scattered on all the paths in the underworld; they also say that it is distributed among the nine or three times nine generations of the spirits which cause sickness, whose roads and paths the shaman will in future know. He will be able to help with ailments caused by them; but he will not be able to cure those maladies caused by spirits that did not eat of his flesh.[42]

The shaman, thus dismembered, not only dies in and of himself, but serves as a sacrament to the spiritual forces of the universe. In this way he mystically unites himself with a sacred order of being, beyond the dimension of this or that person in this particular body.

There is a rite of Tibetan Tantrism called *chod* which follows this same pattern of sacrificial dismemberment. Since in Buddhist doctrine the universe is ultimately made up of one's own thought forms, one must break through the veil of maya that is responsible for our "illusion of separateness." Thus the celebrant summons the terrifying, cannibalistic, blood-drinking spirits in which the mythology of Tibet abounds to come and eat of himself. This is often done in a lonely place, believed to be haunted (and it should be emphasized that by most Tibetans such spirits are vividly and wholeheartedly believed in). One account of this ceremony is as follows:

To the sound of the drum made of human skulls and of the thighbone trumpet, the dance is begun and the spirits are invited to come and feast. The power of meditation evokes a goddess brandishing a naked sword; she springs at the head of the sacrificer, decapitates him, and hacks him to pieces; then the demons and wild beasts rush on the still quivering fragments, eat the flesh and drink the blood.[43]

The Buddha, according to legend, is said to have given his own flesh to starving animals and man-eating demons. And our remembrance, at this point, is drawn irresistibly to the supreme sacrament of the Christian Church.

And as they did eat, Jesus took bread, and blessed, and brake it, and gave to them, and said, Take, eat; this is my body.

And he took the cup, and when he had given thanks, he gave it to them: and they all drank of it.

And he said unto them, This is my blood of the new testament, which is shed for many. (Mark 14: 22-24, King James Version)

We are led, surely, to the conclusion that this pattern of sacramental death and rebirth is universal. It occurs not only among shamanistic hunting societies but also among the planting societies, where it is incorporated into the cycle of the crops, and the dying god is equivalent to the ear of corn that falls into the ground to die, and is born again in the new growth. But it would seem foolish to *derive* the myth from the vegetation cycle, as so many comparative mythologists have done, for it is surely of more ancient status than the neolithic planting cults. As we shall see, this symbolism is not restricted to mythology but recurs spontaneously in the inner experiences of people everywhere. As such, in the Jungian terminology, it has *archetypal* status. As Jung says,

The archetypes are the numinous, structural elements of the psyche and possess a certain autonomy and specific energy which enables them to attract, out of the conscious mind, those contents which are best suited to themselves, the symbols act as *transformers*. . . .

. . . The symbol works by suggestion; that is to say, it carries conviction and at the same time expresses the content of that conviction. It is able to do this because of the numen, the specific energy stored up in the archetype. Experience of the archetype is not only impressive, it seizes and possesses the whole personality. . . .[44]

Surely the symbolism of death and rebirth is the most fundamental of such transformation symbols. In the journals of the mystics, ecstatic experiences are most often preceded by a "dark night of the soul," an experience of aloneness, desolation, and often dying. Many Jungian analysts report episodes of initiation, death, and rebirth in the lives and dreams of their patients. In both private psychotherapy and my own research on psychedelic sessions I have repeatedly found experiences to follow this symbolic form. The real terror—and even suicidal urges—come when one does not know the mythological pattern; i.e., that the experience of deep despair is always the prelude to an invitation to rebirth. In almost every such case I have worked with or researched, the death and rebirth experience is focal, engaging both the most difficult personal problems for the individual and yet at the same time opening the doors to transpersonal experience, to renewal of the self, and to ecstasy.

Dr. Stanislav Grof, a veteran LSD researcher, finds that almost all in-depth LSD experiences hinge around a pivotal point: the sequence of death agonies leading to rebirth. He says,

The encounter with death was always accompanied by a deep existentialist crisis and an agonizing search for meaning in life. It was also the time when deep religious feelings appeared in all the subjects, without regard to their background, education, and previous beliefs.

The subjects experiencing the anguish, despair, pain and loneliness of the mentioned situations referred frequently to such concepts as "Dark Night of the Soul," "pit," "no-exit," "Dante's Hell," or other images of hell from various religions. Especially frequent seemed to be the symbols of the ancient Greeks: Tantalos exposed to eternal tortures in Hades, Sisyphus rolling incessantly his boulder, Ixion fixed on the wheel and Prometheus chained to the rock.[45]

Dr. Grof goes on,

After a certain number of sessions which differed for various subjects, an ultimate total annihilation was experienced in all subjects who reached this stage. It involved the experience of "ego death," final defeat and destruction on all imaginable levels: physical, emotional, intellectual, moral, social and transcendental. The "ego death" was immediately followed by the experience of final rebirth and liberation. The sequence of experiences always had a very definite religious emphasis. A typical symbolism for this sequence would be Christ's death on the cross and his resurrection; Shiva in the role of a destroyer; death and rebirth of Dionysus or Osiris; the legendary Phoenix hatched from the egg in the flames, destroying the parental bird and the nest; sacrifice to the goddess Kali or Astarte, escape from the strangling embrace of the Sphinx and solving her riddle, etc.[46]

The symbolic enactment of death and rebirth, then, whether experienced through a ritual or from within, is the doorway to the transpersonal. At that point the individual leaves behind his private life and concerns and enters a mythological, archetypal realm. And the meaning he finds there is not of social fulfillment but a deeper, more profound one: a place in a larger, eternal order which transcends his local boundaries of time and space.

The shaman is one who personally makes the plunge into the transpersonal. He is, as it were, the delegate of the tribe to the mythological realm. And as we have seen, the symbolism he finds there is of a universal cast. Though his symbols seem dramatis personae of the local mythological landscape, closer inspection often reveals them to be local versions of universal archetypes.

There is a rich symbolism to accompany the genesis of the shaman. Frequently animals or snakes present the call to him. Often he may follow such an animal, which leads him further and further into the wilderness, where he encounters his adventure. Another frequently occurring symbolism is the "breaking of plane." Movement in a vertical direction symbolizes both alteration in consciousness and a moving into a new dimension. One goes either to the underworld or a celestial domain. Professor Eliade has extensively documented this symbolism:

> The breaking of the plane effected by the "flight" signifies . . . an act of transcendence. It is no small matter to find already, at the most archaic stage of culture, the longing to go beyond and "above" the human condition, to transmute it by an excess of "spiritualization." For one can only interpret the myths, rites and legends to which we have been referring by a longing to see the human body behaving like a "spirit," to transmute the corporeal modality of man into a spiritual modality.[47]

The symbolic flight, the "breaking of plane" envisioned in shamanism, may thus be the prototype of the ecstasies described in all the higher forms of mysticism. One of the earliest shaman trances we know of is found in a deep crypt at Lascaux. Here lies a paleolithic shaman in trance, next to him his staff surmounted by a bird, signifying the flight of the spirit.* Poles with birds on them are found in many primitive settings. The totem pole or ritual pole in the shaman's tent indicates this vertical arrangement of universes, of the spirit world that may be reached from this one.

The ritual ascent to a celestial world is described in ecstatic

---

*I am indebted to Prof. Joseph Campbell for pointing out the symbolism of this figure.

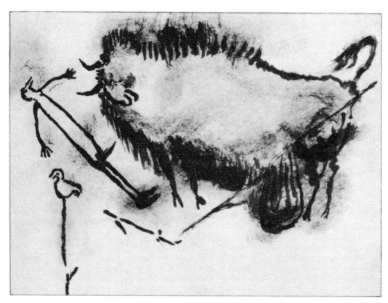

Shaman-like figure with Bird on Pole. (ink copy) Cave of Lascaux, France. Paleolithic: between 30,000 and 12,000 B.C., according to various systems of dating.

Birds on Poles, Symbolizing the Flight of the Spirit

Indian Grave Yard, Bella Coola, Br. Columbia, Canada.

Deserted Village at Cape Fox, Alaska.

Birds on Poles, Symbolizing the Flight of the Spirit

Wooden "Loon" Mask, N.W. Coast, Canada.

accounts the world over. Rainbow symbolism is a frequently occurring motif for the bridge between the worlds. Often shaman drums are decorated with rainbows, and the ribbons used in initiations are rainbow symbols. These symbols occur from Siberia to Japan to Australia. One rather vivid Australian initiation is described as follows:

The master assumes the form of a skeleton and equips himself with a small bag, in which he puts the candidate, whom his magic has reduced to the size of an infant. Then, seating himself astride the Rainbow-Serpent, he begins to pull himself up by his arms, as if climbing a rope. When near the top, he throws the candidate into the sky, "killing" him. Once they are in the sky, the master inserts into the candidate's body small rainbow serpents, *brimures* (i.e., small fresh water snakes), and quartz crystals (which have the same name as the mythical Rainbow-Serpent). After this operation the candidate is brought back to earth, still on the Rainbow-Serpent's back.[48]

The introduction of the quartz crystals or some other permanent substance—iron bones for example—into the initiate's body, is an almost universal motif. Joseph Campbell says of it, "And so here again we see a theme of death and restitution, but with a new body that is adamantine. The Oriental counterpart, which plays a role in both Hindu and Buddhist mystical literature, is the 'diamond' or 'thunderbolt' body (vajra), which the yogi achieves."[49]

Another universal theme, which may have given you a slight subliminal buzz as you read the account of the Australian shaman's ascent, is the "rope-climbing" and killing of the initiate at the top. This is the identical pattern found in the Indian rope trick, widely practiced by fakirs throughout the East. Mircea Eliade has explored the shamanistic origins of this symbolism.[50] Related symbolic rituals have the initiate climbing trees or ladders. The Siberian mythology tells of a great larch whose top reaches the heavens. On every branch is a nest, in which a shaman is placed. Sometimes they are hatched out of eggs. They grow up in the nests of this tree, often suckled by an "animal mother," another widespread motif. The Siberians

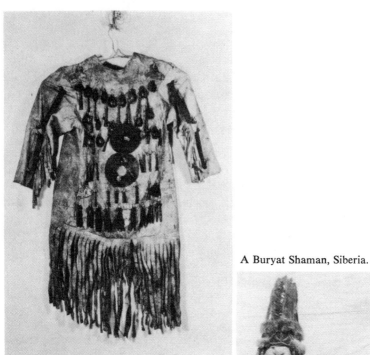

Shaman's Coat, Yakut, Siberia,
Back view.

A Buryat Shaman, Siberia.

The Shaman Costumes   Shaman
costumes display the symbolic features of the archetypical Shamanic
mythology. Iron ornaments symbol-
ize the iron bones of immortality,
as do quartz crystals. The helping
spirits are depicted in the form of
animals: bears, cats, serpents, liz-
ards. The Shaman tree often appears with its roots in the earth and
crown in the heavens. In its
branches, say the Siberian Shamans,
are nests where the Shaman Spirits
hatch to maturity, fed by their animal mothers. (*The American Museum of Natural History, New
York.*)

Shaman's Coat, Goldi, Siberia, Back view.

say that if the shaman is a great one his animal mother has
the appearance of the great elk, if a lesser one, that of a reindeer.

The spontaneous initiation of the shaman is both an archetypal and an individual event. No two are exactly the same,
and yet there are common and recurring features in all of
them. One such theme is the acquisition of "helping spirits,"
supernatural beings who become the shaman's familiars and
the instruments of his power. We remember that this theme
came up in the visionary dismemberment and sacrifice of the
shaman. The shaman acquires power over those spirits who
came to eat of his flesh. These initial encounters with the
spirit are often both violent and intimate. Isaac Tens, a Gits-
kan Indian, described his initial encounter like this:

I went up into the hills to get firewood. While I was cutting up the
wood into lengths, it grew dark towards the evening. Before I had
finished my last stack of wood, a loud noise broke out over me,
chu——, and a large owl appeared to me. The owl took hold of me,
caught my face, and tried to lift me up. I lost consciousness. As
soon as I came back to my senses I realized that I had fallen into
the snow. My head was coated with ice, and some blood was running out of my mouth.[51]

Later, he says,

My body was quivering. *While I remained in this state, I began
tossing. A chant was coming out of me without my being able to
do anything to stop it. Many things appeared to me presently: huge
birds and other animals. . . . These were visible only to me, not to
others in my house. Such visions happen when a man is about to
become a shaman; they occur of their own accord. The songs force
themselves out complete without any attempt to compose them. But
I learned and memorized these songs by repeating them.*[52]

Often the more violent the initial encounter with the "helping spirit," the more power the shaman gains. The violence
seems related to the mythological symbolism of death and
dismemberment. Often, too, the initiate is possessed by a
"nameless dread" or a "strange terror" before the encounter

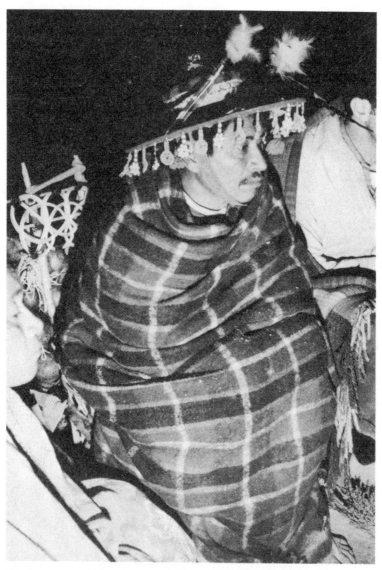

The Huichol Shaman Ramon Medina in Peyote Trance, 1968.
Courtesy Peter T. Furst.

Colas, the great Maráákame (Shaman) **of San Andrees, Cohamiata Greeting the Rising Sun.** *Courtesy Peter T. Furst.*

Shaman Shooting Sorcerer. (The Shaman *Kauyumari,* wearing the deer antlers of the peyote vision quest, shoots the sorcerer *Kieri* with an arrow. Out of his mouth come disease bubbles. In front is a Shaman's basket (with deer antlers), and a peyote button. Yarn painting, original size 2 x 2 feet by the late Huichol Artist, Shaman Ramon Medina. *Courtesy Peter T. Furst.*

Shaman Dancing with Spirits. From the FATIH ALBUM of USTAD MEHMED SIYAH KALEM, The Shaman's relation to his helping spirits may be depicted as ferocious and masterful, as in this Turkish painting, or alluring and seductive, as in Chinese Shamanism. (*The Topkapi Saray Museum, Istanbul, Turkey*).

The Spirit Nartoq. While hunting caribou, Arnaquaq met this spirit which is called Nartoq (the pregnant, or the one with the big stomach.) It rushed threateningly at him but disappeared when he prepared to defend himself. Later on it appeared to him again, but this time it was calm, and said that its name was Nartoq. The cause of its hotheadedness was that Arnaquaq himself was too easily angered. In the future he never need be afraid of it, if only he changed his disposition and abandoned his short temper. It became one of his best helping spirits. Drawn by Arnaquaq. (*Account and drawings from Knud Rasmussen, Among the Caribou Eskimos.*)

The Goblin Woman Manilaq and other Spirits. (*Account and drawings from Knud Rasmussen, Among the Caribou Eskimos.*)

with or possession by the spirit. Psychologically this would seem to point to the totally "other" nature of this confrontation, a direct meeting with what Harry Stack Sullivan called the "not-me;" that nonhuman order of intrapsychic experiencing which seems totally other than oneself.

But the acquisition of these helping spirits is not always brutal and violent; it may be rather of a gentler order of mystical experience. One shaman, quoted by Knud Rasmussen, the great Danish Arctic Explorer shows us an experience of this type:

Although everything was ready for me while I was still in my mother's belly, I tried in vain to become a conjurer up of spirits with the help of others. I never succeeded. I visited many famous shamans and gave them large presents, which they immediately passed on to other people. For it they had kept them for themselves, their children would have died. Then I went out into the solitude and soon became very melancholy. In a mystical fashion I used to break into complaints and become unhappy, without knowing the reason. Then sometimes everything would suddenly become quite different and I felt a great and inexplicable joy, a joy so strong that I could not control it. I had to break into song, into a mighty song that had no room for anything but this word: Joy! Joy! Joy! And in the midst of this mysterious bliss I became a shaman, without knowing how. But I was a shaman. I could see and hear in an entirely new way.

Every real shaman has to feel an illumination in his body, in the inside of his head or in his brain, something that gleams like fire, that gives him the power to see with closed eyes into the darkness, into the hidden things or into the future, or into the secrets of another man. I felt that I was in possession of this marvellous ability.

My first helping spirit became my name, a little *aua*. When it came to me, it was as if the door and roof rose and I received such power of vision that I could see right through the house, into the earth and up into the sky. It was the little *aua* that brought me all this inner light, by soaring over me so long as I sang. Then it stood outside in a corner of the doorway, invisible to everyone, but always ready when I called it.

An *aua* is a little spirit, a woman, who lives down on the shore. There are many of these shore spirits. They run about with pointed skin caps on their heads, their trousers are quaintly short and of bearskin. They have high boots with black patterns and furs of sealskin. Their feet are turned upwards and they seem to walk only on their heels. They hold their hands with the thumbs always pressed against the palms. They hold their arms raised with folded hands, as though they were continuously stroking their heads. They are gay and jolly when you call them, and look like small, charming, living dolls, for when standing up straight they are no taller than an arm's length.

A shark became my second helping spirit. One day I was out in my kayak when it came swimming up to me, turned over on its side and whispered my name. I was very surprised, because I had never seen a shark before. They are very rare up here. After that it helped me with every kind of hunt and was always with me when I needed it.

These two, shore spirit and shark, were my most important helping spirits and they helped me with everything I wished. The song I used to sing when I called them did not have many words and went like this:

> Joy! Joy!
> Joy! Joy!
> I see the little shore spirit,
> My name.
> Joy! Joy!

I could repeat these words over and over again, until finally I burst into tears, the prey to a strange fear.

Then I could suddenly shiver all over my body, as I shouted out again:

> A—a—a—ah!
> Joy! Joy!
> Now I want to go home.
> Joy! Joy![53]

This shaman has consciously aspired to the vocation, but that is not enough. One must play the game of "as-if" and wait. And when the divine seizure comes it may come suddenly and totally other than one's expectations. One is in the grip of the spirit, and as Isaac Tens says, "A chant was coming out of me without my being able to do anything to stop it. . . . Such visions . . . occur of their own accord." The vision may come in the form of a great owl which brutally knocks one bleeding into the snow, leaving no doubt that the spirit is totally other than oneself; or a fierce walrus that seizes one from his kayak, a wolverine, or a shark. And sometimes the call may come in the form of an omen, a series of events, the import of which a mythically unattuned mind might pass right by.

But yet again, the long-awaited moment may come in a song of joy and a little spirit woman with a pointed cap and quaint trousers. And the song she has to teach is one of universal import: that in essence, this universe of terrors, when approached with the right consciousness, may yield an intense joy or a "mysterious bliss." And the little woman is familiar too. She recalls to us stories of the "good people" or "little people" the world over.

The shaman's description of the little woman leaves us with no doubt that he has "seen" her. Whether we consider this an hallucination or an eidetic image, we see that his description is highly visual, not conceptual. Whatever the process within the shaman that sponsors this (as we would term it) "hallucination," it does so in an imagistic rather than a conceptual way.

We can make a deduction here: Whatever process in us (European and American twentieth-century man) is responsible for our imagistic, nondirected, prelogical thinking emerges when our attention is relaxed, not engaged. Also it tends to be "autistic," concerned with ourselves, in an inadvertent, unconscious way. With the shaman it is otherwise. First, his imagery partakes of both the local geography and the local mythology of his tribe: reindeer, seals, a larch tree as the world axis, with its shaman nests, and so on. But his imagery also partakes of the collective, archetypal level of symbolism.

We must assume that the local mythology of shamanism, with its cosmology, symbols, and initiation rites, is derived from individual plunges into the realm of primary meaning, the realm of the archetypes. But at the same time the structure of those individual experiences is mediated by the local mythic symbols, which function as a kind of mythological vocabulary. Through this vocabulary the individual may better understand and relate to his own experiences, and also transmit their import to others.

The shaman obviously has access to dimensions of consciousness usually unavailable to us. Whether in trance or awake, he seems to be able to see things that others do not see. In our culture this condition is regarded invariably as a symptom of psychotic episode. Yet the shaman is not psychotic; he is a fully functional member of his local social order, and, as many investigators have pointed out, often among the most intelligent and creative people of the community. Joseph Campbell says of the effects of the shamanic initiation:

It has been remarked by sensitive observers that, in contrast to the life-maiming psychology of a neurosis (which is recognized in primitive societies as well as in our own but not confused there with shamanism), the shamanistic crisis, when properly fostered, yields an adult not only of superior intelligence and refinement, but also of greater physical stamina and vitality of spirit than is normal to the members of his group. The crisis, consequently, had the value of a superior threshold initiation: superior, in the first place, because spontaneous, not tribally enforced, and in the second place, because the shift of reference of the psychologically potent symbols has been not from the family to the tribe, but from the family to the universe. The energies of the psyche summoned into play by such an immediately recognized magnification of the field of life are of greater force than those released and directed by the group-oriented, group-contrived, visionary masquerades of the puberty rites and men's dancing ground. They give a steadier base and larger format to the character of the individual concerned, and have tended, also, to endow the phenomenology of shamanism itself with a quality of general human validity, which the local rites—of whatever community—simply do not share.[54]

The shaman is, then, a cosmically instructed man. His initiation is appropriate to the outer forms of his existence, yet bears an archetypal stamp. It parallels the mythological sequence of initiation the world over, from the ancient mysteries to contemporary psychedelic experience.

There is an urge to immediate, ecstatic, shamanistic awareness present in the psyches of many, many modern people right now. And many aspiring shamans have gained access to some remarkably potent chemical sacraments, capable of evoking the depths of the psyche. As Timothy Leary urged the would-be, turned-on shamans of the sixties:

Drop-out—Detach yourself from the external social drama which is as dehydrated and ersatz as T.V.

Turn-on—Find a sacrament which returns you to the Temple of God, your own body. Go out of your mind. Get high.

Tune-in—Be reborn. Drop-back in to express it. Start a new sequence of behavior that reflects your vision.

Actions which are conscious expressions of the turn-on, tune-in, drop-out rhythm are religious.

The wise person devotes his life exclusively to the religious search—for therein is found the only ecstasy, the only meaning.[55]

And many people, out of the sixties and into the seventies, are doing or trying to do just that, seek their ecstasy even at the cost of the destructive effects of illegal, impure chemicals.

But beside the archaic, retarded government restrictions on research with these remarkable substances, another major problem is making itself manifest. We have no symbolic vocabulary, no grounded mythological tradition to make our own experiences comprehensible to us. We have, in fact, no senior shamans to help ensure that our dismemberment be followed by a rebirth.

2

The Enactment of Vision

The Mother of the Sea Creatures

The playhouse in which the real visionary work of the shaman must be performed is the neighborhood theater—no matter how modest—a collection of yurts, igloos, or perhaps a more imposing longhouse. To the extent that the shaman fulfills his role as "technician of the sacred," he must make his visionary capabilities available to his friends and neighbors. This he does in healing ceremonies for individuals or ceremonies conducted in behalf of the entire tribe, to solve a collective problem.

To the extent that the shaman is successful it is because he has been able to contact, in a visionary experience, an imagery of more than personal significance. Thus we often find, amongst the features of the local geography—the seals, tundra, and caribou of the Arctic Eskimo, for example— themes of a more general archetypal cast, familiar to mythology the world over.

The following visionary enactment, the visit to "the Mother of the Sea Creatures," is practiced by coastal-dwelling Arctic Eskimos as a remedial ritual when the seal-hunting has been poor. But look through the local mythic and social elements to the archetypal forms beyond, and you will see a mythic structure of great age and power. The following is from Andreas Lommel's translation of Rasmussen's description:

Before the great magician the path through the earth down into the sea opens up of its own accord; he goes down it without meeting any obstacles, as though falling through a tube . . . if he comes to the woman's house and finds that a wind-wall has been built in front of it, this means that she is hostile to men. The magician must then immediately throw himself against the wall, knock it down and trample it into the ground. Her house is like an ordinary human house, only the roof is missing—it is open at the top so that from her place by the lamp she can keep an eye on the dwelling-places of men. All kinds of game—common seals, bearded seals, walruses, and whales—are gathered in a dragnet on the right of her lamp, where they lie puffing and blowing; only for the sharks she has another place, and these live in her chamberpot; that is why sharks taste of urine.

The only obstacle to the shaman's entry is a large dog that lies across the doorway and blocks the path. People say that the Mistress of the Underworld was married to the dog before she was abducted by the stormy petrel. The dog shows his teeth and growls threateningly like a ferocious animal that does not want to be disturbed; often it lies there gnawing at the bones of a man who is still alive; without hesitating or showing fear, the shaman should push the dog aside and leap into the house. Here he meets the father, who grabs hold of him and tries to shut him up with the spirits who are atoning for their sins. He must say promptly: "I am of flesh and blood." Then nothing will happen to him. As a sign of her anger, the Mother of the Sea Creatures is sitting with her back to the lamp, with her back to all the animals she would otherwise send up to the shores. Her hair, washed down over her face and eyes, is untidy and dishevelled.

As soon as the shaman enters he should seize her by the shoulders and turn her face to the lamp and to the animals, he should stroke her hair and smooth it in a friendly fashion and say: "Those up above can no longer help the seals out of the sea by their front flippers." To this the woman answers: "Your sins and the levity of your women with the births (this refers to abortions and the breaking of taboos during pregnancy) are blocking the way." The shaman must employ all his art in order to pacify her anger. As soon as she has been mollified she picks up the animals and drops them one by one on the ground. An eddying springs up, as though a whirlpool were circling in the house, and the animals vanish into the sea. This means good hunting and plenty.

Now it is time for the magician to return to those waiting for him in the camp. They hear him speeding towards them from far off. The roar of his travelling comes closer and closer; with a mighty "pu—a" he emerges behind the curtain, as a sea beast that compresses its lungs and shoots up out of the depths.

For a moment there is silence; no one must break this silence, until the shaman says: "Let us hear." And the shaman continues in the solemn language of the spirits: "Word will rise up." And then everyone in the house must confess the infringements of the taboo of which they are guilty. They interrupt one another saying: "Perhaps it is my fault." Men and women cry out, filled with the fear of bad hunting and hunger; they begin to confess all the wrong they have done. The name of each person in the house is called out, everyone has to confess; in this way they all learn a great deal of which no one had any inkling. Each one hears the secrets of the other. But in spite of all the sins that come to light the shaman often speaks like an unhappy man who has made a mistake. Again and again he bursts out with the words: "I am seeking the reasons in things that have not happened. I am talking like a man who knows nothing." Then suddenly it happens that someone comes out with a secret sin that he wanted to hide, and then the shaman utters a great cry of relief. "That was it!" Often it is the very young women and men who have sinned and are to blame for the misfortune that has come upon the settlement. But if the women are young and step forward weeping, this is always a sign that they are good women. For in confession lies forgiveness. Everyone is filled with a great joy that a disaster has been averted, and they are quite sure that the following day there will be a glut of game.[1]

The visit to the Mother of the Sea Creatures is, as it were, a public dream, and the shaman dreams for the entire community. It seems to contain all the elements that Carl Jung described as belonging to the "big dream." Primitive people the world over recognize two major classes of dream: the first is the kind concerned with the more ordinary events of recent experience, or memorable incidents; but the second is the kind of dream that often seems especially powerful or mysterious, that bestows an initiation of some kind or carries a portent for the entire tribe. These are often referred to as "big dreams."

Now, the visit to the Mother of the Sea Creatures meets the

requirements of a "big dream." Many of the elements of this remarkable vision are archetypally familiar. The dog who guards the entrance to the underworld is a universal motif. We need only recall the dog Cerberus, fearsome guardian of the entrance to the Greek underworld, or Anubis, the jackal-headed god who guides souls through the Egyptian underworld. And in the Mother of the Sea Creatures we meet what Jung called "the dual mother motif." The Great Mother is most often recognized as the source of life, regeneration, and fertility. But she is also the "devouring mother" in her role as the mistress of the underworld. She is the universe, which having given all things life again devours its offspring. She is both bestower of life and that which reclaims it. She is capable of yielding bounty, and hence just as capable of withholding it.

Jung says, "The animal is a representative of the unconscious," and, "All animals belong to the Great Mother, and the killing of any wild animal is a transgression against the mother."[2] And we remember in this regard that the shaman makes only veiled reference to his real reason for wanting the Mother to release the animals: "Those up above can no longer help the seals out of the sea by their front flippers."

In Greek mythology we find that Hecate, mistress of the underworld, is also referred to as a birth goddess and as a "multiplier of cattle." Her consort is the Lord of the Dead, who universally passes judgment and extracts atonement as does the "father" in the shaman's vision. We are reminded too of the myth of the hero, with the ever recurring "night sea journey" motif. The hero's quest of treasure or boon often takes him to the bottom of the sea or deep within the earth. And Gilgamesh, that prototype of the hero, seeks in the depths of the sea for the herb of immortality, the secret of rebirth.

The Mother of the Sea Creatures is a rather unappetizing creature herself, smelling of fish of course, and with hair matted and tangled—in a Greenland version, full of vermin and lice. This "ugly woman" shows up again and again in mythology. The Balinese goddess Rangda is "a monstrous old woman, naked, stripped black and white, with fantastically pendulous breasts, ringed by black fur. Her long hair reaches to her feet. . . ."[3] And the hair of the Gorgons, those terrible women of Greek mythology, consists of tangled serpents.

The ugly woman appears in an Irish legend of the five sons of King Eochaid, which Joseph Campbell quotes in *Hero with a Thousand Faces*. The legend tells us some important things about her. Out hunting, the five sons of the king find themselves lost and in need of water. Fergus is the first to set off,

And he lights on a well, over which he finds an old woman standing sentry. The fashion of the hag is this: blacker than coal every joint and segment of her was, from crown to ground; comparable to a wild horse's tail the grey wiry mass of hair that pierced her scalp's upper surface; with her sickle of a greenish-looking tusk that was in her head, and curled till it touched her ear, she could lop the verdant branch of an oak in full bearing; blackened and smoke-bleared eyes she had; nose awry, wide-nostrilled; a wrinkled and freckled belly, variously unwholesome; warped crooked shins, garnished with massive ankles and a pair of capacious shovels; knotty knees she had and livid nails. The beldame's whole description in fact was disgusting. "That's the way it is, is it?" said the lad, and "That's the very way," she answered. "Is it guarding the well thou art?" he asked, and she said: "It is." "Dost thou license me to take away some water?" "I do," she consented, "yet only so that I have of thee one kiss on my cheek." "Not so," said he. "Then water shall not be conceded by me." "My word I give," he went on, "that sooner than give thee a kiss I would perish of thirst!" Then the young man departed to the place where his brothers were, and told them that he had not gotten water.

The other brothers do likewise, ask the old woman for water but deny the kiss. Finally Niall, the last brother, comes to the well.

"Let me have water, woman!" he cried. "I will give it," said she, "and bestow on me a kiss." He answered: "Forby giving thee a kiss, I will even hug thee!" Then he bends to embrace her, and gives her a kiss. Which operation ended, and when he looked at her, in the whole world was not a young woman of gait more graceful, in universal semblance fairer than she. . . .[4]

It would seem a highly reliable rule of thumb, whenever one confronts such a grotesque hag in dream or fantasy, to give her the kiss, or as the Eskimo shaman does, comb her hair. For to him who is willing to face the appearance of ugliness is beauty given or the life-giving boon bestowed.

This then is the meaning of combing the hair of the Mother of the Sea Creatures. The shaman descends to the matrix of creation, to reenact the archetypal quest of the hero: once again magically to transform the Great Mother from her angry, withholding aspect to her life-giving, bountiful aspect. He ignores the appearance of ugliness and does something nice for her. And only then does she respond in kind, granting the shaman his wish.

Several things about the shaman's journey should be mentioned here. First, the visit to the Mother of the Sea Creatures is a traditional mythologem of Eskimo culture. It is the standard magical procedure when there is a dearth of animals. Yet we notice that it is not merely celebrated as a rite, but *experienced*. The shaman, as emissary of the community, reenacts it personally and, it is believed, actually. This enactment, then, belongs to the symbolic vocabulary of the tribe and is activated in and through the experience of the shaman. The shaman flies personally to the numinous, mythogenic realm, *there* to enact the symbolic drama. This realm, while invisible to ordinary people, is accessible to the shaman. And it is, effectually, a realm more real than this one, since events there are conceived of as being anterior to, and causal of, events in the physical world.

Notice also that the community perceives the symbolic event as intimately bound up with its own social situation, infractions of taboo, and the like. The community performs its response to the shaman's symbolic visionary invocation in this magical litany by a collective confessional of sins. This event is curiously reminiscent of those Christian ceremonies where the congregation communally confesses its guilt and unworthiness. Obviously the important psychological functions of confession —release and atonement—are met in both ceremonies. There is also a revitalization of the power of the communal taboos.

Further, we can see how this enactment functions on the archetypal level. The symbols of local mythology are inflections, derivations, of more transcultural, transpersonal structures. The potency of these symbols resides in their ability to arrest and engage the primary mythic imagination. As such, they transmit the universal meaning of the hero quest and the ancient ritual transformation of the Great Mother archetype from her withholding to her bountiful aspect. The ceremony does this principally within the shaman, but simultaneously within the psyche of each mythically attuned member of the community. There are many levels engaged in this enactment of vision.

Iroquois and Senoi Dream Enactments

From these discussions of the rites of shamanism, we must surely see that primitive people are often both more in contact with and more capable of responding to the living symbols of their mythic imagination than are we, all too often preoccupied with our conscious concerns. Whereas our own style of dealing with the mythic imagination seems to keep its symbols private, autistic, and undeveloped, theirs seems to encourage a public symbolic enactment in which the problems of both the individual and the community are creatively and therapeutically dealt with.

A major vehicle for the primitive's advantage in this regard is the possession of an operative mythology which contains, structures, and expresses the otherwise inaccessible inner level of psychological meaning. Such a mythology constitutes a comprehensive symbolic system, which may function both for internal reference and for social dialogue.

But if we are by now prepared to find primitive man being mythically more attuned than ourselves, are we equally prepared to find him more psychologically astute? In the two systems of dream interpretation and enactment discussed in this chapter we find primitive man's instinctive affinity for symbols combined with some remarkably sophisticated insights into the functioning of the mind.

The American Iroquois and the Malayan Senoi are two pre-literate peoples living at almost opposite sides of the globe, yet there is an astonishing degree of similarity between their ways of dealing with dreams. I have distinguished the four following areas of agreement:

1. The dream is recognized as the only available access or key to an inner life which is *other* than waking consciousness. This inner life is believed to be as real or more real than the waking world.

2. Dreams are recognized as possessing a meaning within the ordinarily chaotic and incomprehensible surface of the dream. One must go beyond this appearance to apprehend the true meaning.

3. The dream and the inner life of which it is the symbol are the key to what "goes wrong" in man: physical sickness of various kinds, psychological problems, moodiness, even inter-personal conflicts and ill fortune. Consequently the dream is the key to therapy.

4. The enactment of dreams is all-important as a thera-peutic technique. Dreams are believed to ask for a making-real. This may be in some cases a literal carrying out of what the dream wants to do, or if this is not appropriate (in the case of an act of aggression, for example) a symbolic enactment or resolution.

We see then that these two preliterate peoples have upstaged psychoanalysis by at least several centuries, and probably much longer. We are dealing with a truly psychological approach to dreams that goes beyond the limitations of any specific mytho-logical system. These four assumptions, appearing in the Iroquois and Senoi as well as in our own psychoanalytic dream theories, would certainly seem to be transcultural, and perhaps basic to almost any system of dream interpretation or therapy.

Let us turn first to the Iroquois. A lake- and forest-dwelling people found in what is now western New York State and upper Pennsylvania, the Iroquois had already assimilated divergent cultural groups into their confederated Five Nations by the time white men came among them.*

One of the first things noticed by the French trappers and Jesuit missionaries who came among the Iroquois in the early 1600s was the presence of dancers wearing grotesque masks with twisted faces and tangled hair. Some of the Jesuits wrote home about these masked dancers, comparing them to the masqueraders of provincial France. We know, then, that the masked societies of the Iroquois existed before the first contact with white men; and such has been their tenacity that they have survived over three centuries of debilitating cultural diffusion.[5] The most important of them was called the "False Face Society." This was a medicine society whose almost exclusive concern was the curing of illnesses. As in most primitive masked societies the wearing of the mask makes one psychically identical with the supernatural being whom the mask represents. There are two legends of origin for the False Faces. One is a mythical epic of the creation, the other a more human, shamanistic type of adventure.

The first involves an interaction between the Great Creator of the World and an enormous flying stone head. As the Creator was walking around inspecting his handiwork, the head flew up to him. The Creator demanded to know who the creature was, and an argument sprang up between them over who had made what, and to whom the earth belonged. They decided to settle the issue by a titanic magical contest, namely, as to who could move a distant mountain toward them. The head tried and only moved it partway. Then the Creator had his turn, but as he was doing it, the head got impatient and turned around to see, whereupon the mountain, rushing up, hit him square in the face, adding injury to defeat. However the Creator, realizing that this titan had great power, assigned

*From west to east the Five Nations were the Seneca, Cayuga, Onandaga, Oneida, and Mohawk. Legend has them organized by the statesman Deganawidah (son of a virgin mother) and his noble and now immortalized counselor, Hiawatha. This great Indian confederacy was ruled by tribal sachems, themselves appointed from special families by matriarchs.

The Iroquois False Face Society.
(The American Museum of Natural History.)

Wooden Mask with Horse Hair.
Late 19th or early 20th century
(The American Museum of Natural History.)

him a task: that of driving out disease from the earth and assisting human beings. The broken-nosed creature agreed that if humans would make portrait masks of him and call him grandfather they would have the power to cure disease by blowing hot ashes.[6]

The other story of the origin of the False Faces, paraphrased from the accounts of some Iroquois storytellers, goes as follows:

As humans went about the earth in the fall men went into the woods hunting. They carried native tobacco and parched corn meal for mush. They were tormented by shy querulous beings who flitted timidly behind trees with their long hair snapping in the wind. Sometimes, a hunter returned to his camp to find the ashes of his fire strewn about the hearth and the marks of some great dirty hand where someone had grasped a house post for support as he leaned over and pawed in the fire. The hunter agreed to stay home while his partner went afield. During the morning, a False Face approached cautiously, sledging on one hip, now and then standing erect to gaze about before proceeding. Going to the hearth, he reached into the ashes and scattered the coals as if seeking something. That night the hunter had a dream in which the False Face requested tobacco and mush. The next day, the hunter set a kettle down for them. The Faces came and taught him their songs and their method of treating patients with hot ashes. In a subsequent dream, they requested him to remember them every year with a feast saying they are everywhere in the forests, bringing luck to those who remember them.[7]

This is similar to the shamanistic formula, is it not? In the wilds or in a dream one encounters a mythical or spiritual being, has a confrontation, and then out of that meeting brings back a special power, something of value to the community. And the shamanistic ability to hold hot stones and ashes without injury is believed to belong to the dancers in the False Face ceremony.

Among the Seneca one is admitted to a particular medicine society either because of a dream, because one has been cured of an illness by that society, or because a clairvoyant has prescribed the ritual of that society for a cure. This would seem to correspond to similar restrictions determining membership in the masked societies of other Iroquois and related tribes as well.

The Iroquois distinguish three categories of illness: (1) problems caused by natural events such as accidents or injuries in battle; (2) those caused by witchcraft, through the spells and charms of sorcerors; and (3) those that are psychic and caused by the resentment of the inner soul, whose basic needs are not being met.

For the last two categories especially the False Face Society is used. The ceremonies may be public or private. For the purpose of expelling the spirits of sickness the eerie band of masked dancers comes prancing and prowling and uttering weird cries to the house, and around it, looking for the presence of spirits—peering into corners and under beds. They blow hot ashes all around and on the patient. And the cure is believed to be effected through power bestowed by the original mythical beings with whom the dancers are temporarily identical.

But it is particularly with the third category of illness that we are concerned here. This sort of illness is not best cured by the kind of ceremony of masked dancers just described, but by another kind: the interpretation of dreams carried on and directed by the medicine societies during the great spring, fall, and midwinter dream festivals.

The Iroquoian concept of dreams is based on the idea of the "desires of the soul." One Father Ragueneau, an early Jesuit observer of the Iroquois in 1649, describes it thus:

In addition to the desires which we generally have that are free, or at least voluntary in us (and) which arise from a previous knowledge of some goodness that we imagine to exist in the thing desired, the Iroquois believe that our souls have other desires, which are, as it were, inborn and concealed. These, they say, come from the depths of the soul, not through any knowledge, but by means of a certain blind transporting of the soul to certain objects: these transports might in the language of philosophy be called "desideria innata" to distinguish them from the former, which are called "desideria elicita."[8]

These two levels of desire appear in metaphysical systems throughout the world. There is a close analogy, for example, in the Tantric concepts of *maya-sakti* (the power of desire born of physical objects), and *cit-sakti* (the power of desire born of consciousness itself). And the Japanese metaphysical concepts of *ji hokkai* (the universe of things, perceived by the senses), and *ri hokkai* (unconditioned consciousness) would seem similar.

The only key to the inner, nonconscious desires of the soul are dreams. As our perspicacious Jesuit observer Father Ragueneau says,

Now they believe that our soul makes these natural desires known by means of dreams, which are its language. Accordingly when these desires are accomplished it is satisfied, but on the contrary, if it is not granted what it desires, it becomes angry and not only does it not give its body the good and the happiness that it wishes to procure for it, but it also revolts against the body, causing various diseases, and even death.[9]

And the anthropologist J. N. B. Hewitt, writing in 1895 on "The Iroquoian Concept of the Soul," describes these inner desires and their relation to dreams as follows:

. . . in addition to the desires and longings of the mind which are in a measure free and voluntary, arising as they do from a previous knowledge of the good or benefit derived from the object desired, and so suggested thereby, the soul has other longings and desires which are innate, hidden, spontaneous, intuitive, and which emanate from its depths not through previous knowledge, but by an innate rapture of the soul or the object it has in view. The soul makes these desired objects known through the medium of dreams.[10]

The inner desires, therefore, are of a different ontological order from one's externally acquired, learned experience— one's "history of reinforcements" as the Behaviorists might say. They are born of an "innate rapture" coming from the depths of the psyche, not from experiences of our ego in time and space.

Jungian psychology makes this same distinction between the desires of personal consciousness and those born within and below consciousness in the depths of the "objective psyche." The experiences that come from this level are often felt to be "other" than one's conscious intentions. Dreams and fantasies may act as a counterpoint to our conscious ideas. As one Jungian analyst says,

The goal-directedness of psychic energy which becomes apparent through the statements and "directives" of our dreams suggests a compensating and complementing entity which appears to exist regardless of the dreamer's awareness and which is more often than not at variance with his wishes and ideas of his own state, sometimes quite disconcertingly so.[11]

This entity, which is suggested by the behavior and nature of our dreams, Jung called the *Self* or the *Other*. And he describes this Self as if it behaved like a living entity operating out of our consciousness, and with an a-priori relationship to it. It is not caused by consciousness; rather it is the base on which consciousness itself rests. As such it is of the order of instinct. Jung says, "This instinct comes to us from within, as a compulsion or will or command, and if—as has more or less been done from time immemorial—we give it the name of a personal daimon we are at least aptly expressing the psychological situation."[12]

Jung also terms the Self the psychological source of the God-image. And we are not surprised to find then that the Iroquois feel that these special inner desires are incited in man by the power of the Sky God, *Tha-ro-hya-wa-ko*. Thus the Iroquois pay the strictest attention to the messages contained in dreams, for to ignore them is to court illness, madness, and disaster by opposing the messages of the god coming from within. As Hewitt says of the power and importance of the dream in Iroquois society,

. . . the dream became the motive and occasion of elaborate ceremonial and other observances, the unquestioned and determining oracle in the most minute or most important civil matters as well as in the most momentous affairs of state and war. This of course was a logical and necessary consequence of the doctrine that the dream is a promulgating of a message of *Tha-ro-hya-wa-ko*, brought to the knowledge of man by the reasonable soul in the form of an innate desire or in a dream.[13]

The dream is thus used for both personal and social *guidance* in Iroquois society. The *orienting* function of the mythology simply serves to underline the need for this type of guidance. Thus the mythology operates to support a system which must be seen as basically psychological in function. The Iroquois mythological context leads the dreamer to expect important revelations from the interpretation of dreams. This seems remarkably close to the Jungian approach:*

> Together the patient and I address ourselves to the 2,000,000-year-old man that is in all of us. In the last analysis, most of our difficulties come from losing contact with our instincts—with the age-old unforgotten wisdom stored up in us. And where do we make contact with this old man in us? In our dreams.[15]

The ancient man within each of us emerges in a remarkably clear fashion in the myths and metaphysics of the Naskapi Indians, hundreds of miles to the north and east of the Iroquois, on the Labrador Peninsula. They call him the "Great Man" within, a source of guidance and knowledge far more ancient and wise than man's conscious self.[16]

The enactment of dream is the most important part of Iroquois dream theory. In the spring, in the fall, and especially in the five-day-long midwinter festival called the "Feast of Dreams," dreams are the focus of attention, interpretation, and enactment. Each person tells a dream he feels to be of particu-

---

*There is another analogy between Iroquois and Jungian psychology. The Iroquois believe that "every species of animals, birds, fish and insects had in the spirit world a type or model for that species, which was many times larger and more perfect than any earthly member of that species which was called the ancient or old one of that race of beings." Their term for this was *oia ro*, which means likeness, imitation of form. This is remarkably close to the Jungian concept of *archetype*. People too were considered to be copies of spirit prototypes, the word for person, *oiron ta*, being a derivative of the word *oia ro*.[14]

lar importance for him. The other members, as audience, respond with their feelings or interpretations. When the dreamer —or others—feel that someone has made the right interpretation, he must pay that person a "forfeit," usually a gift or favor. A bond of friendship is expected to spring up between them as a result of this psychosymbolic transaction.

If the dream expresses a "wish of the soul," everyone takes part in helping the individual to realize his wish. As these wishes are considered of higher ontological status than waking needs and desires, other people go out of their way to help the dreamer realize them. If the wish, as surely must happen much of the time, would infringe excessively on anyone else's rights, or is aggressive, or grandiose, the drama is enacted symbolically, with the audience playing various parts.

These dream dramas are remarkably reminiscent of what is now emerging as the avant-garde in current dream therapy; psychodrama and gestalt therapy particularly come to mind. What is essential to these methods is that the dream be brought to consciousness and dialogue, that it be taken seriously, treated as if it were real. As Jung says, "If we meditate on a dream sufficiently long and thoroughly, if we carry it around with us and turn it over and over, something almost always comes of it."[17] The Iroquoian approach to dreams ensures that this will occur, and not only within the individual himself but also among his friends and neighbors. The dream is valued and treated "as-if" it contained meaning. And then, almost always, meaning emerges.

For our next comparison let us move twelve thousand miles, halfway around the planet, to a preliterate people dwelling in the central mountains of the Malay peninsula, who have never heard of Jung, Fritz Perls, or the Iroquois. Yet the Senoi people, too, developed a remarkably sophisticated dream theory.*

* Senoi is a general term for the folk in the central mountainous region of the Malay Peninsula. The particular tribe studied by Kilton Stewart were called, more precisely, Temiar.

The Senoi, like the Iroquois, have public dream interpreting ceremonies, but also use them as a part of the daily household ritual. Breakfast time functions as a "dream clinic"; dreams of the previous night are told, compared, interpreted. Working with dreams is a vital part of child education and a major area of communication between children and their parents.

In our culture the usual response to a child's nightmare is to say, "Don't worry dear, it isn't real." The Senoi do otherwise. The child is rather told that the dream *is* real but partakes of a different reality from the waking world. And the child is encouraged to go further with the dream, not to repress it or flee from it. Kilton Stewart reports:

The simplest anxiety or terror dream I found among the Senoi was the falling dream. When the Senoi child reports a falling dream, the adult answers with enthusiasm, "That is a wonderful dream, one of the best dreams a man can have. Where did you fall to, and what did you discover?" He makes the same comment when the child reports a climbing, travelling, flying, or soaring dream. The child at first answers, as he would in our society, that he awoke before he had fallen anywhere.

"That was a mistake," answers the adult-authority. "Everything you do in a dream has a purpose, beyond your understanding while you are asleep. You must relax and enjoy yourself when you fall in a dream. Falling is the quickest way to get in contact with the powers of the spirit world, the powers laid open to you through your dreams. Soon, when you have a falling dream, you will remember what I am saying, and as you do, you will feel that you are travelling to the source of the power which has caused you to fall.

"The falling spirits love you. They are attracting you to their land, and you have but to relax and remain asleep in order to come to grips with them. When you meet them, you may be frightened of their terrific power, but go on. When you think you are dying in a dream, you are only receiving the powers of the other world, your own spriritual power which has been turned against you, and which now wishes to become one with you if you will accept it."[18]

In this remarkably sophisticated piece of education, the child learns three important things: first, that the terrifying forms of the dream are in reality his own thought-forms; second, that he may operate as an active as well as passive participant in the process of dreaming; and third, that he may relate to these inner powers in a creative dialogue. Thus the child is instructed in behavioral strategies for dreaming as well as waking consciousness, and his dreams, unlike ours, are cultivated, not allowed to grow wild.

When Stewart visited among the Senoi in 1935, he reported some astonishing things about these highland folk, living in their bamboo-stilt thatched longhouses. According to elders of the tribe, there had been no violent crimes or intercommunal disputes for hundreds of years. There were few or no psychological problems, and everyone seemed remarkably well adjusted and happy.

The Senoi did not practice black magic like so many Malaysian tribes, but did allow neighboring tribes to believe that they were extremely powerful magicians, thus making sure that outsiders had little desire to invade, a remarkably wise psychological strategy.

There were few formal rules and little political structure among the Senoi, as Stewart tells us.

Study of their political and social organization indicates that the political authority in their communities was originally in the hands of the oldest members of patrilineal clans. . . . But the major authority in all their communities is now held by their primitive psychologists whom they call *halaks*. The only honorary title in the society is that of *Tohat*, which is equivalent to a doctor who is both a healer and an educator, in our terms.[19]

They have then, no professional politicians—praise the Lord! The secular authority is grounded in a technician of the sacred, and fortunately he is no priest with a dogma to enforce, but rather a shaman, psychologist, astral traveler.

The interpretation of dreams is so widespread that the *halak* may not hide his psychological incapabilities behind a mask of professionalism, as do so many therapists in our culture. He has the same skills everyone else has, only more highly developed. Stewart says of the development of these *halaks*, "The co-operative reverie (or trance state) is not participated in until adolescence and serves to initiate the child into states of adult-hood. After adolescence, if he spends a great deal of time in the trance state, a Senoi is considered a specialist in healing or in the use of extra-sensory powers."[20] Like the shaman, the *halak* personally enters the mythogenic dream realm, to deal there with the dream forms in their natural, protean state.

The basis of the Senoi psychological system is simple enough, and Kilton Stewart explains it clearly.

While the Senoi do not of course employ our system of termi-nology, their psychology of dream interpretation might be summed up as follows: man creates features or images of the outside world in his own mind as part of the adaptive process. Some of these features are in conflict with him and with each other. Once inter-nalized, these hostile images turn man against himself and his fellows. In dreams man has the power to see these facts of the psyche, which have been disguised in external forms, associated with his own fearful emotions, and turned against him and the in-ternal images of other people. If the individual does not receive social aid through education and therapy, these hostile images, built up by man's normal receptiveness to the outside world, get tied up together and associated with one another in a way which makes him physically, socially and psychologically abnormal.

Unaided, these dream beings, which man creates to reproduce inside himself the external socio-physical environment, tend to remain against him the way the environment was against him, or to become disassociated from his major personality and tied up in wasteful psychic, organic and muscular tensions. With the help of dream interpretations, these psychological replicas of the socio-physical environment can be redirected and reorganized and again become useful to the major personality.[21]

In this theory the Senoi have captured some of the deepest and most valuable insights of psychoanalysis. Particularly im-pressive is the notion that nonconscious, uncultivated experiences and memories can become psychologically destructive. These "systems of tensions" which Stewart describes seem quite analogous to the theory of "complexes," an important cornerstone of Jungian theory. The meaning of these destructive systems becomes apparent, not to the consciousness of the waking state, but rather to that of the dream. And in the dream, present in symbolic form, the dreamer is to dialogue with them, unravel their tensions, use them. Once again we see the functional power of a technique that is willing to *experience* the dream, not simply interpret. "Cooperative reverie," a major technique of working with dreams in a trancelike condition, seems remarkably similar to the Jungian technique of "active imagination," or the guided fantasy techniques used in Gestalt, or Psychosynthesis.

And what would Freud have thought of this little sleight of hand with sexual sublimation?

Dreams of sexual love should always move through orgasm, and the dreamer should then demand from his dream lover the poem, the song, the dance, the useful knowledge which will express the beauty of his spiritual lover to a group. If this is done, no dream man or woman can take the love which belongs to human beings. If the dream character demanding love looks like a brother or sister, with whom love would be abnormal or incestuous in reality, one need have no fear of expressing love in the dream, since these dream beings are not, in fact, brother or sister, but only have chosen these taboo images as a disguise. Such dream beings are only facets of one's own spiritual or psychic makeup, disguised as brother or sister, and useless until they are reclaimed or possessed through the free expression of love in the dream universe.[22]

Thus, too, these remarkably insightful masters of symbol short-circuit the compelling power of the incest taboo (a technique Freud might have thought not quite "proper," perhaps). The fatal attraction is, the Senoi realize, a symbolic, psychological one and should be treated accordingly.

The Senoi, like the Iroquois, value the enactment and making public of messages contained in their dreams. The dreamer is ever to gain from his dreams, or the beings involved in it, a song, a dance, a poem, to be presented to the group. As with the Iroquois, if someone appears in a hostile form in a dream, one is to go to the actual person to see if there is any problem between them. Stewart says,

A child dreams that he is attacked by a friend and, on awakening, is advised by his father to inform his friend of this fact. The friend's father tells his child that it is possible that he has offended the dreamer without wishing to do so, and allowed a malignant character to use his image as a disguise in the dream. Therefore, he should give a present to the dreamer and go out of his way to be friendly toward him, to prevent such an occurrence in the future.[23]

The dream here is trusted as being valid on two levels. First, in that the dream presents a real psychological situation which needs the attention of the dreamer. His enactment of attention to it on the outer level also carries a symbolic message to the inner. Second, the dream is considered to have at least a possible objective validity. That is, since the dream playwright chose the form of this or that person to carry a conflictual content, perhaps it is because there is an objectively real problem between the dreamer and that person. The dream is thus credited with transpersonal perspective, a clairvoyant view of a situation between two people.

One might go on describing the wonders of the Senoi dream psychology, from which we so obviously have much to learn. But I refer the reader rather to Kilton Stewart's brief but highly informative monograph, *Dream Theory in Malaya.**

Perhaps in a few more decades we will have *halaks* of our own, voyaging in their own mythic inner spaces and bringing back things of value for us all. And perhaps too they can show

---

*Since this was published four years ago in Charles Tart's influential and definitive anthology, *Altered States of Consciousness*, it has been a great stimulant to many of us interested in the phenomenology of dream experiencing. Unfortunately, there is not much additional information on these truly remarkable technicians of dream, and the violent turbulence of World War II has left us little to compare to the life of the Senoi community as Stewart observed it in 1935. See also *Pygmies and Dream Giants* by Kilton Stewart.

us all how to wake up a little in our dreams, to educate the inner imagination-self we keep locked in a darkened room like an autistic child. Possibly, also such *halaks* might give our psychiatrists a little competition, make them take off their horn-rimmed glasses and climb on the couch of life with the rest of us.

Black Elk's Vision

In many primitive societies the "big" dream or vision is actively sought after. Among the Plains Indians of North America, a young man seeking to cross the threshold from adolescence into manhood would frequently go into the desert alone, to fast and await such a vision. The vision, like that of the shaman, serves as a psychological initiation. It enables the youth to pass into manhood and at the same time establishes his own sense of a primary mythic validity. The archetypal dimension of such an experience serves to initiate one into a sense of belonging, not only to the social but to a cosmic order. Often the young man emerges from the experience with a sense of personal power, and perhaps also with a new name, which he may keep for the rest of his life.

Surely one of the most remarkable documents of our times is the transcribed account of the "Great Vision" of Black Elk, an Oglala Sioux. The visions and events in the following narrative took place from approximately 1870 to 1890. They were written down by John Neihardt in the early 1930's from his extended conversations with Black Elk. Black Elk, it seems, did not court his vision for personal validation. It came to him unsought, in great pain and the fire of ecstasy. We shall see in this chronicle, then, the genesis of a "greater shaman"; great not only because his vocation was spontaneous, but in the deep wisdom that shines through the forms of his vision and his own response to it. Black Elk was nine years old when this experience came to him, unbidden. Here he describes the events leading up to the onset of the vision.

It was the summer when I was nine years old, and our people were moving slowly towards the Rocky Mountains. We camped one evening in a valley beside a little creek just before it ran into the Greasy Grass (the Little Big Horn River), and there was a man by the name of Man Hip who liked me and asked me to eat with him in his tepee.

While I was eating, a voice came and said: "It is time; now they are calling you." The voice was so loud and clear that I believed it, and I thought I would just go where it wanted me to go. So I got right up and started. As I came out of the tepee, both my thighs began to hurt me, and suddenly it was like waking from a dream, and there wasn't any voice. So I went back into the tepee, but I didn't want to eat. Man Hip looked at me in a strange way and asked me what was wrong. I told him that my legs were hurting me.

The next morning the camp moved again, and I was riding with some boys. We stopped to get a drink from a creek, and when I got off my horse, my legs crumpled under me and I could not walk. So the boys helped me up and put me on my horse; and when we camped that evening, I was sick. The next day the camp moved on to where the different bands of our people were coming together, and I rode in a pony drag, for I was very sick. Both my legs and both my arms were swollen badly and my face was all puffed up.

When we had camped again, I was lying in our tepee and my mother and father were sitting beside me. I could see out through the opening, and there two men were coming from the clouds, headfirst like arrows slanting down, and I knew they were the same that I had seen before.* Each now carried a long spear, and from the points of these a jagged lightning flashed. They came clear down to the ground this time and stood a little way off and looked at me and said: "Hurry! Come! Your Grandfathers are calling you!"

Then they turned and left the ground like arrows slanting upward from the bow. When I got up to follow, my legs did not hurt me any more and I was very light. I went outside the tepee, and yonder where the men with flaming spears were going, a little cloud was coming very fast. It came and stopped and took me and

*Black Elk sees these figures in a much briefer earlier vision.

turned back to where it came from, flying fast. And when I looked down I could see my mother and my father yonder, and I felt sorry to be leaving them.

Then there was nothing but the air and the swiftness of the little cloud that bore me and those two men still leading up to where white clouds were piled like mountains on a wide blue plain, and in them the thunder beings lived and leaped and flashed.

Now suddenly there was nothing but a world of cloud, and we three were there alone in the middle of a great white plain with snowy hills and mountains staring at us; and it was very still; but there were whispers.[24]

And then the most remarkable, numinous vision unfolds itself to young Black Elk's wondering eyes. I would love to quote it for you in entirety, for it is surely of the primal stuff of mythic revelation. But it seems better to refer you to the original source material. What I should like to do here, however, is to summarize the major parts and then move on to my central concern: What is to be done about such a vision?

Black Elk sees four groups of twelve horses, each a different color, each from a different direction. The horses are *numinous*: with "manes of lightning and thunder in their nostrils . . . with eyes that glimmer like the daybreak star and manes of morning light." The horses, after dancing through the sky amongst the thunderclouds, conduct Black Elk to the "Grandfathers." He says,

Then as we walked, there was a heaped up cloud ahead that changed into a tepee, and a rainbow was the open door to it; and through the door I saw six old men sitting in a row.

The two men with the spears now stood beside me, one on either hand, and the horses took their places in their quarters, looking inward, four by four. And the oldest of the Grandfathers spoke with a kind voice and said: "Come right in and do not fear." And as he spoke, all the horses of the four quarters neighed to cheer me. So I went in and stood before the six, and they looked older than men can ever be—old like hills, like stars.

The oldest spoke again: "Your Grandfathers all over the world are having a council, and they have called you here to teach you."

And then Black Elk says,

His voice was very kind, but I shook all over with fear now, for I knew that these were not old men, but the Powers of the World.[25]

As young Black Elk sits in that cloud-borne rainbow lodge, the Grandfathers begin to teach him. And a remarkable symbolic pageant unfolds. Black Elk is presented with several mystical tokens: a cup (the power to make live), a bow (the power to destroy), an herb of power (to heal), a sacred pipe with eagle's wings, and a bright red stick that flowers and becomes like a tree filled with singing birds.

There is then a procession which leads Black Elk to four difficult ascents, the events facing him and all his people. The first ascent is "green," the next "black," then an awful one in which "the nation's hoop is broken and the people are scattered." It begins with a terrible blue man, source of sickness and death, whom Black Elk must ceremonially slay. But the blue man's effects are felt, for the journey grows more terrible. On the third ascent,

all the animals and fowls that were the people ran here and there, for each one seemed to have his own little vision that he followed and his own rules; and all over the universe I could hear the winds at war like wild beasts fighting.

And on the fourth ascent,

It was like rapid gun-fire and like whirling smoke, and like women and children wailing and like horses screaming all over the world.

These symbolic events are both representation and prefigurement of the awful collective destruction of the American Indian.

Then Black Elk says,

. . . a song of power came to me and I sang it there in the midst of that terrible place where I was. It went like this:

> A good nation I will make live.
> This the nation above has said.
> They have given me the power to make over.

And then a horse, all faded, skin and bones, appears, and Black Elk is commanded by the Voice to use his herb of power.

Then the poor horse neighed and rolled and got up, and he was a big, shiny, black stallion with dapples all over him and his mane about him like a cloud. He was the chief of all the horses; and when he snorted, it was a flash of lightning and his eyes were like the sunset star.[26]

The magical, renewed stallion sings a great song of power. "His voice," says Black Elk, "was not loud, but it went all over the universe and filled it. There was nothing that did not hear, and it was more beautiful than anything can be. It was so beautiful that nothing anywhere could keep from dancing." Everything dances together to the stallion's song, and then Black Elk says, "And when I looked down upon my people yonder, the cloud passed over, blessing them with friendly rain, and stood in the east with a flaming rainbow over it."

How can we help but remember a similar event, following upon a terrible destruction, celebrated in another mythology for thousands of years,

And God said, This is the token of the covenant which I make between me and you and every living creature that is with you, for perpetual generations:

I do set my bow in the cloud, and it shall be for a token of a covenant between me and the earth.

And it shall come to pass, when I bring a cloud over the earth, that the bow shall be seen in the cloud:

And I will remember my covenant, which is between me and you and every living creature of all flesh; and the waters shall no more become a flood to destroy all flesh. (Gen. 9:12–15, KJV)

Then, following this eternal mythological sign of covenant, Black Elk begins to see in what he calls "a sacred manner . . . the shapes of all things in the spirit, and the shape of all shapes as they must live together in one being." And in this unitive, sacred seeing, Black Elk's vision encompasses not only his own people and their tragic plight, which has been the substance of the vision, but the connectedness of all people, all things. "And I saw that the sacred hoop of my people was one of many hoops that made one circle, wide as daylight and as starlight, and in the center grew one mighty flowering tree to shelter all the children of one mother and one father. And I saw that it was holy."[27]

Black Elk leaves the rainbow lodge of the Grandfathers, and as he goes he hears the sun singing as it rises, a marvelous cosmic song. And then he is home. "Then I saw my own tepee, and inside I saw my mother and my father bending over a sick boy that was myself. And as I entered the tepee someone was saying: 'The boy is coming to; you had better give him some water.' "

This is indeed a potent vision to be contained within the frame of one little nine-year-old Sioux Indian boy. As Black Elk himself says, "I was very sad; for it seemed to me that everybody ought to know about it, but I was afraid to tell, because I knew that nobody would believe me, little as I was, for I was only nine years old." Then he adds, ". . . as I lay there thinking of my vision, I could see it all again and feel the meaning with a part of me like a strange power glowing in my body; but when the part of me that talks would try to make words for the meaning, it would be like fog and get away from me." This, then, is surely what we have defined as "primary meaning," a meaning totally other than words. And just as surely, this is a vision of more than personal import; its meaning is transpersonal.

Black Elk does not know how to communicate his awesome vision, so beyond his personal powers and ability to describe. Whirlwind Chaser, a medicine man, notices something is strange with the boy. "He sat down and looked at me a long time in a strange way and then he said to my father: 'Your boy is sitting there in a sacred manner. I do not know what it is, but there is something special for him to do, for just as I came in I could see a power like a light all through his body.' " There are many signs that this is a vision of power, from the intense physical symptoms Black Elk experiences to what

Whirlwind Chaser sees when he looks at him. But Black Elk is still afraid. He says, "While he was looking hard at me, I wanted to get up and run away, for I was afraid he might look right into me and see my vision there and tell it wrong and then maybe all the people would think that I was crazy. For a long while after that, whenever I saw Whirlwind Chaser coming, I would run away and hide for fear he might see into me and tell."[28]

Notice that Black Elk is not only concerned that people will think him crazy, but also—and perhaps this is more important —that Whirlwind Chaser might "tell it wrong." While too young to "understand" the vision, Black Elk feels fully its awesome, sacred power. He does not want it misunderstood or altered in any way in the act of revelation.

We move now to eight years later. The intervening time has been a very troubled one for the Sioux, with frequent broken treaties and battles with the *wasichus* (white men). The little tribe to which Black Elk belongs is continually on the move, fleeing either white soldiers or hostile Indian tribes. Black Elk has told no one of his vision. But it comes up again within him, irresistibly.

"I was sixteen years old and more," he says, "and I had not yet done anything the Grandfathers wanted me to do, but they had been helping me. I did not know how to do what they wanted me to do." He feels that his vision requires something of him, but does not know how to do it. But at this point there is more than merely a conscious decision to do something about it. Black Elk says,

A terrible time began for me then, and I could not tell anybody, not even my father and mother. I was afraid to see a cloud coming up; and whenever one did I could hear the thunder beings calling to me: "Behold your Grandfathers! Make haste!" I could understand the birds when they sang, and they were always saying: "It is time!" The crows in the day and the coyotes at night all called and called to me: "It is time! It is time! It is time!"

Time to do what? I did not know. Whenever I awoke before daybreak and went out of the tepee because I was afraid of the stillness when everyone was sleeping, there were many low voices talking together in the east, and the daybreak star would sing this song in the silence:

> In a sacred manner you shall walk!
> Your nation shall behold you!

I could not get along with people now, and I would take my horse and go far out from camp alone and compare everything on the earth and in the sky with my vision. Crows would see me and shout to each other as though they were making fun of me: "Behold him! Behold him!"[29]

Surely this is more than a conscious preoccupation with an idea, it resembles more an obsession, coming from deep within, or as we might think in our own cultural terms, the onset of a psychotic episode. But the Siberian shamans would call it *amurakh*, the frightening, numinous onset of the sacred vocation.

The fear was not so great all the while in the winter, but sometimes it was bad. Sometimes the crying of coyotes out in the cold made me so afraid that I would run out of one tepee into another, and I would do this until I was worn out and fell asleep. I wondered if maybe I was only crazy; and my father and mother worried a great deal about me. They said: "It is the strange sickness he had that time when we gave the horse to Whirlwind Chaser for curing him; and he is not cured." I could not tell them what was the matter, for then they would only think I was queerer than ever.

I was seventeen years old that winter.

When the grasses were beginning to show their tender faces again, my father and mother asked an old medicine man by the name of Black Road to come over and see what he could do for me. Black Road was in a tepee all alone with me, and he asked me to tell him if I had seen something that troubled me. By now I was so afraid of being afraid of everything that I told him about my vision, and when I was through he looked long at me and said: "Ah-h-h-h," meaning that he was much surprised. Then he said to me: "Nephew, I know now what the trouble is! You must do what the bay horse in your vision wanted you to do. You must do your duty and perform this vision for your people upon earth. You must have the horse dance first for the people to see. Then the fear will leave you; but if you do not do this, something very bad will happen to you."

So we began to get ready for the horse dance.[30]

Would that many a modern-day psychotherapist had the wisdom of Black Road. Not all departures from normality are pathological. Rather, they may be presentiments of a more important reality trying to emerge through the tangled nets of our conscious cares and concerns into awareness and fruition.

The Jungian analyst Edward Whitmont says in regard to our ubiquitous mental disturbances, "The question one must ask above all with any neurosis is not, 'How do we eliminate it,' but rather, "Whither does it want to go?' "[31] What comes to us from the primary, mythic level of the psyche may be at variance with our conscious preconceptions, but it requests— no, demands—to be taken account of by us. And often, it would seem, it wishes to be taken on its own terms, not translated into ours. And the substance of Black Elk's vision is indeed the primary stuff, not only of myth, but of religious, mystical revelation. As Jung says of the emergence of such numinous, archetypal revelations from within in the course of therapy,

> To the patient it is nothing less than a revelation when something altogether strange rises up to confront him from the hidden depths of the psyche—something that is not his ego and is therefore beyond the reach of his personal will. He has regained access to the sources of psychic life, and this marks the beginning of the cure. . . . As a religious-minded person would say: guidance has come from God.[32]

Jungian analysts feel that the emergence of such archetypal material signals the onset of a natural curative process from within. And they are not the only witnesses to this remarkable process; this is also the finding of many investigators using psychedelics in therapy or research. The drug in and of itself has no power to cure, it is simply a psychological amplifier.

But the most remarkable improvements take place with the reaching of the inner level Masters and Houston have called the "symbolic" level, where intensely meaningful rituals and dramas, often of archetypal reference, unfold themselves. Some subjects reach the even deeper "integrative" level of the psyche. Of this level Masters and Houston say, "In our experience the most profound and transforming psychedelic experiences have been those regarded by the subjects as religious."[33] And the research findings of Stanislav Grof involving thousands of patients, both in Czechoslovakia and here, verify this. There is a curative magic in finding one's meaningful place in the archetypal, cosmic order.

In Black Elk's Great Vision the vision itself is the occasion both of his sickness and its cure. Black Elk's father had given the attending medicine man, Whirlwind Chaser, his best horse for "curing" Black Elk. But Black Elk knows differently. "I knew it was the Grandfathers in the flaming Rainbow tepee who had cured me; but I felt afraid to say so."[34]

But why then does Black Elk's sickness return, those eight years later? What more does it want?

Black Elk's vision, like a "big dream" with a more than personal import, is meant for more than Black Elk, even though it appears in and through his psyche. It is a vision of trans-personal meaning which asks to be let into the minds and hearts of his stricken people, where it may further work its healing. In an essay on "Mythogenesis," Joseph Campbell says of this vision,

The elements (the bricks) of this marvellous dream—the tree at the world center, the crossing there of the two roads, the world hoop, the world mountain, the guides, the world guardians, and their tokens, magical powers, etc.—are such as are known to mythologies of many orders. The landscape and the animals involved, on the other hand, the colors and virtues of the four directions, the attitude toward nature and the supernatural, the high roles of the buffalo and the horse, the peace pipe, spotted eagle, etc., are of the architecture of the mythic world of the North American plains heritage. The intuition that gave rise to this vision in the mental sphere of a nine-year-old boy was personal, however: personal in the same sense that no one else had ever had it, though collective indeed, not only in the sense that its imagery was archetypal, but also in the sense that its prophecy was of the destiny, not merely of this boy, but of his folk. It was the foresight of an impending crisis, subliminally intuited, together with a statement of the way it was to be met.[35]

We have been speaking of this vision as if it possessed a willful power of its own, and not without reason. Black Elk would have said that the "Grandfathers" wanted him to do something. But as students of mythology we are perhaps not entitled to share his mythological perspective. However, we should point out that the vision, in and of itself acts *as-if* it wishes to be enacted. Black Road's diagnosis is, then, as we should say, "right on."

There follows, then, a public enactment of Black Elk's Great Vision. A marvelous mythological pageant it must have been. Black Elk describes the preparations.

There was a man by the name of Bear Sings, and he was very old and wise. So Black Road asked him to help, and he did. First they sent a crier around in the morning who told the people to camp in a circle at a certain place a little way up the Tongue from where the soldiers were. They did this, and in the middle of the circle Bear Sings and Black Road set up a sacred tepee of bison hide, and on it they painted a bow and a cup of water, on the north white geese and the herb; on the east, the daybreak star and the pipe; on the south the flowering stick and the nation's hoop. Also they painted horses, elk and bison. Then over the door of the sacred tepee, they painted the flaming rainbow. It took them all day to do this, and it was beautiful.[36]

In short there is a careful, painstaking attempt to render faithfully Black Elk's supernatural vision on this physical, earthly plane. Black Elk also is prepared. First he takes a sweat bath and is ceremonially purified. Then,

That evening Black Road and Bear Sings told me to come to the painted tepee. We were in there alone, and nobody dared come near us to listen. They asked me if I had heard any songs in my vision, and if I had I must teach the songs to them. So I sang to them all the songs that I had heard in my vision, and it took most of the night to teach these songs to them. While we were in there singing, we could hear low thunder rumbling all over the village outside, and we knew the thunder beings were glad and had come to help us.[37]

The dramatis personae are, of course, the members of the tribe: six old men for the Grandfathers and numerous maidens, warriors, and their horses. They carry sacred objects: the healing herb, the holy pipe, a white goose wing to represent the cleansing wind (we see how beautifully mythically attuned these people are), the flowering stick, the nation's hoop. Black Elk carries only a red stick (red is symbolic of health, re-generation). Then the dance begins, and we can imagine how young Black Elk must have felt to see his sacred dream take tangible form upon the earth.

> They will appear—may you behold them!
> They will appear—may you behold them!
> A horse nation will appear.
> A thunder being nation will appear.
> They will appear, behold!
> They will appear, behold!

There are four sets of four riders on black, white, sorrel, and buckskin horses. There is drumming and the singing of sacred songs, and the horses are prancing as the parade is marshaled.

Surely this is no ordinary event, but a numinous, portentous one, and the cosmic forces seem to join in the drama.

Now when we were all in line, facing the west, I looked up into a dark cloud that was coming there and the people all became quiet and the horses quit prancing. And when there was silence but for low thunder yonder, I sent a voice to the spirits of the cloud, holding forth my right hand, thus, palm outward as I cried four times:

"Hey-a-a-hey! hey-a-a-hey! hey-a-a-hey! hey-a-a-hey!"

Then the Grandfathers behind me sang another sacred song from my vision, the one that goes like this:

"At the center of the earth, behold a four-legged.
They have said this to me."

And as they sang a strange thing happened. My bay pricked up his ears and raised his tail and pawed the earth, neighing long and loud, and the whites and the sorrels and the buckskins did the same; and all the other horses in the village neighed, and even those grazing in the valley and on the hill slopes raised their heads and neighed together. Then suddenly, as I sat there looking at the cloud, I saw my vision yonder once again—the tepee built of cloud and sewed with lightning, the flaming rainbow door and, underneath, the Six Grandfathers sitting, and all the horses thronging in their quarters; and also there was I myself upon my bay before the tepee. I looked about me and could see that what we then were doing was like a shadow cast upon the earth from yonder vision in the heavens, so bright it was and clear. I knew the real was yonder and the darkened dream of it was here.

And as I looked, the Six Grandfathers yonder in the cloud, and all the riders of the horses and even I myself upon the bay up there, all held their hands and palms toward me, and when they did this I had to pray, and so I cried:

"Grandfathers, you behold me!
Spirits of the World, you behold!
What you have said to me, I am now performing!
Hear me and help me!"

Then the vision went out, and the thunder cloud was coming on with lightning on its front and many voices in it, and the split-tail swallows swooped above us in a swarm.[38]

The people of the village run to fasten down their tepees, but the marvelous ceremonial is not rained out. Black Elk says,

. . . the hail and rain were falling yonder just a little way from us, and we could see it, but the cloud stood there and flashed and thundered, and only a little sprinkle fell on us. The thunder beings were glad and had come in a great crowd to see the dance.[39]

We certainly have no relevant explanatory models to account for the cooperation of natural forces in mythological events. But our own mythology, on the other hand, is full of such accounts.

Black Elk's vision, then, is a great success, in this mythogenic enactment that instructs us so well how ritual emerges from myth. At the end of the ceremony the sacred pipe is passed around the village "until every one had smoked at least a puff." But their euphoria is not from what is contained in the pipe, but from living in a myth and from the sacred celebration. Black Elk says,

After the horse dance was over, it seemed that I was above the ground and did not touch it when I walked. I felt very happy, for I could see that my people were all happier. Many crowded around me and said that they or their relatives who had been feeling sick were well again, and these gave me many gifts. Even the horses seemed to be healthier and happier after the dance.[40]

And then he says, and this is testimony to the therapy that may be contained in myth,

The fear that was on me so long was gone, and when thunder clouds appeared I was always glad to see them, for they came as relatives to visit me. Everything seemed good and beautiful now, and kind.

Before this the medicine men would not talk to me, but now they would come to me to talk about my vision.

From that time on, I always got up very early to see the rising of the daybreak star. People knew that I did this, and many would get up to see it with me, and when it came we said: "Behold the star of understanding!"[41]

The initial experience of such a vision may itself be healing or life-transforming. But often our dreams and visions may ask for more: perhaps to break through into the field of time and space, to wear there, even briefly, a tangible, solid form. In this way are the dimensions of within and without woven together. The human psyche is an intermediary between two worlds. It may choose to close itself off to their relationship, separating its own mythic imaginings from the daylight world. But then, it seems, there is something missing from each.

We know how often in human doings the world of myth has come to knock at the doors of our consciousness, asking for admittance. And we are also finding out how bleak our three-dimensional world can be without the magic light of myth shining into it. The shaman is the full-time specialist who ensures that the doorway be kept open, that vision may seek enactment.

3

Priests, Scientists, Yogis

If we are to find some way in which we can enact our visions in the contemporary world, as does the shaman in his society, we cannot merely imitate him. We must first become grounded rather firmly in the reality of our three-dimensional world, our technological society, our global village. Only from the actual necessities of the social, physical environment can we initiate a vision-quest which will in any way prove relevant for us.

The fabric of the reality we now find around us is spun out of history, woven on the loom of technology, and patterned by myth. We may watch teenage Guru Maharaj-ji on TV and compare him to Bishop Fulton Sheen. We may jet to Benares to find our guru; and when we are there we may offer him LSD, as Richard Alpert did, to compare chemical with traditional ecstasy. We can verify people's dreams and altered states of consciousness by devices that read EEGs, EMGs, and GSRs. And many contemporary psychologists are telling us we can speed up the ageless quest of the voluntary control of internal states by biofeedback devices.

The priest, the scientist, and the yogi all are technicians of different aspects of our reality. They seem to be rather different creatures from one another, yet, as we shall see, there are echoes and reflections of each in the doings of the others. It is also interesting to note that each of these roles is a further development of tasks which originally belonged to the shaman: the perpetuation of myth, the manipulation of reality, and the pursuit of physical self-control and mystical ecstasy.

It would seem foolish to return to a contemporary shamanism without some in-depth consideration of what priest, scientist and yogi have discovered in their more specialized disciplines. As I have suggested, each of these roles corresponds to a different "stage of mythic engagement." We see them also corresponding to very specific social conditions and historical dynamics.

I start with the oldest of these specialists, the priest.

Belief and Orthodoxy (Stage 2)*

As many students of myth have pointed out, mythology throughout most of the world has been read in a rather playful, mythopoetic way, from the Orient to the ancient Greeks. It has especially been insisted in our literal-historical Judeo-Christian tradition that myth equals literal reality. Joseph Campbell says of this that

among the poets, artists, and philosophers, such direct belief in the literal truth of a poetically conceived mythology was impossible. They knew that, just as they were themselves coining and developing myths, so in the remote past the inherited mythology had also been composed—under the influence of divine inspiration, no doubt, yet by the hands and labors of functioning poets.[1]

Campbell portrays the relative amount of "mythopoetic" consciousness present in an individual as the determiner of three separate modes: the *poet, prophet,* or *priest.* Each is dealing with mythic inspiration. But taking the inspiration too literally, the poet becomes prophet, whose utterances may be defined as "poetry overdone," and who founds a cult based on the literalization of myth, paving the way for the priest, who with his orthodox interpreting does the myth, as it were, "to death."[2]

Mythic identity is ecstatic but unstable, and the individual who partakes of this intense level of experiencing almost always sinks back into what Jung called "symbolic elaboration," where ecstasy crystallizes into a belief or myth that can be dealt with by ordinary consciousness. We remember that the Buddha, perhaps the wisest of visionaries, following his il-

*For the *Stages of Mythic Engagement* see p. 24.

lumination concluded that what he had experienced could never be taught. (But there he was, still possessed of a physical body and a sizable life expectancy. What else could he do?) The ecstatic vision asks us for enactment in the objective world. And mythic identity leads most often, even when we wish it not to, to orthodoxy.

Marghanita Laski, in her book *Ecstasy*, refers to the "over-belief" that is often present before an ecstatic experience and afterward provides the structure of its integration. She mentions that in the cases of both Saint Augustine and John Wesley the elements of their religious experience were there beforehand. Saint Augustine does not become a Buddhist but a Christian, which he had been contemplating anyway. And Wesley was already a minister when he had his revelation. The ingredients of the final belief system may be originally present, but the experience of ecstasy is needed to activate and consolidate them, making them experientially real.

We might say that when a religious experience is actively and sincerely sought after, the mythic meaning that emerges in its ecstatic realization is most likely to vivify and inform the existing belief system—if indeed it provides an adequate symbolic "vessel" for the experience. We remember that shamans have very typical adventures, part of the mythology of their tradition. Zen Buddhists likewise have *satori* experiences, not shamanistic encounters or Christian ecstasies. On the other hand, as in the case of Dorothy, when no experience is being sought but one comes unasked, we see that it may take its form from her unconscious problems and conflicts, fragments of her belief systems and past history. The effort involved in religious exercises, mediation, and inward questioning seems to develop a "symbolic musculature" for handling a powerful primary experience. Lacking this, the individual may indeed become psychotic, since all parts of the unprepared psyche are equally "supercharged." What should be emphasized at this point is that whenever an encounter with the mythic takes place, whether in schizophrenia, religious ecstasy, or psychedelic experience, there is always the dual presence of both the "overbelief" and the personal formula in the ensuing symbolic drama and the emerging mystical belief.

My observation has been that monotheistic and heavily orthodox belief systems exert a very powerful stabilizing and organizing effect upon the psyche. There is a polarization within the psyche between the central God-authority archetype and all the other parts. The monotheistic pattern seems more likely to produce powerful ethical and legalistic systems, intense confrontations between conscious and unconscious, and a stronger ego.

The polytheistic orthodoxies on the other hand, seem to allow the psyche more of its own innate polymorphous perversity. Sharp distinctions between good and evil are much harder to make. And though the deities of the polytheistic pantheon are prone to squabble, there are never enmities of the scope of that conflict between the Lord of Light and the Prince of Darkness. The pre-Christian Romans never attacked the indigenous mythologies of the people they conquered the way they did after Christianization. Polytheism seems much more open, both in culture and in psyche, to fostering a live and let-live atmosphere. Perhaps this is one reason why in our times of the reopening and unfolding of human capacity for pleasure, we may let a few of those myths—the banished gods, and most especially goddesses—back in the door. After all, what's wrong with a "graven image" as long as you don't mistake the symbol for what it hints at, the finger for what it points to? Religious persecution, as well as religious evangelism, is the disease of the literal-minded.

Most of us have been trained by our literal Judeo-Christian heritage to think of our myths as either literally true or not true at all. The paranoid schizophrenic then, who projects his inner mythic drama on the outside world, is conforming to our cultural pattern. He has no training in turning the attention within to the living landscape and there allowing his energies to enact their symbolic play, the meaning of which is psychological, not literal. Hence, too, the plight of our callow shamans, who having ingested a few milligrams of freeze-dried mythology and feeling that they can fly, walk out of windows. But can we really, as do the press and anguished parents, blame this tragedy on the drug? Are these people not equally the victims of a culture which has never been able to distinguish the difference between the mythic and the real? Experiencing and perceiving mythically for the first time, these neophyte shamans have never had a chance to learn how to deal intelligently or creatively with the mythopoetic consciousness. Like Dorothy and Levy-Bruhl's primitives, they have been living in "participation mystique," never learning to differentiate between the objectively real and the "glosses" that arise from the mythic and personal levels within. Surely this is another sign of the incredible deficiencies in our approach to education. Would even a very small child among the Senoi make a similar mistake?

Following the unmistakable and widespread opening of the mythic imagination occasioned by psychedelic drugs in the 1960's, we seem to be coming (the inevitable sequence) to a more stable relationship with the symbolic phantasmagoria released into the collective mindscape. Cults of various kinds —witchcraft, yoga, astrology—are once again flourishing after years of neglect. And our susceptibility to mythic identity seems undiminished.

A major movement among the disaffected young, who have recognized that it is impossible to stay high all the time, yet cannot go back to the old patterns of existence they feel they have rejected once and for all, is the Jesus movement. On the one hand, this is attractive because it offers firsthand experiential religion. Tied in with both rock and soul music, it talks to feelings, not thoughts. "Charismatic" phenomena, such as "the gift of tongues" and testimonials, are prevalent among these groups. And the enthusiasm generated is understandable when we remember that "enthusiasm" literally means "being filled with spirit." Also there is much talk about Jesus as a personal friend and guide within, a phenomenon which certainly must have been present among those early followers of

Christianity, the secret wellspring of their strength through adversity and torture. For this, on the psychological side, we cannot help but wish them well; and this experience of the "guide within" fulfills a psychological need which is one of the basic functions of myth.

But what about the orientation side of their beliefs? They seem to have regressed a few thousand years. There is no conception whatever of the distinction between the poetical, psychological, and metaphoric functions of myth on the one hand and their literal actuality on the other. Most of the movement seems to share the belief of early Christianity and the most literal of the fundamentalist sects that Doomsday is near.[3]

There are many scriptures in the Bible that prophesy the signs of the end of the world. First, there will be famines (Matthew 24:7); members point to the hunger that already exists in Biafra, India, Pakistan and some parts of the United States. There will be earthquakes (Luke 21:11); to document this sign they point to California, Japan, Chile and Peru. The recapture of old Jerusalem is interpreted as another sign (Zechariah 12–14 and Ezekiel 36:16–18). Wars (Matthew 24:6), rioting (Luke 21:25), and the peace movement (I Thessalonians 3:5) are other events that Jesus people claim are signs of the end.[4]

The Bible then, as for Jehovah's Witnesses, is the literal "Word of God" which contains prophecies about the end of the world. It is not a spiritual text for symbolic instruction. One of the things that has horrified liberal and intellectual churchgoing parents of these offspring, who might otherwise have been pleased by their "return to the fold," is this fundamentalism and dogmatism. But do we really have a right to be surprised? Literalism is one of our oldest traditions, stemming back to the messianic beliefs of a little tribe of Semitic nomads wandering about the deserts of the Middle East. And our level of mythological sophistication seems still to be where theirs was twenty-five hundred years ago.

The front page of the second section of the *New York Times* for May 7, 1973, carried a story that is very characteristic of our time. I summarize the relevant essentials below. The account was headlined ABDUCTIONS FROM RELIGIOUS SECTS STIR INCREASING CONCERN AND MORE CHARGES.

Mr. M., a middle-aged professional man, with help forcibly seizes and abducts his son Marcus M., who is walking along the street on his way to where he is presently living. Marcus is a recent convert to the "Children of God," a new-age fundamentalist Christian sect. The article is not specific as to why force is necessary, but the implication is that his father fears Marcus is truly "off his head"; he has proven unresponsive to other types of persuasion. For three days what amounts to a "marathon" encounter is held, employing· the services of a Mr. P., who specializes in this sort of thing, a process he calls "deprogramming." Mr. P. works entirely with converts to the abounding fundamentalist and mystical sects (or more correctly, *for* the disgruntled parents of the converts), and claims to have "recovered," with his assistants, more than six hundred youths. Eventually, after several escape attempts, Marcus finally breaks down and agrees that the Children of God had perhaps "distorted the Bible" (ie., his relation to the orthodox mythic belief system has been shaken).

Thus the efforts of some well-meaning parents to rescue their offspring from what we might term "an incursion into the mythic realm." Their goal seems to be to get their son back to some semblance of membership in our conventional social reality. The issue in this case seemed to be not so much *what* Marcus believed, but *how* he believed. The article mentions that "Mr. M., a 48-year-old budget analyst, remained calm during this period [of the marathon] but his wife, *whose hobby is astrology* [my italics] was visibly anxious and said she was taking tranquilizers." The article also quotes one of the deprogrammers as saying that "the arms of the protection of God are around me," and the other as claiming that he was "saved from drugs by accepting Jesus." The deprogrammers come on by quoting more scriptural passages than the convert has available and by interrogating him mercilessly about his articles of faith.

What we have seen here is an extremely common panic response among the socialized members of a human community when one of their number leaves the consensually valid reality for a nonordinary mythic relationship to it. Mr. M. claimed the Children of God had "psychologically kidnapped" his son. "I had to do what I could for him," he said, "I'd have done anything." But is "deprogramming" really the answer to our problem? If so, we may expect a booming business for this profession and an incorporation of "metaphysical mugging" into our daily way of life.

There is an interesting issue here between Marcus and his mother's styles of mythic involvement. Is astrology a more plausible cosmic conception than a radical Christian orthodoxy these days? Apparently so. The question, though, would seem to be whether the sacred is contained in the profane or vice versa. Mrs. M. is a dilletante who no doubt does her housework. Marcus is the mystic whose mythic seizure has evidently been rather total. His parents' reaction is not unlike that of Saint Clare's family, who tried to abduct her physically when she ran away from home to join Saint Francis's band of world-abnegating saints; or the legend of Saint Thomas Aquinas, whose family allegedly locked him in a room with a whore to dissuade him from joining the Dominican order.

Our present goal, should not be to perfect our deprogramming methods, which I fear may be our first impulse, but rather to understand the dynamics behind these potent myth-embracing behaviors. What is it in Marcus, what in his mother, what in each of us, that is still susceptible to a myth in these enlightened times?

The great mythic orthodoxies of our planet seem to be in a process of withdrawl. These traditional socially grounded forms for both satisfying and restraining man's living, dynamic requirements for mythic meaning have been disanchored and depotentized. With throwing off their stifling sense of existential and moral confinement, though, we have at the same time lost the benefit of their stabilizing influence on the mythic imagination. The need in man which has ever gazed past the confining circumstances of his private life toward an eternal order of meaning is still as active as ever. Yet the organized churches, venerable stewards of our great myths for centuries, are in a senile decline.

Having been shown by Darwin that the Garden of Eden is most likely not literally true, we have thrown out our entire mythological orientation, with its psychological guiding functions as well. Somehow it would seem that if we had been a little less literal all along, the revelations of science about the actualities of our physical universe would have been less shattering to our mythology.

Science and Myth (Stage 3)

Anyone who has ever interacted with the scientific academy in a more than casual way knows that we have replaced our old mythic orthodoxies with a more modern secular one. There are doctrines and dogmas, sectarian divisions, official and heretical ways of thinking. Though science is ideally supposed to withhold final commitment from its hypotheses about the nature of reality, in practice it seems to offer to many a picture of the universe no less orthodox than those mythic systems we are in the process of banishing.

I feel there are two levels on which we must consider the impact of science on man. The first is the more obvious collective level, at which we see a previously undreamed-of breakthrough in our understanding of and control of physical reality. In the past two centuries we have advanced far more than in the previous two millennia in this regard, and the horizon ahead looks almost limitless. Our ability to subordinate and utilize the physical universe seems to grow equally with our technological skill. In these past few years, a mere moment in his long history, man the manipulator has come into his own.

But a second level we must consider is the personal, psychological one. How does the approach to reality which we call science function within the living nervous system of individual human beings? And how does this new world-transforming way of looking at reality fit into the functioning of a psyche which has been preoccupied with spirits, gods, and demons for a major portion of its probably one or two million years of existence? Each of us experiences this life through the medium of a body, an organic entity which we neither designed nor created, but which is the living, tangible manifestation of millions of years of an evolutionary process. And our genealogy includes not only ancestors we recognize as human (even the squat and hairy ones we would prefer not to), but stretches back to origins in primal seas—crustaceans and mollusks, and finally that shapeless yet most accommodating ancestor of us all: the amoeba. Our modern consciousness is a bright flower, enjoying its day in the sun, but our roots are dark and deep.

Onto this living nervous system we impress the artificial systems of our conscious learning. In the beginning the un-tutored child-psyche in each of us thinks magically, unitively, and does not distinguish and classify as does the socially imprinted adult. Traditional, socially bound mythologies have taken advantage of these innate properties of the psyche to graft on forms that speak to that sense of mystical unity, to the image-prone imagination. Effective myth binds the forms without to the forms within.

It is on this level that I am particularly concerned with comparing science and myth. And we must ask ourselves how science functions as myth. To the extent that our imagistic, animistic world view has been replaced by a mechanistic, empirical one, science must now be in the position that mythology has occupied for thousands of years. And there is a difference between science as methodology, as an operating manual for technicians and researchers, and science as a world view, taught to our children in school in much the same way as myths of origin and the history of the gods have been for countless generations.

The first issue to which I call the reader's attention is a vital one, perhaps at the root of many corollary issues: I have mentioned that one of the child's primary impulses is to conceive of the universe as alive. In both egocentrism and animism the world is considered to be a living extension of oneself, and oneself of the world. Yet we find in the most widespread contemporary scientific outlook a complete negation of this. The universe obeys certain mechanical laws, but in essence it is inert, dead. I do want to emphasize that this is not the opinion of our most advanced scientific minds, but rather, at the level with which this discussion is concerned, the picture of the world that science has communicated to everyman.

This way of conceiving of the universe is not new. It reaches as far back as Democritus, Greek contemporary of Socrates, who taught: "By convention coloured, by convention sweet, by convention bitter; in reality only atoms and the void."[5] The philosophical history of science shows a dialogue between this view and those thinkers, epitomized by Kant, who thought there must be an a-priori principle of rationality in nature no less than in man. "Empiricism," in the beginnings of the history of science, was used as a term of derogation, referring to those styles of knowledge that drew only from experience, and not with reference to principles. But with the advent of positivism and the influential work of Ernst Mach at the end of the last century there was a shift in the other direction. Mach taught that scientific theory, far from being an approximation of some a-priori principle underlying the workings of things, was merely a convenient summary of experiences. His influential opus *Die Mechanik* is thought of as the founding work of positivism and is simultaneously a reaffirmation of the mechanical nature of the universe.

The second issue involves theory. In empiricism there is the tacit recognition that theory is a rather dangerous borderline activity. Whenever the mind leaves pure observation and begins to formulate the reasons for things, or the connections that exist between them, it runs the risk of describing more its own inner dynamics than the objective behavior of reality. Any theory that seems "too right" may easily be satisfying the mind's hidden wishes for symmetry or lawfulness rather than truly representing the behavior of particles of matter. We all know subliminally that there is a facile mythmaker in all men, who is often an evangelist besides and would like nothing better than to reveal to humankind the secrets of the universe. The history of science is full of scandals where myth seized the mind and disrupted the delicate yoga of unbiased observation and reporting. We need only think of the great hoaxes, such as Piltdown man, or the great evangelists, proponents of the remarkable and miraculous, seizing the attention of the mythic man in each of us, yet also earning the scorn of the more dedicated, ascetic scientist. We think of Immanuel Velikovsky with his theory of planetary collision and catastrophe, or the strange fanatic Hans Horbiger with his mythic-surreal doctrine of eternal ice, which was evidently rather influential on Hitler;[6] or Wilhelm Reich, who moved from a respectable and limited study of the characterology of bodily tensions to capturing and evangelizing about the "cosmic orgone energy," secret of life, that eventuated in his imprisonment. And our popular imagination seems to have fallen in love with the "chariots of the gods," an hypothesis of extraterrestial superscientific influence in the workings of human history. (Surely those pyramids could not have been built by men!)

Myth, as we have seen, is the shadow of the scientist, and the relationship between them seems to be inversely proportional. Michael Polanyi, the Oxford philosopher-scientist, mentions the passionate quality that attaches to successful discoveries and assertions, scientific or otherwise.

We have on record the outcries of dizzy exultation to which Kepler gave vent at the dawning of discovery, as well as those of others at the false dawn of supposed discoveries. We know the violence with which great pioneers like Pasteur have upheld their claims against their critics and can hear the same angry impatience expressed today by fanatical cranks like Lysenko.[7]

The abstract processes of scientific methodology are one thing; the presence of a scientific point of view in an individual human psyche is something else. We are living persons, not detached observers of life. Polanyi, in his excellent book *Personal Knowledge*, distinguishes between *explicit knowing* and *tacit knowing*. "Tacit knowing," he says, "is more fundamental than explicit knowing: we can know more than we can tell and we can tell nothing without relying on our awareness of things we may not be able to tell."[8] And what we know, explicitly or tacitly, exists in the greater field of our "being-in-the-world." Combining the methods of science with those of phenomenology, Polanyi says we must come inescapably to the conclusion that "all knowledge is ultimately personal."

A scientist may be no less dogmatic, no less orthodox than a fundamentalist Christian. To the extent that his belief systems are structured to accept certain possibilities and reject others, the specific content of his world view is irrelevant. What is important is that his belief system is more or less resistant to change, more or less charged with energy, and more or less likely to bend incoming data to fit the system (mythic assimilation). And we must recognize finally that the stance of the confirmed skeptic is no less a mythological human posture than that of the true believer.

Any theory or belief which proposes to interpret or explain the totality of things seems to activate the covert functioning of a psychological dynamism. This is recognizable in religious beliefs especially, but also seems to be active in philosophical belief systems, ideologies, reformist movements. Personal experience comes increasingly under the influence of a central idea. This idea or cluster of ideas comes to dominate thinking, planning, personal behavior. It may be socialism, Scientology, astrology, macrobiotics, psychoanalysis, skepticism, Buddhism. And there are atheists who pursue the spread of their beliefs religiously. Jung's analysis of Freud's monomania seems to illustrate this point rather well. There was nothing religious in the *content* of Freud's beliefs, but rather in the *way* he held them. The sexual theory became for Freud an all-consuming doctrine which subtended his understanding of everything from Egyptian history to the sculptures of Michelangelo.

In an autobiographical account of his interactions with Freud, Jung quotes him as saying,

"My dear Jung, promise me never to abandon the sexual theory. That is the most essential thing of all. You see we must make a dogma of it, an unshakable bulwark." He said this to me with great emotion, in the tone of a father saying, "And promise me this one thing, my dear son: that you will go to church every Sunday."[9]

Jung was rather astonished by this, and particularly by the use of the term dogma, reserved for articles of religious belief. He says, " . . . until then I had not considered sexuality as a precious and imperiled concept to which one must remain faithful. Sexuality evidently meant more to Freud than to other people. For him it was something to be religiously observed."[10] Perhaps there is no adequate Freudian explanation of this behavior pattern. But Jung, appropriately enough, constructed a Jungian one.

I was bewildered and embarrassed. I had the feeling that I had caught a glimpse of a new unknown country from which swarms of new ideas flew to meet me. One thing was clear: Freud, who had always made much of his irreligiosity, had now constructed a dogma; or rather, in the place of a jealous God whom he had lost, he had substituted another compelling image, that of sexuality. It was no less insistent, exacting, domineering, threatening and morally ambivalent than the original one . . . the sexual libido took over the attributes of a *deus absconditus*, a hidden or concealed god . . . the lost god had now to be sought below, not above. . . .

Freud never asked himself why he was compelled to talk continually of sex, why this idea had taken such possession of him. . . . Although for Freud, sexuality was undoubtedly a *numinosium*, his terminology seemed to define it as a biological function. It was only the emotionality with which he spoke of it that revealed the deeper elements reverberating within him.[11]

Even in this great psychoanalytical mind, then, delusion was wont to occur. Certainly if this foible had been related to one of his own areas of theoretical expertise, Freud might have been able to diagnose his own problem. But it was not, and he had no psychological models to deal with his own behavior. Having disposed of religion in three of his major books,* Freud probably never expected it to emerge, not in the content but in the style of his beliefs.

There are in man "deep structures" of which he is little aware, yet which pattern and shape his entire experiencing. One set of these receives the imprints of the syntactical structures of the language and other social systems to which he is exposed in childhood. But there are others. Some relate to our images of all women, of all men, of authorities, of nature, of religion. Of these archetypal, deep structures, that which is receptive to those input patterns which might be called "religious" is central. Jung became specifically concerned with this archetype, which he called the *Self*, and its manifestations. To its influence he ascribed the universality of religious experience.

When there is no religious orientation, Jung hypothesized, the religious archetype is still active but remains primitive—because uncultivated—and unconscious. Its powerful valence is attracted to any life activity or belief which assumes a central role for an individual. Its functioning is then unconsciously cathected to that system, lending it a religious intensity, with the corollary phenomena of fanaticism, dogmatism, orthodoxy, and so on. The religious archetype may be, in fact, most dangerous when not bound to outer religious forms. It may emerge in a monomania, in a fanatical intensity of personal style, in an obsession, a fetishism, or in those peculiarly distorted, fragmented religious seizures we often find in delusional schizophrenia.

Some modern men are capable of a convenient split which enables them to be scientists on weekdays and go to church

Totem and Taboo, Moses and Monotheism, and *The Future of an Illusion* might be seen as a variety of attempts to come to terms with his personal feelings about religion, as well as exercises in psychoanalytic theory.

on Sundays, expressing beliefs of Mormonism or Catholicism which are logically absurd in view of their scientific knowledge. For others the contradictions between a mechanistic, impartial universe and the internal pressure to find a meaning in life is intolerable. And the results are alienation, depression, and the existential emptiness with which we are all familiar.

Here we come to a crucial issue of the relation between engagement and disengagement. Science has disengaged myth from man's perception of the universe in order to enable him to see what is there more clearly and to gain the control necessary for his own security and survival. At the same time, guilty as ever of throwing out the baby with the bath, we have disengaged the positive, guiding, nurturing aspects of mythic-religious experiencing. Literal, scientific orthodoxy has made mythic orthodoxy impossible. But need it also displace the psychological functions?

Science has, in a broad sense, created "myth" as we currently experience it. By disapproving of any assertions about the nature of the universe except those confirmed by the experimental testing of hypotheses, it has relegated to the realm of myth anything that is not science. Thus all religious beliefs, theological models of the universe, myths of creation and origin, are in the same boat with fairy stories and wish-fulfilling fantasies. In this regard Joseph Campbell's whimsical definition of myth as "other people's religions," takes on significance. Science insists it has provided us with a baseline belief system against which all other beliefs, models, and explanations of reality must be measured. In this way the sacred and the profane have been further divided and we have begun to insist that all religious vision is equal to myth and belongs to the childhood of man. Science is the ultimate secular consciousness. Science believes that it alone shows us the difficult-to-accept but alas-too-true actuality of things —the ultimate, undeluded perception which is the supreme goal of Freud's "reality principle." Science belongs to the realistic maturity of man's growth, beyond the wish-fulfilling myths of childhood. Robert Ornstein in *The Psychology of Consciousness* speaks both of the personal nature of all knowing and of the highly conservative nature of scientific knowing:

Personal consciousness is a continual selection and construction, at each stage becoming more and more conservative. As a refinement of the active, personal mode, science is one of the most restricted and sure forms of knowledge available to man. Our senses limit; our central nervous system limits; our personal and cultural categories limit; language limits; and beyond all these selections, the rules of science cause us to further select information which we consider to be true. By a slow, conservative process of construction, science gradually builds a stable lore of knowledge. Science is the very essence of the analytic mode, one of meticulously charting causes and effects, of radically restricting the conditions of observation in order to attain precision. It constitutes another highly specialized development of consciousness, at once its most conservative, yet its most reliable.[12]

For the dedicated scientist, science shows "objective reality." But as Michael Polanyi reminds us, "all knowledge is ultimately personal." Operative within a living nervous system —a human psyche with its ancient roots—science, like any belief system, functions as myth. Now here is the point: there is convincing evidence that, as myth, the view of the universe that science has presently bestowed upon us is inadequate. Alienation and existential despair, on the one hand, combined with our contemporary frenzy to embrace a bizarre variety of religious cults on the other, amount to a rather impressive clinical picture. Our secular myth leaves us personally, psychologically, unsatisfied. That in man which has generated the variety of his religious forms is ever yet susceptible to them, and still requires that sacred mode of experiencing which I have recurrently introduced throughout this book.

Man's recent visit to the moon could have been for us either a cosmic-mythic event, culmination of the ages of our poetic rapture with this magical, celestial body, or a dry technological or political achievement, beating the Russians at setting foot on a dead planet. For most of us, I fear, it was the latter. The awakening and engagement of our mythical sensibilities was somehow precluded, not enhanced, by the precision and complexity of the technology. The overwhelmingly scientific secular consciousness of the announcers, the NASA technicians, and the astronauts themselves spoke to the same level in us. I overheard one woman exclaim in dismay while listening to the so often banal commentary, "Why couldn't they have sent a poet up there?"

The plain truth of the matter is, of course, that a poet couldn't be trusted to drive a space ship—to remember that extraordinary complexity of details. But maybe they could have asked one along for the ride; maybe they could have included a professional ecstatic as part of the crew, whose entire job would have been to tell us what it *felt* like to be there—I have found my attention seized at two points especially in our space program. One was when one of the earlier astronauts on a spacewalk in deep space became ecstatic, joyously mad, literally "spaced out." If you remember, there was a little difficulty in getting him back to the ship. "At last," I thought, "an appropriate human response to cosmic space."

Another item of interest has come to light recently: several of the astronauts, after their return from space, have undergone rather interesting personality transformations. There have been "personality breakdowns," family problems, religious conversions, and one of the astronauts (Ed Mitchell) has become deeply involved in ESP research.

I am especially interested in these particular events because they are signs that (as some among us had hoped and others feared) modern man has not been able to subdue and eliminate his mythical consciousness. I would find it tragic if man were able to visit the mysteries of deep space without ecstasy or personal transformation. These men, of course, have been selected for their psychological stability and computative intelligence, their resistance to daydreams and myths. They are exemplars of the scientifically trained and indoctrinated modern human being. Yet somehow the mystery dimension of what they were doing broke through the purely cerebral level of their discipline, whether fleetingly or permanently only time will tell. Following their spaceflights several astronauts have mentioned their regret that the incredible concentration and responsibility demanded of them left no time for inner flights of joy and wonder. Like the machinery of which they were a part, they were required to be precise and infallible.

Scientific enlightenment, unlike the religious variety, seems to have done away with our sense of wonder, rather than regenerating it. But must it be so? My suggestion is that this predicament is more a result of the style of our science than of any inherent contradiction between science and wonder. An event of cosmic magnitude which for many has now passed into the realm of the commonplace may serve to illustrate this point.

In the oldest great metaphysical systems of the world we find a truth perhaps more basic than all the others: this all-too-solid-seeming world of forms and events that we coinhabit is an illusion. We find this recognition in the Platonic tradition, in the best of the Christian mystics, and in its oldest form in the Hindu cosmology. The surface of things is a maya, a dancing veil, ever different, ever the same, behind which hides "the true nature of things."

What is the true nature of things? The Katha Upanishad puts it vividly: "Whatever there is—the whole universe—vibrates because it has gone forth from Brahman, which exists as its ground. That Brahman is a great terror, like a poised thunderbolt. Those who know It become immortal."[13] The recognition of this mystical truth seems inseparable from every major form of religious illumination, satori, or moksha. Like the wish-fulfilling gem in both fairy tales and sacred stories, this truth has many facets. In it may be seen the corollary that we are all aspects of the same underlying force, a part of everything; and that one must not confuse the temporary with the permanent nor cling to what must pass. These are among the deepest of men's religious insights.

For countless generations mankind's philosophers and mystics have been haunted by this truth: the vision of the one underlying energy beneath the separate forms of appearance. Philosophers have argued it (but who listens to them?). Yogis have gone beyond argument into the ardors of manifesting this principle in their own personal lives. And this was indeed the supreme insight of the Buddha. But for the greater part of humanity it has functioned as a myth, both in the positive and the pejorative sense: a potent idea, which opens the mind to what is beyond the senses, yet remains ultimately an unproven assertion.

The formula $E=mc^2$ is a religious truth. And that epiphany at Alamagordo not so many years ago should have been greeted on all sides by sacred celebrations. Once and for all let the skeptic behold: *All matter is energy!* The too-heavy substantiality that you take so seriously is an illusion, a transient shimmering dance of pure spirit. Our life, then, is a metaphor, a symbol play. In that atomic explosion the truth of the philosophers and the yogis was indeed made manifest in our midst. A tiny bit of the maya-illusion was unraveled back to its origins in the blinding white light. And if, instead of generals, the grandstands and the sidelines at Alamagordo had been filled with alchemists, monks, and yogis whose lifetime efforts had brought them to the dawning point of this truth, the blinding white light might have brought illumination indeed, and the thunderclap recognition.

But what might have been called (if the reader will allow me a flight of fancy) "the sacred Maya-Sakti-Vajra process," is called "the Bomb." And its celebrations are in the hands, not of technicians of the sacred, but rather men of the narrowest secular consciousness; men with imaginations like steel traps: politicians and generals. The epiphany has brought most of us, then, not enlightenment but restless dreams. What might have served as a crowning planetary celebration, a cosmic-mythic Fourth of July, was used for human destruction. One day we will perhaps dedicate the bomb to Shiva, that men may mix wonder with their horror at the presence of such cosmic destructiveness in our midst.

Sir John Woodroffe, the distinguished Tantric scholar, felt that science could be, like yoga, a sacred activity.

To-day Western science speaks of Energy as the physical ultimate of all forms of Matter. So has it been for ages to the *Sāktas*, as the worshippers of *Śakti* are called. But they add that such Energy is only a limited manifestation (as Mind and Matter) of the almighty infinite Supreme Power *Mahā-Śakti* of Becoming in "That," *Tat*, which is unitary Being, *Sat*, itself.[14]

The physical universe is the tangible form of the great *Sakti* Energy which is the true being of us all. As such, the lowliest entymologist with his magnifying glass is performing an act of sacred inspection upon the body of the Great Mother. So too, is the geologist on a broader scale; the astronomer still further. Chemists would be not really so far from alchemists, and the nuclear physicists are those who have perhaps come closest to the ultimate mystery. And their "way" is a different but parallel sacred path to the way of the yogi.

"Obeisance be to Her who is pure Being-Consciousness-Bliss, as Power," is the invocation in the *Yoginihrdaya Tantra,* "who exists in the form of Time and Space and all that is therein, and who is the radiant Illuminatrix in all beings."[15] Is it not possible to conjoin somehow the mystery of mythic experiencing with the penetrating vision of science at this level? We may think of a few wise and gentle souls who have made such a mystical marriage in themselves: Einstein surely, and Teilhard de Chardin, who made his meticulous paleontology also sacred anatomy. And this consciousness is present to a degree perhaps in any act of observation and description lovingly engaged in. The best of our naturalists were all mystics who were drawn to the formless in those myriad forms. Finding crystals in the earth, observing fish or the flight of birds, watching the behaving of microbes or the being of stars, can be sacred activities when matched with the sacred frame of mind.

The eighteenth-century scientist-visionary Emanuel Swedenborg was led from his remarkably advanced scientific work in mineralogy and anatomy to a study of more ultimate things. He began to find, in the relationships and forms of natural events, spiritual principles. He saw in the complexities of the physical body the shaping influence of the spirit. The natural world he found to be the final emanation of a ray of creation extending from God through higher levels, celestial and spiritual, into the natural. Events in this world of appearances are metaphors for an ultimately more real, sacred order of being, ciphers of a psychospiritual language.

Science and myth need not be antagonists. We can use our technology and methodology to extend the worlds of our vision rather than vitiate whatever we gaze upon. Can we not move from our stuporous hypnosis by the apparently heavy solidity of things to the vision of the dance? And if indeed the universe has been developing us for new eyes through which to behold itself, as some have said, can we not be worthy of the show?

Yoga—Suspended Engagement (Stage 4)

Through innumerable myriads of forms, through innumerable myriads of eyes and sense-organs of creatures, through innumerable myriads of microcosms, Mind knows Itself to be the Dreamer of Maya's Kingdom. But until the Mirage of Being is scattered by Bodhic-Enlightenment, the Many know not the One.

W. Y. Evans-Wentz, *Tibetan Yoga*

For perhaps three thousand years men of indomitable will, some naked and alone in the forest, some in caves, and some perched on tiger skins and surrounded by devotees, have single-mindedly striven to awaken from "Maya's dream" to behold the One behind the illusion of separateness. As the distinguished Orientalist quoted above so clearly says it, "Maya is the Magic Veil, ever worn by Nature, the Great Mother . . . which veils Reality. It is by yoga alone that the Veil can be rent asunder and man led to self-knowledge and self-conquest, whereby illusion is transcended."[16]

Yoga is the prototypic philosophy of disengagement. From it have come many others, which in bewildering variety have spread throughout the East from Ceylon to Japan. Yoga, though, is not philosophy alone, but method. Its basic assumption is that when man has truly recognized that being, as he experiences it, is a mirage, then his only recourse is to seek liberation from the state of mind that remains fascinated under the spell of illusion.

But this realization of the presence of "the One behind the Many" is not at all easy, and the truth our physicists demonstrated at Alamagordo was sought in the only way available, through a personal discipline which would culminate in a revelation. What we have proven physically to be a fact is what the yogi sought psychologically. And when a single high-powered individual had made the difficult crossing, pierced the veil, he became the living manifestation of that most difficult to obtain of all metaphysical truths, and was surrounded by other seekers still only partway there. Hence the endless chain of gurus and their *chelas*, the tradition of personal transmission of ultimate truth; for only in the unswerving devotion of the single person could Bodhic-enlightenment occur. The practice of total submission to the guru is thus a symbol of the transience and unreality of personal attachments (the many) in the face of the One, of whom the guru is the exemplar.

Likewise the yogic *ascesis*, the ascetic detachment from the desire-self, is practiced not because the flesh is inherently evil (as in Christian asceticism) but rather as a metaphor for cosmic detachment, the freedom from all illusion to which the yogi hopes to attain. Desires are the living cords of bondage, snares of entrapment from which he must ever free himself. Thus the practice of yoga involves disengagement both from the world as it appears and as one is drawn to it.

There is a curious complementarity between this Eastern philosophy of disengagement and our present Western immersion in materialism. We see on the one hand a tradition which regards the basic fabric of reality as insubstantial, and on the other, one all too apparently caught up in its actuality. As the ancient Greeks might have predicted, in such a polarized situation what must occur is an *enantiodromia*, an exchange of opposites. This indeed seems to be what is happening in the world at the present time. No less obvious than the export of secular technology to the East is the influx of a remarkable variety of spiritual disciplines to the major Western technological societies. As Jung says, "By an inevitable decree of fate the West is becoming acquainted with the peculiar facts of Eastern spirituality."[17] And this is not an idle intellectual curiosity but a psychological compulsion, an irresistible mutual attraction between the introverted sacred technology of the East and the extraverted secular one of the West.

I experienced the actuality of this all-too-neat-sounding hypothesis a few years ago when acting as host to a representative of the Dalai Lama to the Western Hemisphere. Partway through a delightful conversation which lasted several hours, I came to the realization that while I was continually turning the conversation to the variety of Tibetan mystical practices (*tum-mo*, the yogic discipline of generating psychic heat; and *lon-gompas*, special messengers who run, in trance, over great distances, mountain passes, and so forth), my Oriental guest was asking me about politics, land prices in New York State, and the engine in my sports car. And I do not think this was merely politeness on either part—rather a fascination bordering on the compulsive.

We are, in fact, so attracted these days by the spiritual disciplines of the East that compulsion has mastered our discrimination. We have many suddenly devout Western yogis who may have donned orange robes but have never bothered to find out the difference between a Vendantist and a Krishna devotee, between a Zen and a Nichiren Buddhist. The psychological compulsion, originating as it does from beyond and below consciousness, makes us seize mindlessly upon some orthodoxy, strange and alluring because of its utter differentness, without concern as to its social-cultural history or its philosophical genesis. The question then arises, inevitably, of the appropriateness of Westerners taking up the wholesale practice of spiritual disciplines grown thousands of miles away, under different skies and out of alien cultural soil. Or to put it more bluntly, can some kid from Bronx, New York, or Berkeley, California, "give up his ego" in the same way as the naked forest-dwelling Indian sadhu? Is the ego the same? Is the psyche the same? I offer here my own personal experiences with a yogic *sādhana*,* in the hope that they may be of some use in answering these questions.

For several years I had been interested in both yoga and Zen, made occasional visits to ashrams and *zendos,* practiced hatha yoga several times a week, and meditated half or three-quarters of an hour daily. I felt I was getting some benefit from these practices, but also a growing urge for something more, an intensive practice more like that in a full-time ashram. I wanted to reverse the roles of the profane and sacred in my life, so that the sacred dimension should be of primary importance.

Unfortunately it was difficult for me to enter an ashram with family obligations, so I chose a modified course. I began to practice a yogic *sādhana* under an Indian teacher. This involved a daily program of austerities and practices: rising before dawn, purifying the *apāna*† from the psychic system by drinking warm water and defecating, ritually "greeting the sun" (in Sanskrit phrases) as it rose; then, later, *prānā-yāmas* (alternate nostril breathing), about ten *āsanas* (postures), meditation, and a period of psychic visualizations

---

Sādhana includes the concept of "method," "way," "practice."
†*Apāna* is one of the four *vayu* or "winds" located in the body, particularly associated with the lower digestive tract.

(designed to right the imbalances in my "astral body").

The morning *sādhana* took about two and one-half hours, the evening one about an hour. In addition I was required to abstain from meat, fish, eggs, tea, coffee, cigarettes, alcohol, pot. Sex was to be practiced only once a month (on the night of the full moon). Moreover, I was to withhold the imagination from that playful speculation which occurs when one encounters an attractive member of the opposite sex, and avoid association with people, or social groups, that emitted "lower *chakra** vibrations." Fasting was also required one day a week.

In short, the *sādhana* involved a complete sacrifice and revision of the most intimate details of my life. Casual, profane reality was to be replaced by a sacred discipline. Obviously, to carry out (or even be interested in) a program of this sort, there must be a rather strong impulse toward it. And a part of me certainly rejoiced in the order, control, and abstention present in this sacred discipline. I did feel, often, a remarkable clarity while breathing and chanting in the predawn light. But why am I not doing it now?

As my wife described it (and she had joined me in my *sādhana* a while after I started it), she was not sure she wanted to "give up her desires." Both of us began to feel a noticeable diminution in the zest for life that makes it a joy as well as a burden. Outside the *sādhana* we had little energy for anything else, including enjoying each other, creative projects (which had been an important part of our lives before), and the tasks of living (child care and so on). I had expected to have more energy as a result of my practice. I had less.

There was also the problem of psychic upheavals. I felt my teacher had not sufficiently prepared me for these, nor was he able to help me deal with them when they came up (and they did, all right). There was no question that the yoga was affecting our psychic systems; this was unmistakable. The

---

*The *chakras* are psychic centers, in the Kundalini yoga system seven in number, situated throughout the body. The "lower" chakras are depicted as related to the "lower" human urges of sexuality and aggression.

issue was to deal with what came up, which was often rather chaotic, primitive, and regressive material. I have no doubt that an ashram or monastery may be an ideal therapeutic community to cope with these energies, but in daily life they are dangerous and disruptive when they move beyond certain limits. Any instructor whatever who teaches yoga to ordinary people in this hemisphere should be aware of this fact.

By its classic definition, as we have it from the yoga Sutras of Patanjali, "Yoga is the intentional stopping of the involuntary movements of the mind substance."[18] *Citta,* mind substance, is alive in exactly the same way as biological life, and like all living things it is ever restless, ever changing. Its most frequent occupation is to represent the forms of the world outside, so that we may have an inner model of the world without. An instantaneously plastic "substance," it immediately accommodates to the forms of the physical universe that pass before the eyes and enter through the ears. Under most circumstances, *citta* is engaged with the world of physical forms.

Here then is the necessity for the *method* of yoga. For at some time a long time ago, some inwardly attuned explorer took that first step, the attempt to still the movements of the *citta,* to withdraw the senses from the world of outer forms. Have you ever tried it? If you have, you know what that intrepid first explorer found: the "mind-stuff" goes right on moving, representing, recalling, planning. With an extended time of sensory withholding, *pratyāhāra,* and concentration, *dhāranā,* the activity may be somewhat reduced and the mind partially stilled. But what happens when you begin again the next day? The same thing all over again. The living mind-substance is ever resistant to discipline, "like a drunken monkey" as one text facetiously but realistically puts it.

The yogi's task, then, is not an easy one. He must stop the involuntary representations which the *citta,* left to its own devices, ceaselessly produces. This is the psychomental root of man's attachment to illusion. And not until these movements have been stilled can the mind reflect the formless nature of the indwelling *purusha.** A Zen metaphor portrays the process more vividly: the mind is likened to a pool of water. So long as the surface is agitated it cannot reflect the image of the moon. Only when the water is completely calm can the reflection attain any clarity. Likewise, the mind-stuff, when agitated breaks the experienced universe into fragmented reflections of the truth. Only when it is stilled by meditation can it reflect the unitive vision of pure consciousness (*moksha, purusha, samadhi, satori*).

Experimental psychology has unintentionally verified some of the basic descriptions in yoga of the behavior of the "mind-stuff" (*citta*), though with a rather different terminology. Through an extensive variety of experiments psychologists have explored the effects of sensory deprivation, or as some have called it, "afferent isolation." Stimulated by some of the peculiar effects observed by high altitude pilots, as well as people in oxygen tents, iron lungs, and solitary confinement, psychologists began to study systematically the effects of diminished sensory stimulation over prolonged periods. The results have been verified in hundreds of replications. Withheld from the ordinary varied, patterned contact with sensory data that we take for granted, the mind begins to function in a different manner. Cognitive skills such as problem-solving and reasoning diminish. Restlessness, anxiety, and irritability increase, along with an accelerating cycle of spontaneous mental activity (fantasies, hallucinations, delusions).[19] The type of thinking that seems to become dominant is characterized more by "primary process activity" than "secondary processes." Fantasies become increasingly compulsive and display bizarre content, dreamlike logic, and vivid imagery, often of hallucinatory intensity.

A few implications of these studies have become inescapable, even for those psychologists who prefer to resist all and any

---

*In the yoga cosmology the universe starts with a divorce between *purusha*, the principle of pure unconditioned consciousness, and *prakriti*, the principle of energetic manifestation. Ordinary thoughts (*citta*) belong to *prakriti*, they are spontaneously active.

implications about "consciousness":* First, ordinary sensory experience seems to exert a stabilizing effect on conscious processes, maintaining a level at which cognitive processes such as reasoning, problem-solving, and directed thinking are possible. Second, reduction of sensory input seems to facilitate the emergence of otherwise "unconscious" psychological energies characterized by archaic content, spontaneity, lack of directedness.[20] Third, sustained sensory deprivation is not possible for ordinary individuals without severe regression, panic, loss of reality boundaries, and so forth.[21]

The yogis also noticed a long time ago that enforced sensory withdrawal and discipline cause an instinctive resistance by the mind substance. Their portrayal of the mind is of a living thing with its own powerful natural attraction for both representing and desiring the world of outer forms. He who thinks that by practicing a little meditation he can still the mind had better think again, for he is dealing with an adversary of infinite resources and ancient cunning. The *citta*, living psychic energy, desires the world of forms. And when one meditates for an hour, perhaps, and achieves a little clarity, a little stillness, this is only the most momentary victory. One has temporarily stilled the outermost level of psychomental activity (*cittavritti*). But when the artificial tension of concentration has been lifted, *cittavritti* resumes its polymorphous, glimmering dance, perhaps with a little additional animation by way of vengeance for lost time.

Yoga psychology recognizes the origins of psychomental activity as being in "the unconscious," as have the psychodynamic schools of personality. The origins of the ever-changing mental states (*cittavritti*) are to be found in the *vāsanās*, defined roughly as "subconscious latencies," which are inaccessible to direct contact or control. As Eliade says,

The *vāsanās* constitute an immense obstacle—for they are in the highest degree elusive, difficult to control and master. By the very

*Notably Behaviorists, who have decided that since consciousness is not behaviorally describable it must be excluded from psychological methodology.

fact that their mode of being is that of a "potentiality," their own dynamism forces the *vāsanās* to manifest, to actualize themselves under the form of acts of consciousness. Thus the yogin—even if he has long years of practice to his credit and has passed through several stages of his ascetic itinerary—is in danger of finding himself defeated by the invasion of a powerful stream of psychomental "eddies" precipitated by the *vāsanās*.[22]

Thus the spontaneous mental activity observed by our psychologists in the sensory deprivation studies is just an intimation (our first inkling?) of the depth and power behind psychic energy. Yogis have found from years of dedicated attempts to "stop the involuntary movements of the mind substance" that this is the hardest of all tasks: so hard that, as a variety of texts have it, many lifetimes of yoga are required to reach complete liberation. The energy that ceaselessly comes bubbling to the surface of waking experience rises from inaccessible depths within.

But the goal of yoga is to bring about complete cessation of movement, and all else is subordinated to this task. Hence the life of asceticism, abstinence, constant discipline. Only by a ceaseless holding still of the surface movements (*cittavritti*) can the deeper sources of the movement (*vāsanās*) be affected. And even then, as Eliade says, a yogi of considerable attainment may still be overwhelmed by a rushing in of energy from the unconscious. Indeed, this is not infrequent, and the lore of yoga is full of accounts of casualties "along the path." It is generally recognized that in the practice of asceticism (*tapas*) and continuous concentration (*ekāgratā*), by forcing back the natural flow of energy, which travels from unconscious sources within to interact with the forms without, an artificial situation is created not unlike the damming up of water behind a barrier or the sealing of a pressure cooker. And as with the pressure cooker, while the goal of intensifying the process within the vessel is served, there is simultaneously the danger of the process getting out of control, or explosion.

This engagement of the deeper levels of the psyche, then, is a consequence of *disengagement* from ordinary sensory experience. And so it has been portrayed in the numerous mystical scriptures of human kind. The world of the senses and pleasure is antithetical to the world of spiritual realities and must be overcome to permit entrance to the deeper, sacred reality.

But this deeper engagement is not to be taken lightly, for one has activated the entire realm of the mythological within, demons as well as gods, hell as well as heaven. Moreover one's own psychic structure is exposed and vulnerable, with its secret attractions for and entanglements with the *vasanas* or archetypes within. The literature of yoga warns the initiate against this activation of the psychic realm, for here are temptations and struggles far beyond the range of ordinary people and experiencing. This is the realm of the *siddhis*, supernatural powers, the realm of magic and demonic forces. "One must be vigilant," says the Katha Upanishad, "for yoga can be both beneficial and injurious."[23]

In Zen it is recognized that before satori one encounters a phase of intense psychic activity, hallucinatory experiences and so on (*makyō*). In Tibetan yoga they speak of the "steep path," by which one attempts to reach full enlightenment in a single lifetime. But it is also a fully accepted possibility that, because of the intensity of concentration, psychosis may be the result rather than enlightenment. The psychic system, supercharged far beyond its ordinary levels, may take its revenge by becoming autonomous (a condition we usually refer to broadly as "schizophrenia"). And I remember an incident that happened in a New York zendo several years ago during a *sesshin* (an intense period, usually several days, of continuous meditation), when a young woman who had been working very hard, perhaps too hard, at her *zazen* fell into the delusion that she was the *roshi*, and walked around acting like that elderly Japanese man. She was in a state of what might be called "delusional psychosis" for quite some time afterward, and only with difficulty returned to "reality." She reminded everyone (maybe even the roshi) that this quest for enlightenment must be taken in deadly earnest, and that it involves the transformation of the deepest aspects of ourselves, a complete revision of our experiencing.

The yogi recognizes that the engagement with this deeper level (of the *vāsanās*) is indispensable to his quest. That is, the mind cannot really be stilled until the deep-seated origins of his desires, or the psychic energies that course through his system, have been engaged and arrested. Amid the most violent psychic turbulencies he is to go on. Like the Buddha facing the legions of demonic forms, he is to sit firmly, neither fearing nor desiring, aspiring only to that state beyond all states. He is to reject the forms within, as the forms without, as illusion. He is to reject the magical opportunities, the fantastic powers (*siddhi*), as but more tempting snares, which increase with his increasing strength to resist them.

For the yogi then, there are no compromises. His objective has been to force life to reveal its illusory nature, and the incredible psychic phantasmagoria aroused within by his practices are a confirmation of this. They are the *samskāras*, illusion-producing psychic forces in their concentrated and revealed form.

It is evident that this lifelong, ceaseless struggle is against one's natural tendencies, and the dangerous consequences of yoga are a result of the intensity of this artificial constraining of the natural flow of psychic energy through the personality. It is also obvious that for a task of this magnitude nothing less than total commitment will do. One committed to yoga is locked into a life-and-death struggle with his own nature. Various texts and teachers reflect the violence of it; they speak of "killing the ego" and "exterminating one's desires." And the psychic energy responds in kind. Like any organic life it responds to deprivation and torture by thrashing wildly, getting sick, going crazy.

Yoga, no less than any spiritual system, also has the corollary danger of psychic inflation (mythic identity). One identifies immediately with the guru, or the model of the fully liberated soul. This tends to give an inflated perspective in which personal problems, deficiencies in relationship, and reality orientation in general are treated as "illusion" (willfully ignored). Visions of holiness and perfection supplant the obvious deficiencies of concrete reality.

Speaking of *maya, karma, clear white light,* and *astral bodies* as if they knew at first hand what they were talking about, self-styled yogins perambulate about this hemisphere, condescendingly advising their friends concerning illusion and reality, higher states of consciousness, and enlightenment generally. I know perfectly intelligent people whose first impulse these days, when their car breaks down, is to attribute it to "bad karma" rather than to look under the hood. The problem is that we tend to identify with the mythic-spiritual goals of this process rather than with its day-to-day reality. People take up yoga and become certain that this will end all their problems, unaware that it may also intensify or incubate them. We all admire what we know of "enlightenment," but how many of us are truly ready to face the awesome realities of exterminating our desires?

We must learn to face the personal consequences of our transpersonal preoccupations. Do you practice yoga? If so, then how do you feel? Do you perceive reality as an unmistakable illusion from which you must extricate yourself at all costs? If not, you are lacking the first, classic requirement of the yogi.*

I have found from my period of intensive practice that I am not at all sure I wish to "give up my desires." Sometimes they are more than siren songs—rather, keys to new dimensions in reality, the living, plastic substance of creativity. I know I want to shape them and talk to them, but am increasingly unsure about "exterminating" them.† I suggest that anyone who wishes to practice yoga consider seriously whether, indeed,

---

*Buddhism, particularly Zen, counteracts this overidentification with the goals of the process by an emphasis on the here-and-now aspects of consciousness. In one paradigm, the act of meditating is itself enlightenment.
†In India it is recognized that in order to practice yoga successfully one must either have this all-consuming desire for enlightenment or else have lived out the majority of one's life as a householder, then coming to a natural—not artificial—giving up of desires (*verag*).

he or she wishes to do away with all desires, or is perhaps rather looking for something else, for which yoga as yet seems the only available alternative.

I feel that there are several ways to regard the meaning of our current fascination with Eastern spiritual systems. First, most of us have just about "had it" with orthodox systems, dogmas, doctrines, and creeds. Yoga and related systems de-emphasize these in favor of practice, and the orthodox elements which do exist in these systems are so unfamiliar that we do not feel them yet as constraints. Most of the systems are psychologically oriented, relying on practical methods of working with consciousness rather than on traditional rituals of worship of an authoritative but invisible deity. God is to be found within our consciousness, and as most of us since the advent of science have despaired of finding "him" outside, this is a logical change in emphasis. Science has desacralized outer reality but has not had this explicit effect in the inner realms.

Secondly, for those of us who have been brought up in an orthodox Jewish or Christian atmosphere, myth may have served more as the vehicle for our repression and guilt than as a source of ecstasy and wonder. The alien system, with its liberated gods and goddesses, more universal morality (relativity of good and evil, and so on), and sometimes explicit celebration of eroticism, is a welcome, lighthearted change after the weighty burdens of historical Judeo-Christian morality. One's religious or mythological beliefs form a kind of a metaphysical backdrop against which the dramas of life are played out. My indoctrinated cosmic scenery showed absolute good and absolute evil forever in conflict, with every choice one made somehow in the balance. This life was preparation for an afterlife, and every action one performed moved the balance toward heaven or hell. One must not make mistakes, for there were no second chances. Life was very heavy and very serious, as one's only chance to make good must be. Even when I had intellectually rejected the literal orthodoxies of my childhood, this somewhat gloomy atmosphere was not banished but hung around subliminally, subtly permeating my experience of the world in a way I could not, perhaps, have named.

The sacred reality of one's childhood indoctrination is entwined with an archetype and not easily expelled. Intellectual decisions do not really affect it, at root; nor do scientific beliefs. What may be needed to transform it, revitalize it, is another, perhaps complementary, alternative mythic system.

Now compare the Judeo-Christian picture to the metaphysical backdrop offered by the Hindu cosmology. We have not only one chance to make good, but many. The universe is endless, *yugas* and *kalpas* (thousands and millions of years) of duration. Morality is relative, and good and evil both are forms of desire. The destructive forces of being do not dwell in a permanent underground with wailing and gnashing of teeth, with the archdemon tempting us ever to stray from the path, but exist rather in the form of a dancing god, Shiva—terrible and yet marvelous, god of destruction but also patron of yoga, disengagement. Reality is a play of illusion, and we too are such stuff as dreams are made of. We have passed through thousands of life-forms, thousands of transmigrations from one form to another. So why get panicky and rush things? Why get judgmental? Why be so guilty?

Most Westerners I have met who believe in reincarnation seem to enjoy the prospect, reveling in the thought of this immortality through myriad transformations. Whereas in orthodox Hinduism and Buddhism, reincarnation is taken for granted as an all-too-unpleasant fact; the precise goal of religious practice is to free oneself from the "endless round of suffering." But we of the Western tradition, it seems, like Faust, are eternal seekers of experience: adventurers, not renouncers. And the possibility of an eternity of adventure in a thousand disguises seems too good to be missed.

For me, the Hindu mythic cosmology partially replaced, or perhaps more accurately, expanded my previous Judeo-Christian one. As it gradually did this, I felt a great weight lifted. As *sacred* as the Judeo-Christian version, it is more playful, creative, colorful. And grounded, as are all of the world's great mythological and religious traditions, in the source realm of the archetypal psyche, it touched in me (as I believe it has in many) the genesis of my way of looking at the universe, of experiencing reality.

I do not wish to imply that we should substitute one traditional mythology for another. Rather my sense is that we should make friends with them all, a little. Each system generated by the mythic imagination can function as a wonderland of human wisdom. And I suggest that we consult personal feeling in regard to all our metaphysical urges. Finding in myself an affinity for Vedic cosmology, I must inquire within: what in me is so responsive and attuned to these mythic forms? What is it that is so enraptured by these symbol stories?

To bypass this inner questioning and become a Vedantist is, as Jung says, "to indulge our Western acquisitiveness." In doing so we once again confirm that " 'everything good is outside,' whence it has to be fetched and pumped into our barren souls."[24] By becoming Vedantists, or Nichiren Buddhists, or Krishna devotees we show how susceptible to orthodoxy—as well as myth—we still are. But my feeling is that this is an atavism. Orthodox religion is behind, not ahead of us. What is required is a new orientation to this ever recurrent, ever demanding dimension of the mythic within. Jung takes us close to this sense.

Instead of learning the spiritual techniques of the East by heart and imitating them in a thoroughly Christian way—*imitatio Christi!*—with a correspondingly forced attitude, it would be far more to the point to find out whether there exists in the unconscious an introverted tendency similar to that which has become the guiding spiritual principle of the East. We should then be in a position to build on our own ground with our own methods.[25]

Jung simultaneously warns us against pure imitation and yet also reaffirms that in our attraction to these systems is a call that cannot be neglected—an invitation, as he says, to build on our own ground. It is toward furthering this building that I devote the following and concluding chapter.

The great fact that Eastern spiritual systems have understood and developed, but which we have neglected, is what Jung calls "the self-liberating power of the introverted mind." When consciousness turns its energy back upon itself, the inevitable result is to render visible its otherwise inaccessible subjective patterns. When one has engaged those patterns and energies directly, they no longer act unconsciously and compulsively, structuring our conscious experience whether we like it or not. It is this freedom from the compulsions of our own subjective factors that the Eastern texts refer to as liberation.

As Jung says, "nothing in our religion encourages the idea of the self-liberating power of the mind." (Is it not obvious, then, why in an age when psychology is replacing religion people should be attracted to religions based on psychological premises?) The Western religious approach has been to consider God as something totally outside and beyond the self.

In the same way Western man is Christian, no matter to what denomination his Christianity belongs. For him man is small inside, he is next to nothing; moreover, as Kierkegaard says, "before God Man is always wrong." By fear, repentance, promises, submission, self-abasement, good deeds, and praise he propitiates the great power, which is not himself but *totaliter Aliter*, the Wholly Other, altogether perfect and "outside," the only reality. If you shift the formula a bit and substitute for God some other power, for instance the world or money, you get a complete picture of Western man—assiduous, fearful, devout, self-abasing, enterprising, greedy, and violent in his pursuit of the goods of this world: possessions, health, knowledge, technical mastery, public warfare, political power, conquest, and so on. . . . You cannot be a good Christian and redeem yourself, nor can you be a Buddha and worship God.[26]

Western man's instinctual and temperamental bias is to regard ultimate meaning as outside himself. If Jung is correct in hypothesizing that man's entire reality orientation hinges on his religious outlook, our dominant social and cultural forms are an outgrowth of our extraverted style of mythology.

Having come to our present spiritual impasse, we find ourselves looking high and low for God (or ultimate meaning) under stones, through microscopes, or with our giant telescopes into his traditional abode, the sky. And finding no empirical evidence of his presence (footprints, perhaps?) we conclude, like Khrushchev, that there is no God, for if there were the astronauts surely would have seen him.

The core of the impasse is that while the pressure of the religious urge comes ceaselessly from within, our characteristic orientation has been to look outside for what we seek. The *enantiodromia*, the instinctual reversal which comes at the apex of such a one-sided search, is then to embrace the opposite: the Eastern assumption that God is within.

Now this sounds all well and good, but there are problems. First, while attracted to the inwardness of the Eastern systems, we yet seize upon them in our typically extraverted way, applying them to ourselves energetically from without and demanding the cooperation of the within. We decide to "become a Buddhist" or whatever, and expect the full cooperation of the psyche in our endeavor. People take up Zen, and because it offers the image of attaining a preternatural calm and centeredness, fully expect that reward for their endeavor. They do not consider that the psyche may react, not in obedient and tractable fulfillment, but as it often does to the excesses of the conscious viewpoint, with rebellion or compensation. Moreover, there may be added to this reaction all the intensity of energy withheld from its normal expression by meditation or asceticism or whatever. Need we be surprised when a young woman's reward for her intense Zen practice is not enlightenment but a paranoid psychosis?

And this brings us to a rather subtle methaphysical issue. As Jung explains it,

If, through introspection and the conscious realization of unconscious compensations, it is possible to transform one's mental condition and thus arrive at a solution of painful conflicts, one would seem entitled to speak of "self-liberation." But, as I have already hinted, there is a hitch in this proud claim to self-liberation, for a man cannot produce these unconscious compensations at will. He has to rely upon the possibility they *may* be produced.[27]

Here, then, is the value the Western religious approach has to offer the Eastern, for *its* one-sidedness. The transformation (or liberation) of the self requires the cooperation of that aspect of the psyche which is ontologically *other*, not simply an extension of one's own will. Jung says,

It is a curious thing that Eastern philosophy seems to be almost unaware of this highly important fact. And it is precisely this fact that provides the psychological justification for the Western point of view. It seems as if the Western mind had a most penetrating intuition of man's fateful dependence upon some dark power which must co-operate if all is to be well. Indeed, whenever and wherever the unconscious fails to co-operate, man is instantly at a loss, even in his most ordinary activities. There may be a failure of memory, of co-ordinated action, or of interest and concentration; and such failure may well be the cause of serious annoyance, or of a fatal accident, a professional disaster, or a moral collapse. . . . The co-operation of the unconscious, which is something we never think of and always take for granted, is, when it suddenly fails, a very serious matter indeed.[28]

As was mentioned earlier, the dedicated yogi is not interested in a good relationship with his inner psychic forces. He wishes to engage and destroy them. His goal is set beyond "psychological health," at complete enlightenment, even if it means becoming a little crazy in the process. It is unlikely that one could try to lead an ordinary life while engaged in this kind of struggle. So the yogi casts off those worldly responsibilities and attachments which would be destroyed in the thrashing about, and goes to a monastery or wanders naked and alone in the forest. He is willing to risk everything on the supposition that, behind the illusion, he *is* everything already. One's psychic states, moods, dreams are not to be related to, but to be treated as hindrances, parts of oneself that are refractory, undisciplined: epiphenomena of the central process of coming to "enlightenment."

As Jung says in this regard,

I know that *yoga* prides itself on being able to control even the unconscious processes, so that nothing can happen in the psyche as a whole that is not ruled by a supreme consciousness. I have not the slightest doubt that such a condition is more or less possible. But it is possible only at the price of becoming identical with the unconscious. Such an identity is the Eastern equivalent of our Western fetish of "complete objectivity," the machine-like subservience to one goal, to one idea or cause, at the cost of losing every trace of inner life.[29]

It is part of our traditional mythological heritage to respond to the living psychic realm within as "other," an approach which may have its positive as well as negative aspects (when treated too literally). And the Eastern tradition has its own excesses. It is willing to treat not only psychological problems but physical sickness and even accidents as symptoms of one's spiritual inadequacies (bad karma, the just deserts of one's own actions in previous lives). But are *we* truly psychologically ready to leave lepers, schizophrenics, and starving children to their own devices, confident that their infirmities are a tangible and just manifestation of what they spiritually deserve?

I believe that here the way of the shaman captures something vital for our own tradition that the way of the yogi has missed or forgotten.* It is the technique for relating to, rather than vanquishing, the living substance of one's psyche. The shaman's symbolic dialogue with mythic beings and events preserves the idea that there is a positive virtue, a magic in the forms of maya's dreams. In this way it affirms life rather than insisting on closing its accounts for good. The shaman is willing to act in the play of life, not engage in a sit-down strike till removed from the stage.

But at the same time, what can we learn from our preoccupation—or flirtation—with yoga? As Sam Keen suggests, "It is possible to separate the idealistic metaphysics and the presuppositions of Eastern spirituality from yoga practices and

---

*The Siberian Tungus word *shaman* may well be related to the Sanskrit *Sramana*, yogi, ascetic.[31] The two traditions are also interconnected in the Buddhism of Tibet, where the prevailing shamanistic *Bon-po* religion merged with the yogic Buddhism of Padma Sambhava.

make use of its technology of body awareness and control."[30] And I think the lovely multidimensional myths of the Hindu tradition have much to say to us as well.

Shamans, priests, scientists, yogis, each has something to tell us, something important about the way to live our lives. And we are their spiritual as well as physical descendants. A race, like an individual, throughout its life history learns by its excesses, moving and then compensating, polarizing, struggling—and then perhaps recognizing the secret ties that unite the opposites.

We need the wisdom and courage of the best of our ancestors, who were willing to meet and speak with the depths of the spirit. We can treasure their conversations, for they are the true riches of our cultural heritage. But we must also have a dialogue of our own.

4

Myths of Relationship
and Integration

The great shamans seem to have the power to reach beyond the visible universe to the causal dimension from which it emanates. There, in the bright realm, they dream the timeless myths that otherwise only slowly filter down into the smaller dreamscapes of our sleeping world. With eyes open to three dimensions and bodies caught in time, the fourth, most of us are asleep to imagination, the fifth, and its workings show themselves only dimly in our dreams.

When Black Elk saw his Great Vision a hundred years ago, he saw not only into the tragic plight of his own people, but through and beyond it to the larger mythscape, a glimpse of the planetary predicament. As he and his people walked their terrible third ascent,

all the animals and fowls that were the people ran here and there, for each one seemed to have his own little vision that he followed and his own rules; and all over the universe I could hear the winds at war like wild beasts fighting.[1]*

And so it seems, not only in the physical but in the psycho-spiritual worlds. Our great myths are heaps of broken images, and our spiritual sight seems unable to penetrate beyond the personal level, the little vision. This may indeed be the most basic fact the contemporary spiritual seeker has to take into account. We may be moving, at least for a while, into a time of

*At this point in his narrative to Neihardt, Black Elk evidently remarked: "I think we are near to that place now and I am afraid something very bad is going to happen all over the world." Neihardt adds, "He cannot read and knows nothing of world affairs."

individual rather than collective mythology. We have been used to myths only of the collective variety, validating the myth of the individual only when it would fit into the larger one of the sociocultural framework. But the changed emphasis we might now have to take into account is on the personal journey. The collective myths are fragmented, dismembered, and the responsibility for finding a meaningful place within the universe falls back on the individual.

When shamans are dismembered, as we now collectively seem to be, they look forward to the prospect of recreation, of being born anew. And it may very well be that like them we will gain the mastery of those same primordial forces that have been devouring us, fragmenting our collective identity, breaking our mythic images. The pieces are, in fact, all around us now, and perhaps our present task is most like that of those spirit healers who reconstitute the shaman; or that of Isis with her helpers, looking for the pieces of her beloved brother-husband Osiris. We may join in the task and find that in the process of helping to reassemble the god we are also recreating ourselves.

I believe I have found a few pieces here and there, but I am not foolish enough to think that one person can find more than a few. I use this last chapter especially to show and tell what I have found. Mythic fragments may turn up in the strangest places these days, it seems: in comic books, in science fiction, in pills and pipe dreams, in sexual fantasies, in social movements and unorthodox life-styles.

Lacking an official structure, the mythic imagination stirs around in our depths, producing dreams, fantasies, ideas. Some people are well-tuned receptors, accustomed to listening and looking within. Others are poor at it—so accustomed only to looking at the world outside, and listening to cultural noise that the myth cannot appear to them. Or if it does, it comes as an obsession or nightmare. And often it appears in a costume or a collective movement before it appears to consciousness in other ways.

Out of a variety of rather modest, unassuming contexts I

have worked out the five following themes. These I feel are not so much myths, in and of themselves, as mythogenic patterns, foci of images, feelings, and energies particularly important for our present situation on both outer and inner levels.

1. Whole Earth—Whole Body
2. Dialogue: The Two Snakes of Aquarius
3. The Sorcerer's Apprenticeship
4. The Myth of the Crippled Tyrant
5. The Mythic Androgyne

We shall see in these mythic themes a kind of interpenetration, so that each in some way is a reflection or a complement of the others. Even as I have had trouble trying to organize neatly my thinking and writing about them, so I suspect they resist logical compartmentalization. While I have been very conscious of working largely from fragmentary glimpses, I also feel I have begun to intuit the presence of much larger dynamics moving beneath the surface of things. What I give you here is a pastiche of impressions, intuitions, insights. Cumulatively, I believe they point to some rather important directions for our evolution and our dreaming.

1. Whole Earth, Whole Body

The best of our myths speak to both our inner and outer levels. They remind us that the two dimensions may not really be so far apart as we had imagined, after all. We have very recently developed an intense concern for the ecosystem, a concern really for each and every living part of the biosphere of this little planet we live on. It seems to me no accident that Freud made an almost precisely analogous discovery about the nature of the psyche not so very long ago. He pointed out the neglected fact that all parts of the self must be in relationship for the organism to be healthy. If one part has been blocked off or repressed, or become atrophied, the whole psyche—and body as well—suffers.

On both the planetary and the personal level, it seems, we

are learning that we must have a mutual collaboration of parts to be healthy. We are reminded now forcibly that this small planet upon which we dwell is a living organism like ourselves. All the life forms we encounter upon it, ourselves included, are integrally related; we cannot afford to be without the services of rain forests, starfish, or bacteria. If one part of the system becomes possessed by its "little vision"—oversteps its place in the relationship and moves in a unilateral manner—we have war or ecological crisis, cancer or psychosis.

We need most desperately as human beings to outgrow such incredibly self-centered philosophies as that which Tamerlane, the Mongol warlord, caused to be inscribed on his tomb: WERE I STILL ALIVE MANKIND WOULD TREMBLE. Tamerlane is reputed to have ridden his horse to the top of a pyramid made of ninety thousand human heads. These trophies came all-too-unwillingly from his "enemies"; but how one human being can acquire ninety thousand enemies I leave to the reader's imagination.

Where, in this man and in many of our ancestors, was that innate empathy for other sentient beings that comes almost as reflex to many of us now? Is it possible that we never learned the ability, said by Piaget to emerge at age six in most children, to imagine oneself in the other's place?

We are all interrelated, brothers under the skin indeed, not only to other men, but to beasts, fish, mollusks, the very coral of the sea. There seem to be innate vibratory frequencies between all living things, as we are finding out or perhaps remembering. Cleve Backster, an ex-FBI interrogation expert, one day decided to interrogate the geranium plant on his table. Much to his astonishment, he found it responsive to his feeling-toned thoughts. His subsequent research, meticulously carried out, has shown that communication exists, probably on the cellular level, between almost all living organisms. The potted plant by the window may be flinching when you rage, or may gasp silently when you drop that lobster in the pot.[2]

What then does this mean? Must we all become like those devout Jains who refuse to swat flies and try to walk as little as possible, so as not to tread—even unwittingly—on worm or ant? I think most of us find such an existence inconceivable, or ludicrous. Our lives are nurtured through the death of other beings, and there seems to be little we can do about the fact. It is a fundamental principle of life in this universe as we know it. And has India, by making sacred the lives of cattle, managed significantly to decrease the amount of human suffering that takes place there?

I think our awareness needs a sense of relationship more than misplaced sympathy. We cannot stop eating, but why have we forgotten how to ask a blessing or give thanks for what we eat? Joseph Campbell points out that the ritual religions that grew up in the earliest human communities, the Paleolithic hunting societies, are concerned with apologizing to the animals because they must be killed, and both asking and helping by magic the return of the essences or spirits of the buffalo, the caribou, into new bodies so that once again they may enjoy the privilege of earthly life—and once again serve as sacramental food.[3]

The best ecologists I know burn with a kind of religious zeal. There is more to their discipline, they realize, than mere biology; they have become the spokesmen of a spiritual principle, of a multidimensional quest which involves the well-being of us all. Maybe they are entitled to a slightly religious aura. They are the guides, the Moses and Aaron, who offer to lead us out of our present wilderness, our place of exile from nature.

But when did the exile as such begin? There are two myths, I believe, that show us the origins of our departure. The most familiar is, of course, the biblical expulsion from the Garden. As if in a self-fulfilling prophecy two and a half millennia long, we have been gradually but inexorably exiling ourselves from the garden of the natural order. From the patriarchical legal principles of the Old Testament Hebrews through the flagellants of the Middle Ages and into the Protestant ethic and the Industrial Revolution, we see an unmistakably developing trend of alienating and subduing nature, both outer and inner.

The other myth is also Middle-Eastern, and perhaps a thousand years older. Like the Hebrew myth, this Babylonian creation story features a masculine creator God, Marduk. A conflict develops, as in many creation cycles, between the elder parent gods and their offspring. The newer gods ask Marduk to champion them against Tiamat, the Mother Goddess, the great tumultuous Sea. She is enraged because they have caught and imprisoned her counterpart, the creator god Apsu. In a violent confrontation, Marduk slays the Mother Goddess:

> They marched to war, they drew near to give battle.
> The Lord spread out his net and caught her in it.
> The evil wind which followed him, he loosed it in her face.
> She opened her mouth, Tiamat, to swallow him.
> He drove in the evil wind so she could not close her lips.
> The terrible winds filled her belly. Her heart was seized.
> She held her mouth wide open.
> He let fly an arrow, it pierced her belly.
> Her inner parts he clove, he split her heart.
> He rendered her powerless and destroyed her life.
> He felled her body and stood upright on it.[4]

Contemplating the giant corpse of the Mother Goddess, Marduk is overtaken by a kind of creative impulse which momentarily supplants the destructive. He dismembers the corpse and creates and orders the world as we know it, much as Jahweh does in the Old Testament version.

Now there is a violation and reversal of a few truly archetypal patterns in both these myths, which may show us something about our present situation as well as that of a few thousand years ago. Primordially, it is the female gods who create and from whom life springs. Male gods, like their human counterparts who do not give birth, do not usually create except in their role as consort of The Goddess. Second, in all the older Goddess-worshiping traditions it is man the hero who must be slain and dismembered. In his sacramental death he falls back into the being of the Great Mother whence he came and from whom he may be born again. It is she who is Creatress, Devourer, and Matrix from which new birth springs.

But in these Middle-Eastern myths we see what is most

likely a rewriting of earlier myths to provide a masculine, patriarchal emphasis.[5] These are myths of the man's world, the world of the conquest of nature, of heroism and aggression. And as Erich Neumann has pointed out, it is to increase his consciousness that man the hero asserts himself against being reabsorbed by the mother, who in her devouring aspect usually appears as a monster, serpent, or dragon which must be slain.[6] And we have indeed gained consciousness in these last few thousand years, and with it an unprecedented mastery over Mother Nature. But like Marduk, we have dismembered her to make our heroic creations.

The ecology movement seems to be a sudden awakening to our childish, heroic *hubris*. We see around us environmentally the horrible outcome of "slaying the mother." It seems to me that in our brutal attempts to "improve on nature" we may not notice that our reconstruction has left us with a monster much like that created by Dr. Frankinstein. In the medieval Jewish myths of the Golem and in Mary Shelley's work, we seem to be warned of the effects of interfering with processes the wisdom of which was millions of years in the learning. We see, for example, the effects of atomic radiation or thalidomide on genetic patterns; we see the ecological disasters that can occur from interfering with the life cycle of a single species. And here is the worst possibility of all: having thus slain the Great Mother, we may also have forfeited our most precious natural privilege, the right of returning to her for sleep, for gestation, and rebirth.

As with the planetary body of the Great Mother, so with our own bodies, it seems. We look about us at the physical shapes of our fellow men, or read the works of Wilhelm Reich or Alexander Lowen, and know we have also executed a kind of dismemberment on ourselves. The price of our gain in consciousness has been a cutting off, an armoring, a rigidifying of the body.

It seems to me no accident, then, that simultaneously with the ecology movement we have begun to initiate a renewed concern for our bodies. We had been so busy *doing*, we had forgotten that the precondition for pleasurable *being* lies in having a relaxed and integrated body. And such movements as "sensory awakening," the renewed interest in yoga, massage, Bioenergetic Therapy have the simple but compelling objective of putting us back in touch with our physical natures. Thomas Hanna has written convincingly of the revolution that must take place in our philosophy of living when we realize the full potentials of "embodiment." A "somatic revolution" he describes is in fact taking place as we outgrow the life-inhibiting effects of the Protestant ethic and its product, *homo laborans*, man who does nothing but work.[7]

In such books as *Zen in the Art of Archery*[8] or Michael Murphy's delightful *Golf in the Kingdom*[9] we see a new approach to the way the body can be used in athletics: not simply as an instrument to compete, contend, and, vanquish, as in the heroic model, but tuning in to its delicate processes as it plays —to meditation in action. Physical activity can be a very sensitive mirror of the psyche, especially in actions requiring delicacy and control. Inner conflict, egotism, or apprehension show up in the way one coordinates eye to hand, shoots an arrow, or hits a golf ball, as Shivas Irons, Murphy's golf guru, shows him. And don Genaro, that marvelous slapstick "master of equilibrium," standing on his head suddenly, leaping over cataracts, uses his body as a mythical instrument to tune Carlos Castaneda's secular consciousness to the presence of the miraculous.

The resurgence of interest in Oriental martial arts underlines this shift in our collective attention from simple performance to consciousness of physical action. We are moving from *what* you do to *how* you do it. Fighting may be done as a spiritual exercise, and maybe this way of ritualizing and exercising our aggression is better than pretending we don't have any. In the mythology of the Oriental martial arts the most highly developed spiritual athlete is also the best warrior. And even in the cultural wasteland of TV we have "Kung Fu," and a hero who meditates on the mysterious *Tao* as he kicks— or lectures—his numerous and barbarous enemies.

The aggression we have traditionally vented in our conquest

of the environment must be turned within. When the kings of yesteryear had a creative urge, they went out and conquered a country. Nowadays we must find a more modest scale for our creative impulses. We cannot afford to humor those charismatic mad geniuses who drag us into their Cecil B. De Mille dramas as supernumeraries. The concept of conquering and reorganizing outer territory has been the most destructive single urge in human history. But really, the only piece of Mother Earth to which any of us can lay undisputed claim is his own body.*

The world of ourselves, body and psyche, is an appropriate territory to invade. And as we begin this self-invasion we find we are facing a realm as full of resources—and dangers—as the one outside. We need not have only conquest in mind, though, as does the Christian ascetic or the yogi. There are other ways of exploring the self, without continual conflict and aggression, that appear more likely to yield a productive outcome.

Our most recent orientation to our physical bodies seems to have gone past the conquest philosophy of many of our classic spiritual traditions and become more *relationship*-oriented. Self-torturing ascetic disciplines are not very popular these days. Perhaps we recognize in them an analogy, on the inner level, to the Inquisition of the Middle Ages. The self, or the body, is interrogated as one deals with a devil or heretic. And of course the poor tortured thing becomes anxious and tense.

A friend spontaneously shared with me the following insight which came to him while engaged in long-distance running: As he was running he became aware how he was pushing his body. He realized how it had never been able to live up to the expectations he had had for it. At this moment a sense of compassion unexpectedly dawned. He realized the body was doing the best it could, that it was limited by being physical matter, and could not really live up to the soaring expectations of his spirit. As he realized this suddenly a kind of detachment

---

*I was both surprised and pleased to see Jerry Rubin at a Humanistic Psychology conference recently. He has redirected most of his considerable creativity from the political theater to work on his own body.

came, and the body seemed to run effortlessly on, functioning perfectly. This was an ecstatic, liberating feeling, and he felt from this new, altered state of consciousness that his body would do anything he asked of it.

Our Middle-Eastern mythologies, from the dualistic Manichee and Gnostic traditions to the Hebrews, treat the body as an untrustworthy, limiting, rather shameful thing ("the stump" as some Gnostic sects unflatteringly called it). This attitude has become second nature to us now, and persists even when our conscious values may have changed. The body is to be flogged, driven. If it does not run fast enough, *make* it run faster. And treated like a beast of burden it responds by slumping, resisting.

But in release from the oppressive atmosphere of that unconscious assumption—in a moment of lucid awareness, a kind of mini-satori—a new relationship with a touch of compassion replaces the old. In this moment the body shows in a burst of joy and speed that it prefers this new relationship. It is not *made* to run, but *allowed* to.

This little anecdote seems to me representative of a radically new way of regarding the self. It is a life-affirming change that begins to see physical existence, even though bound about by limitations—sickness, old age, and death—as a positive sojourn, a privilege to be enjoyed, not a cosmically imposed time of suffering. Our yoga, it seems, may be not to escape the "wheel of incarnation," but to affirm suffering and limitation as the prerequisites to the ability to experience incarnate existence fully.

As we gradually regain this lost sense of connectedness with our physical selves, perhaps our attitude toward the body of the planet we live on may change. Of one thing I am sure from personal experience. When I am disembodied, out of touch with myself, I am out of touch with the world of nature, and I can remain numb and content in the city of men. But when I am embodied, and the sap-energy of life flows strongly within, I am not happy unless I am among trees and brooks and mountains, or by the sea. I hope they still are there for my children's children.

Our mythological frame of reference can no longer be the single culture in which we dwell. The scope of our responsibility and our loyalty must move beyond the local social boundary to the planet we inhabit together. Captain Edgar Mitchell has told of the overwhelming sense of compassion and unity that came in seeing the earth from the vantage point of the lunar spacecraft. Wrapped in a mantle of cloud, she swam in loveliness through the sea of space. It is our choice to violate or to grace the beauty that is hers.

And really, as we have found in these past few hundred years, the whole earth is simply a larger version of our local culture, tucked away, for all we know, in a galactic backwater. There is overwhelming good sense in avoiding the provincial assumption that we are the only intelligent life in the universe. The *Chariots of the Gods* theme is interesting,[10] not because of its amassing of anomalous facts, but because it echoes a mythic theme knocking at the doors of our consciousness: the universe is not only filled with life, but is itself alive. Our stewardship of earth may be a part of a much larger order of things. And if our collective mythic fantasy and Erich von Daniken are correct about the visits of extra-terrestrial, highly evolved beings, how do we feel about having them visit our home? Its a mess: garbage all over the place; we've been peeing in the water, and family arguments going on in every corner of the house. Surely our prestigious intergalactic visitors ought to feel much as we do upon visiting a slum or backwoods trailer camp. The impression we give is unavoidably one of unawareness of our stewardship—the awesome responsibility of caring for a planet that has been placed in our hands.

2. Dialogue: The Two Snakes of Aquarius

If there is one central realization that must come out of our current ecological, bodily, and psychological crises, it is that *dialogue* is an indispensable part of being in a universe where all is interrelated. Unilateral action, or authoritarian action, is an invitation to disaster. We see this need for dialogue coming up on every level of human relationship we explore: man/nature, man/other men, man/himself, man/woman, parent/child. The breaking of relationship, the refusal of openness to exchange, means disaster in ecology, psychology, politics, marriage.

There may never have been a generation in which so many people have reacted so violently to authoritarianism. I have seen this intimately in my own practice of psychotherapy, where for many people the presence of authoritarian figures, symbolic or real, seems to drive them into either a kind of catatonia or a frenzy of rebellion and anger. But in the larger theater it is there as well. WHAT WOULD HAPPEN IF THEY DECLARED A WAR AND NOBODY CAME? asked one insightful poster in the sixties. The presence of authority immediately seems to evoke the radical. And even the sacrosanct courtroom has seen its mythic authority/radical comedy: the drama of the Hoffmans, Abbie vs. the judge. The old kings used to claim their authority came from God. But who can do that nowadays? Certainly not the judge, nor the man in the White House.

Interestingly enough the astrological symbol of one of our emerging mythologies, the "Aquarian Age," gives us the following diagram as its calling card:

The Piscean age, whose two millennia of conflict have been obvious enough, showed us this:

In the second diagram we see two forces parallel but turned away from each other, while in the first the two lines undulate parallel to each other, in relationship.

Could it be that this is indeed the symbol of dialogue, of relationship, that is emerging as our dominant mythic theme in the current age?* We can see the two lines as spirit and matter, conscious and unconscious, man and woman, innocence and experience. What seems most essential in any of these dual forms of relationship is that each aspect keep aware of the movement and being of the other, that the channels between the two dynamisms be kept open.

I hope to show, in subsequent sections of this chapter, a number of variations on this same theme: how dialogue might be applicable to a variety of human concerns. The central and unifying dialogue, though, as I perceive it, is between ordinary consciousness and the mythic imagination. It is here, it seems, that each of our previous modes has failed; neither mythic identity, religious orthodoxy, science, nor yoga allows for an interplay between consciousness and myth. There is only a fixed relationship, the premature conclusion of a struggle, or a unilateral victory.

In the first two stages (identity, orthodoxy)—which have been prevalent throughout the major part of man's history— the primary imagination has been unquestionably dominant. From the proclamations of shamans or possessed oracles to the edicts of the pope, the word of the Deity has been taken as prior in importance to the reasoning of men. Until the most recent period of our history, mythic forms have held men's imagination firmly enthralled, demanding homage and wielding authority. Consciousness, reason, self-determination have been correspondingly disadvantaged, because the mythic dynasty derives its power from a direct affinity with deeply potent unconscious energies.

But in the other two modes the principle of consciousness has unequivocally declared itself against the unconscious, against its own dangerous myth-susceptible tendencies. This is only achieved, in both cases, by a vigilant discipline and by

*I am indebted to Dr. Edward Whitmont for very cogently pointing out this symbolism (in his lectures at the C. G. Jung Foundation, New York, 1968).

a categorical resistance to myth. Science is the praxis of outward vision, the discipline that on principle rejects the seductive mythic gloss for the hard, cold actuality beyond the projection. And yoga is the praxis of inward vision. Recognizing, as does science, the almost ineluctable subjectivity of ordinary experience, yoga withholds the flow of consciousness from mixing with outer reality, so that the subjective factor must display its illusory, mythic nature within. Both of these modes lead to the control and transformation of reality: science of the outer, yoga of the inner. In both cases power and control are gained to the extent that vision and attention are disciplined.

Jung has pointed out the similarities of science and yoga, observing that while the direction of their attention is opposite, there is similarity in the method. As he says,

> The extroverted tendency of the West and the introverted tendency of the East have one important purpose in common: both make desperate efforts to conquer the mere naturalness of life. It is the assertion of mind over matter, the *opus contra naturam*, a symptom of the youthfulness of man, still delighting in the use of the most powerful weapon ever devised by nature: the conscious mind. The afternoon of humanity, in a distant future, may yet evolve a different ideal. In time, even conquest will cease to be the dream.[11]

Carrying either of these disciplines to its extreme as an instrument of consciousness is artificial, working against and alienating the natural flow of psychic energy. At the extreme each leads to its own kind of fanaticism—and sterility. In the *opus contra naturam*, the work against "undisciplined" nature, contact is lost with the nurturing, creative aspect of nature as well.

As in the *koan* of Zen, we are confronted here with a paradox, a seemingly insoluble problem which yet demands solution. We cannot, most of us, allow ourselves to become identical with the mythic energy within, becoming shaman, saint, or madman. Nor can most of us really accept the culturally conditioned, historically outdated faiths of our fathers.

Simultaneously, we are seeing the all-too-apparent psychological limitations of the desacralized scientific world view, yet cannot relinquish the astonishing gains it has yielded. And again, there is an undeniable culture-wide attraction to Eastern disciplines, together with rather compelling evidence that we had best not become literal imitators.

Where, then, does this leave us?

Jung has a method to suggest for when we are faced with such impasses, and the method itself may contain our answer. To begin with, he suggests that the presence of a conflict, of a pair of opposites that split the mind, is an invitation to a *dialogue*. The mind must be willing to accept the presence of the conflict and—what is less easy—the suffering it implies. As he describes it,

At first no solution appears possible, and this fact, too, has to be borne with patience. The suspension thus created "constellates" the unconscious—in other words, the conscious suspense produces a new compensatory reaction in the unconscious. This reaction (usually manifested in dreams) is brought to conscious realization in its turn. The conscious mind is thus confronted with a new aspect of the psyche, which arouses a different problem or modifies an old one in an unexpected way. The procedure is continued until the original conflict is satisfactorily resolved. The whole process is called the "transcendent function." It is a process and a method at the same time. The production of unconscious compensations is a spontaneous process; the conscious realization is a method. The function is called "transcendent" because it facilitates the transition from one psychic condition to another by means of the mutual confrontation of opposites.[12]

This method of the *transcendent function*, as Jung describes it, involves both the turning inward of the attention which is the basis of yoga, and also treating the within as "other" (without becoming identical with it as yoga does). There is both introversion and extroversion in this method.

The introversion required here is unlike that of classical yoga, which does battle with the inner psyche, subordinating it to the will. And the extroversion is unlike that of Western religion, which places ultimate value in the "wholly other." The inner, "other" self is to be neither coerced nor propitiated. Instead the relationship must be described simply as a dialogue. This, then, is our method for establishing a working relationship between the primary, mythic imagination and consciousness. We are being forced inescapably to the conclusion that neither can do without the other. What is required is a third thing, neither this nor that, but something born of relationship between the two. As in yoga, there is a praxis here. But the *method* leaves open the possibility of a response: the *process* that emerges from beyond the control of consciousness. Nor is whatever revelation comes from within to be treated as unimpeachable divine authority. Rather it is responded to by consciousness, in turn, with its own criteria of reason, practicality, and so forth, and then attention may again be attuned within to listen for the psyche's response. And so on.

An emerging variety of methods that involve this form of dialogue with the self is, I think, our first intimation of a new technology of the sacred, the fifth stage of mythic engagement. Using Jung's idea of "the transcendent function" as a model, I find that there are also a number of developing non-Jungian psychological systems and techniques that seem to employ this same basic approach.

Now the psychology I am referring to is not that of rats, mazes, and numbers. These practitioners are increasingly and by preference referring to themselves as "behavioral scientists." Psychology, as I see it, is an inquiry into the logic of the psyche, or as Webster archaically but nicely defines it: "that branch of knowledge which deals with the human soul; that knowledge of the mind which we derive from a careful examination of the facts of consciousness; the natural history of the mind."[13]

There is a growing left-wing psychological movement in this country (or is it rather very far to the right?) which seems to be returning to this older sense of psychology, examining the "facts of consciousness" and the "natural history of the mind" rather than accepting the dominant dogma, which sees this field as only "the measurement and control of human behavior."* There are those among us who, while trained in the best tradition of the academic behavioral scientist, yet feel that consciousness may not be defined out of existence, nor dreams explained away. It is these people who have presently moved from an exclusively laboratory technology into the areas called loosely "humanistic" and "transpersonal" psychology. And they are exploring problems which have been off limits for decades: altered states of consciousness, fantasy and the creative use of the imagination, inner "depth" experiences of a mystical nature, psychedelics, meditation, and so forth.

In addition, there are furry, beaded, and bearded amateur psychologists on every street corner these days, who for all their apparent disorientation have visited places in inner space which Aldous Huxley marveled to see, and B. F. Skinner would not believe to exist. If this most widespread of inner "tripping" has abated as we moved from the revolutionary sixties into the slightly more moderate seventies, it is not because of government regulation but because these explorers of the psyche have taken up everything from Zen macrobiotics to astral travel— all disciplines with a psychological as well as mythological gist.

As we observe the veritable cornucopia of psychospiritual disciplines erupting into the collective mindscape, we may well ask what is happening. People drift through phases of yoga, astrology, Tarot, macrobiotics, palmistry, and then back to "speaking in tongues." Accusations of flagrant dilettantism are leveled on every side; and there is no question that modern man is acquiring a cafeteria taste in spiritual and mystical systems.

But may not a clue to our development be found in this sheer variety and restlessness of attention? We no longer have the narrow concentration of our ancestors in pledging ourselves to a single system. We are through with the confinements of orthodoxy. Rather, we seem to be playing in a much more childlike way in this remarkable, colorful psychic efflores-

*Definition of psychology found in the introductory section of most college textbooks.

cence.* And as we play, we try something on for size (a bit carelessly to be sure, considering the venerable age and dignity of many of these traditions), matching up its psychosymbolic forms with our personal ones. By the time you have finished a semiserious flirtation with Zen, astrology, and the *I Ching*, you may begin to feel like a dilettante yourself, tantalized by the mysteries but still unredeemed. But I suggest that something else may be going on as well: a process not explicitly conscious, yet working in relation to consciousness. *The psyche has been developing a mythic vocabularly for inner dialogue.*

As you focus attention on a mythic system, half playfully, half seriously measuring its symbolic forms against your own intuitions, you are engaging in a kind of dialogue. Let's say that you have taken up astrology. What do you do first? Find out your own "sign" and the "signs" of all your friends; then you go on to explain your problems in relationship (no wonder your father is so bullheaded, he's a Taurus); and if you go far enough you may get into the complicated intricacies of a horoscope: ascendants and houses, aspects between planets, and so on. Astrology offers a remarkably rich and complicated mythological symbolism.

By playing the conscious mind against these mythic forms, the self is widening the area of contact between consciousness and the mythic imagination. I have found personally that dreams readily pick up on the images of one's conscious preoccupations, especially if they are images with a deep symbolic or archetypal dimension. While psychedelics have opened the floodgates wide to the inner mythic realm, such mystical preoccupations as we have been discussing, even if rather half-hearted and casual, are paving the way for a more studied communication. As Andrew Weil has pointed out in his cogent book *The Natural Mind*, when the excitement of the psychedelic "opening" has mellowed a little the natural flow seems

---

*William Irwin Thompson, quoting David Spangler, suggests that in our present time a sort of "sunset effect" is taking place as our elder myths disappear over the cultural horizon. They appear, as never before perhaps, in a full spectrum of vividness and color. The collective imagination reflects the sunset in its profusion of systems, from Pentecostalism to Satanism.[14]

to be toward taking up a spiritual discipline.[15] Each person searches in his own way for something that will allow a more complete, long-term engagement of the mind-boggling flood of mythic meaning that comes from within with the systematic consciousness of every day.

Most of the new forms of psychotherapy that have emerged in the last decade or two use dialogue as an explicit technique. Gone are the couch and the one-way monologue of psychoanalysis. Modern therapists prefer to face their patients and talk. And in psychodrama or gestalt therapy one is encouraged to get in touch with split-off parts of oneself through dialogue. The conscious self practices being or indwelling the other person or character or part of a dream with which one has been having trouble.

From my own experience, this is a very powerful technique. When one is able genuinely to experience the other perspective, there is at once a loosening of the rigidity with which one was trapped in the previous point of view. The other, in this approach, is treated as "thou," not an "it" to be feared, attacked, or pushed out of the way. And in such systems as Transactional Analysis one is to work toward confronting the other person in an equal relationship: adult to adult, not parent to child or any of the other unequal, role-determined modes.

Wilson Van Dusen, a clinical psychologist, describes how he began to have direct dialogues with the split-off autonomous personalities inhabiting his psychotic patients.[16] Often he would learn things from these conversations that had never emerged before. It seems that one can be afflicted by an hallucination or other psychic force for years without ever once questioning it or asking it to speak for itself. Van Dusen, from years of conversations with these intrapsychic entities, distinguished two "orders." A "lower" order, which were usually quarrelsome, tried to control or dominate the patient's mind and were reluctant to communicate. The "higher order" appeared more seldom, but were always open to dialogue and seemed to respect the patient's wishes and best interests.

In his talks with hallucinations, Van Dusen was impressed by how much these entities knew beyond what was available to the patient. One such hallucination

appeared to a man as a lovely woman who entertained him while showing him thousands of symbols. Though the patient was a high-school educated gas-pipe fitter, his female vision showed a knowledge of religion and myth far beyond the patient's comprehension. At the end of a very rich dialogue with her (the patient reporting her symbols and responses) the patient asked for just a clue as to what she and I were talking about.[17]

Van Dusen felt his experiences were similar to the descriptions of spirits reported by Emanuel Swedenborg, the great eighteenth-century Swedish visionary. Swedenborg kept a more complete and meticulous diary of his inner experiences than any other intrapsychic explorer in history. He began to have dialogues with his dreams and intuitions. He found himself guided into learning ways of inner focusing, listening, and special yogalike breathing techniques. He would often feel spirits emerging through parts of his body. His spiritual diaries record his conversation with the autonomous presences he encountered. Encountering the "lower order" he would usually discover them to be vain and shallow. To the "higher order" he was an unfailingly receptive listener, feeling that through them he was receiving an influx of divine wisdom.

From his inner dialogues Swedenborg assembled a multidimensional theology of considerable depth and wisdom. While it is grounded in the Judeo-Christian scriptural system, yet it envisions a transparency to matter and its relationship to the spirit which rivals the deepest insights of Buddhism and the discoveries of modern physics. The human ego is poised between two orders of spiritual forces. It functions mainly as a receptor to these forces. Evil is equivalent to exclusive self-interest, being closed off. Regeneration, spiritual growth, is opening oneself both to the influx of divine spirit within oneself and to its presence in other people.

The lower-order hallucinations described by Swedenborg

and Van Dusen remind us rather forcibly of spirit possession as described by countless cultures and in our own medieval tradition. Recently, in fact, there has been a rather startling resurgence of belief in demonism and spirit possession. Not long ago in a therapy group I worked with a young man who for days after having seen the film version of *The Exorcist* had felt himself to be followed by invisible presences and heard voices just nudging at the edge of his consciousness.

In dealing with such manifestations, it seems to me far wiser to try first the approach of dialogue rather than the traditional exorcism. In the latter, the priest immediately assumes what is bothering the patient must be an evil spirit, and begins to heap foul abuse on it and demand that it depart.* If you do this before other strategies of relationship are tried, you very soon have a devil indeed. Whether we assume these are split-off parts of consciousness or objective entities, as our ancestors believed, the net effect is the same. A little sensitivity and tact work wonders on the inner as well as outer level.

Pierre Janet, the great French psychologist of the last century, describes a very interesting case of a man seemingly possessed by the Devil. He would blaspheme against the Deity, writhe, and grimace. Fortunately, since it was the nineteenth and not the seventeenth century, he was institutionalized rather than tortured or exorcised. Janet tried unsuccessfully to hypnotize him, only to be mocked and jeered at by the Devil. Finally he slyly slipped a pen into the hand of the possessed man, who then began to do unconscious writing. Janet directed questions to the writing hand, thus:

"Who are you?"
"I am the Devil."
"Ah, very good, very good! Now we can talk."

---

*The medieval rationale for this practice was that the Devil had an overwhelming pride. The more one could abuse and insult the possessed person, the more likely was the Devil to abandon the premises. But in actual fact it seldom worked this way. (See Aldous Huxley's *Devils of Loüdon* and Oesterreich's *Possession*.[18]) These violent nondialogues often developed into almost interminable stalemates.

Janet indeed talks to the Devil, who proves to be a vain and arrogant fellow but not entirely unresponsive to persuasion. He challenges him to show how much he can do to poor Achille, the afflicted man, against his will. The Devil easily does one thing after another (raising his hand, stomping his feet, and so on). Finally Janet challenges him to put the patient into a hypnotic sleep, which the Devil obligingly does. Janet then very quietly questions Achille, who is in a "somnambulistic trance," and learns about a guilt-inducing incident, an infidelity to his wife, which evidently precipitated his madness. Through a variety of psychotherapeutic and also fantasy(!) techniques, Achille is cured, and the Devil departs without recourse to holy water or horrendous-sounding abusive commands in Latin.[19]

The following *mondō* or dialogue between a Buddhist priest and a fox spirit possessing a woman in Japan seems also rather conversational and practical compared to the high bombast of the Christian exorcism:

"Who are you?" he asked, "and why are you molesting this woman?"

"I have nothing against her myself," replied the fox, "but I am compelled by a certain person to torment her and if possible kill her."

"Who is this person?" demanded the priest.

"He is an ascetic," replied the fox. "Another woman paid him three yen to send me on this errand. I am sorry about it, but I have to obey orders. . . ."

The fox, it turns out, is a rather decent chap who used to live under a rock on a mountainside and was captured by the ascetic through magic. The magician was in the employ (as happens in Voudon as well) of the jealous wife of a man who was seeing the possessed woman on the side. The exorcism is accomplished in the following rather amusing fashion: "The priest, after threatening the fox with a portrait of the Emperor Meiji, which reduced it to an abject state of shame and terror, eventually cajoled it into leaving the woman's body by promises of a place in the retinue of the deity *Inari*."[20]

The fox is not banished to an infernal region of wailing and gnashing teeth, but offered a nicer place in the mythic universe with the deity Inari, sacred to foxes.

The subliminal psyche seems to be quite susceptible to suggestion. Denounce a demon, tell him who he is in vile epithets, and you have ensured his continuing demonism. But you may also be simply tapping a part of the self that has been repressed, or a creative impulse, for that matter, which has become vexed for being so long misunderstood or ignored by the ego.

The realm of the psyche seems to respond to us much as we approach it. If we come armed for conflict, inner troops are marshaled and battle indeed takes place. But we may also go as pilgrim, sightseer, wayfarer in disguise. We can seldom really pass within unnoticed, but a humble and unassuming pose is usually the best passport in any strange country. There are wildernesses to be tamed within, and hostile beings we may encounter, but even these respond better to a touch of the silk glove than to the slap of the gauntlet. I find myself doing Hatha Yoga these days, not to lose my desires, but to loose them. The same *āsanas* (postures) that were developed three thousand years ago to still the passions may also awaken them. And some of Lowen's Bioenergetic exercises can be very well integrated with yogic *āsanas*.

Science fiction has seemed to pick up our theme of self-conquest rather than galactic conquest these days. Like Michael Valentine Smith in *Stranger in a Strange Land*,[21] the heroes have gained or are working on *siddhi*—personal magical powers, the ability to sit unnoticed at the bottom of a swimming pool for hours, to influence matter telekinetically, to read minds.

Macroscope is an amazing science-fiction epic which starts out technological and ends up archetypal.[22] The quest of the book is to find the one being who can look into and master the "macroscope," a clairvoyant telescope-microscope fabricated by an earlier, highly advanced civilization. This remarkable device not only allows one to peer into any corner of the physical universe, but contains, ultimately, unfathomable depths of universal knowledge. As one looks into it, the mind is led to follow a simple sequence of symbols which grows increasingly more complex, the logic of which is however inescapable. Following the sequence helplessly, the mind eventually boggles; the ego disintegrates. As the story unfolds, there are more and more blown-out superscientists and mathematicians wandering around. A search is instituted for the ultimate genius, the one being capable of perhaps assimilating the awesome knowledge of the macroscope: a man named Schön.

As it turns out Schön has hidden within the identity of one of the other characters in the book, a rather unassuming person called Ivo Archer. From here the story really gets interesting. What has been needed all along is not some intellectual supergenius, but someone with feeling, intuition, and compassion. The makers of the macroscope knew full well how destructive its awesome knowledge could be in the wrong hands. Hence they built in this little safety device, which short-circuits any mind that tries to penetrate its mysteries without willingness to undergo transformation—to meet with the archetypes.

In this story then which is clearly a metaphor for the discovery of the psyche, the characters are led through a series of encounters with transpersonal mythological powers. Intellect is not what is required, though it may be helpful, but rather feeling and intuitive sensitivity as well. Our inner adventure may be a dialogue as well as a struggle, a penetration of mysteries which, because they unfold within us, most profoundly change our view of who and what we are.

3. *The Sorcerer's Apprentice*

"We are men and our lot is to learn and to be hurled into inconceivable new worlds."

"Are there any new worlds for us really?" I asked half in jest.

"We have exhausted nothing, you fool," he said imperatively.

"Seeing is for impeccable men. Temper your spirit now, become a

warrior, learn to see, and then you'll know that there is no end to the
new worlds for our vision."

Carlos Castaneda, A Separate Reality

Cleansed and ripe for vision
I rise,
a bursting ball of seeds in space.

Which of the four worlds of crystal
will open for me?
I have sung the note that shatters structure,
and the note that shatters chaos,
and been bloody.

I have been with the dead,
and have attempted the labyrinth.
Bathing beneath the flow,
I smoke with images.

For the storm is looking for a wordless Man
who would pierce his tongue for the wind.
Who would sing, Holy! Holy!
I am the ring of bones beneath the tree,
I am the hunter of the healing wind.
Who would balance his song
against his sanity.

J. B., from "Caves and Hunters"[23]

In children's comic books, those treasure-houses of the
mythic imagination, an interesting dialogue has recently
emerged. It is between two comparable figures: the mad scientist and the magician. Almost always they are fighting. The
mad scientist has been around for some time. His archetype
by now is familiar to most of us. He is power and knowledge
run mad. He invents diabolical devices, creates complex and
inhuman plots for enslaving the human race and so forth. He
is out of touch with ordinary human qualities such as sympathy, compassion, or the enjoyment of everyday things.

Now, power is also the goal of the magician. This is the

Dr. Strange. Comic book magician whose arch-enemy is Yandroth, a power-mad scientist. While Yandroth's weapons are technology and intellectual control, Dr. Strange's powers are those of magic: ESP, psychic control, visualization. *(Courtesy Marvel Comics Group. Copyright© 1973 by Vista Publications Inc., Marvel Comics Group, 625 Madison Ave. N.Y., N.Y. All rights reserved.)*

prototypic symbolic role of the man whose power transcends ordinary limits of time and space. From the *sorcière* of *Les Trois Frères*[24] to the Yaqui sorcerer don Juan we see the same quest for power and control in a universe of limitation. The magician, though, does not manipulate reality directly.* As we have seen with the shaman, he relies upon his contact with a supernatural dimension to cause effects in the physical world. The technician of the sacred relies upon the myth to change reality. The secular technician manipulates it directly, and tries at least to exclude commerce with myth.

The scientist really is a magician of a very powerful order. So it has seemed to every technologically less advanced civilza-

*There is really somewhat of a debate on this issue among anthropologists. For example, homeopathic magic seems to attempt to work directly upon reality. The majority of shamanistic practices, however, rely upon the presence of supernatural agencies.

Dr. Strange Vanquishes Yandroth. The magician is seen as hero, who banishes the one-sided, power-conscious scientist to an appropriate fate—to fall endlessly through the dimension of dreams. As Dr. Strange so aptly says it, "Perhaps it is a fitting fate for one so absorbed in controlling the material universe that he could not recognize the existence of the Spirit!" *(Courtesy Marvel Comics Group, Copyright© 1967 by Vista Publications Inc., Marvel Comics Group. 625 Madison Ave. N.Y., N.Y. All rights reserved.)*

Men of Fantasy and Illusion. Rock groups, particularly in the 1960's were aware of the magic being released through their music. They seem in many ways like the Celtic Bards who were known as magicians as well as poets and musicians. *("Country Joe and the Fish," Courtesy Vanguard Records, New York. Photo by Joel Brodsky.)*

tion we have overwhelmed around the planet. Their own indigenous systems of power and reality tend to wither in the face
of our magic-wielding tools. Why, then, does the figure of the
magician reappear for a return bout with the reigning champion, the planetary favorite? I believe the figure of the scientist as madman may provide the key. In his *hubris* of power,
like the evil magicians in fairy tales, he has lost contact with
nature, his own as well as that around him. The compensatory
cloak-wearing figure of the archaic magician contains the missing dimension—the mythic quality the scientist has lost in his
symbolic asceticism.

The scientist is only the magician of the daylight world. He
has lost touch with the nocturnal world of the imagination,
where self-luminous forms and beings dwell and where the
mind participates in constructing the universe it perceives. He
is only in touch with his abstract logic or his experimental
design, and is thus an exile from the mythological; his magic
belongs to the universe seen only in one specialized state of
consciousness.

Carlos Castaneda, a scientifically trained anthropologist,
continues to visit Don Juan, a Yaqui Indian sorcerer, to learn
the mechanics of "nonordinary realities."[25] He feels, somehow,
as do we, that the world view into which we have been indoctrinated is good for some things but not for everything. He
wants to reach through and beyond for knowledge in the
dimension of myth and magic.

Now traditionally, magicians are not only manipulators of
reality but evokers of wonder as well. Among the Celts or
the Finns, for example, they were bards, magical singers often
referred to as "men of fantasy and illusion." In this older view
our daylight world is only one of many. There is the tradition
of "this world and that," and a constant commerce between
them. The other is the "bright world," the world of mystery,
as compared to this one of mundane realities.

Carlos's quest, then, carries him away from science and
into the wonder-filled world of the magician. The success his
adventure seems to have with us shows it is our quest as well.

When the technical mastery of reality has become prosaic, we are irresistibly drawn to mystery again. The four books of the Castaneda tetralogy are in fact a continuous dialogue between the scientific *Weltanschauung* and the magical world of the sorcerer. It seems to go on endlessly. And Carlos sometimes lures, sometimes drags us along. His myth is our myth, the finding of that lost sense of wonder. And his failing is ours too: ever and again asking for explanations, formulas to explain mystery. Don Juan seeks to plunge Carlos again and again into concept-shattering experiences that will dissolve his Aristotelian world view. And for the briefest of moments his wonder is aroused, he is transfixed by awe; but then his ineluctable networks of reasoning and conceptualizing cloak the primary moment. He is like most of us.

The sorcerer's apprenticeship is a quest to learn again the mechanics of the mythic imagination, to acquire a technology of the sacred. Witchcraft and a host of other cults, freed from the threat of organized persecution by the churches, are again flourishing. I find among my circle of friends these days several apprentice sorcerers, astrologers, diviners. The tendency is, of course, to learn from a teacher versed in the vocabulary and dynamics of a particular mythic system. And we have had some very bold explorers who have entered cultures not as voyeurs, "objective" observers, but as participants, living the utterly different reality of an alien symbolic universe.

Maya Deren, an American filmmaker and writer, went to Haiti to film Voudon dance and ceremony but ended up living in a Haitian village, caught up in the living myths and practices of the religion. She says,

. . . this book was written not because I had so intended but in spite of my intentions . . . (this) is, to me, the most eloquent tribute to the irrefutable reality and impact of Voudon mythology. I had begun as an artist, as one who would manipulate the elements of a reality into a work of art in the image of my creative integrity; I end by recording, as humbly as I can, the logic of a reality which had forced me to recognize its integrity, and to abandon my manipulations.[26]

Ms. Deren was lured by the power of living in a myth into the most intimate experience of Voudon, possession by a spirit *loa*. She later called this numinous experience "a white darkness, its whiteness a glory and its darkness a terror."[27]

The following account is taken from the experiences of a contemporary psychic explorer who will be referred to herein as J.B. Poet, adventurer, traveler in inner as well as outer dimensions, he was taken as apprentice and initiated by a Dogrib Indian shaman in 1963. His account has not been published elsewhere, and the materials in this text are taken from his personal notes and taped conversations with him. "S." in the recurring dialogue is myself.

J. B. NARRATIVES AND DIALOGUE

My encounter with shamanism took place in the area near Great Slave Lake and the Mackenzie Range. I was working at a fishing camp, the kind rich men from the States fly up to for enormous sums of money. There was a group of Dogrib Indians there who worked as guides. I had heard that they were mushroom eaters and I became interested in them for that reason. I had been into peyote down in New Mexico and I was excited by the prospect of experiencing something new. I even allowed for the possibility of learning something.

The head man of the Indians was named Adamie. I had heard stories about him, and I became curious. I began checking with the guides every day to see if he had arrived yet at camp. While working on the boat dock one day I noticed an Indian I had not seen before watching me. He was about sixty years old and weatherbeaten. His face was a dendritic river basin, deep furrows carved in almost perfect pattern. As he approached I felt my spine involuntarily quiver. I lost sight of everything except his deep-set black eyes. I heard his voice say to me, "You have been looking for me. I am at the house farthest north in the village."

Up till that moment my stay at this place had been a detached fantasy—a drifter's game to be played for two or three months until I had my fill of the river and its fish. Now, suddenly I began to feel a sweaty fear of survival urging me to get the hell out of that wilderness. But that was crazy. Just because an old Indian, tatooed by wind and cold, had spoken to me was no reason to run. I did a lot of running then, but I usually had better reason than this.

THE FIRST SEANCE—THE CALL

I went to visit Adamie at his house. There was a seance going on. Adamie was shamanizing, curing a sick woman.

Suddenly the drumming seemed louder and louder. The pitch became unbearable. It screamed like thunder over the lake. Animal cries cut through the darkness as Adamie leaped up. The metal that hung from him rang like a thousand bells gone berserk. I was pulled into a state of turmoil. I saw great birds smash through the room. A force was pulling me into the dance and frenzy. Time was lost. I wanted to jump up from my place and scream wildly. Blood filled my head till I felt like it was bursting out of my eyes and mouth. I stared at Adamie and felt my body convulse violently. I turned my gaze on the others in the room. They were distant and embalmed. My bones began to lose their adhesiveness—swirling light passed through my body. My mind made one last grasp at solidity. I screamed.

The chaos ended as suddenly as it had begun. Adamie fell by the woman's side and began murmuring. Then he was silent. Those around me started to get up and move towards the door. I couldn't move. The dirt floor held me like a cradle and swayed me gently. Someone lifted me with pleading and frightened sounds and half carried me to the door. Once outside I began to regain my footing. The ground shifted from the vertical back to the horizontal plane. It was almost daylight. I started back to the lodge, Eddie, one of the guides, giving me a hand. "Poor Joe, poor white man," he whispered. "All those good Indians there and you the one that gets called. Sometimes I wonder if those spirits know what they're doing. You don't even know nothing about it."

The days after the ceremony were days of shadows. Something had entered me and I felt as if I were being watched and motivated by some force outside myself. My will was being drained from my body, and I often felt the nauseating dizziness associated with loss of blood. It was like jumping up too fast after lying down too long —thrown off by the sudden shift in altitude.

A manic excitement eventually overtook me. I managed to get through my chores. All my excess energy was channeled into a "hash" pipe I was carving from a piece of hardwood. I became intensely concerned with every detail of its making. Each cut in the wood was carefully made and had to be exact. My fingers became sensitive to the precise needs of the wood. I felt its history run through the knife and into the palm of my hand. I took care with my work as I had never done before in my life. It seemed as if my very existence was tied to its outcome.

When the pipe was finished to my satisfaction I put it carefully into my leather pouch with some tobacco and went looking for Adamie. I didn't want to go, but something insisted on an answer to my present condition and it seemed that Adamie would have that answer. I worked my way slowly to his house like a fox trying to hide his tracks. I backtracked, dodged, and circumvented my destination till by a miracle of will I found myself at Adamie's door. I didn't knock, I just walked in.

Adamie was sitting in an old chair by a small wood stove in the center of the room. The room was almost barren except for a table filled with odds and ends of fishing tackle and a mattress on the floor in the corner. The hiss of two gas lanterns was the only sound that greeted me. Adamie looked up at me, and his face came alive with a gap-toothed, grandfather smile. He clapped his hands several times and began to laugh.

"How's that woman?" I blurted. "She's well," Adamie answered, continuing to laugh gently. His laugh was feather on my feet; it tickled and was painful. "I . . . I brought you this," I said, offering the pipe from my pouch.

"Why have you come here?" he demanded.

"To learn," came out of my mouth without me wishing it.

I placed the pipe on the table to occupy myself in the fragile silence my words had created. I feared that something terrifying was about to smash that wordless world.

"What are you thinking now?" Adamie's voice cracked through the hiss of the lanterns.

"That you're an old, ugly Indian, and what the hell am I so afraid of." I stunned myself with my honesty.

Adamie smiled. He motioned me to sit down on the floor near his chair. He got out of the chair and sat down next to me.

We talked for a long time, or at least I did. Adamie asked me question after question: What was Edmonton like? And New York? Where had I fished? Where was my home? Who were my people? He kept me talking till he had emptied me of everything that had come to be my identity.

"You have been so many places and seen so much. What do you think I could show you?" he asked.

"You could show me how to fish the lake for a start, and maybe . . . well . . . how you healed that woman."

"And is that why you brought me the gift?"

"I don't know exactly," I answered.

THE INSPECTION OF SOUL

"I would look at your soul," Adamie said flatly and finally.

"Help yourself, Adamie." I was feeling too spaced-out to be taken aback by his request.

S. Might as well give the nice old Indian man what he wants.

J. Right. What else do you say when someone asks you a question like that?

Adamie instructed me to lie down with my hands at my sides. He began to chant, walking slowly around me. Lying there I felt pleasant, and trusting, perhaps slightly amused.

Adamie's chant was cool and smooth and felt like a lover's body wrapped in silk. And as the chant fondled the mind, the silk grew warm and I threw the covering away and reached for the sources of heat inside the flesh of the lover, inside the flesh of the chant. Till my hand touched the fire—till I was the fire. A giant wind sucked the breath from the fire and I gasped in the darkness.

(Someone floated with no will, in black space. "I" no longer existed in the darkness that fell heavier than sleep. There are no recollections, no metaphors to express the suspended emptiness.)

I felt a gale blow across me, and a shiver which began at my mouth rippled my entire body. I heard Adamie chanting, and the sounds pulled my eyelids open.

"How long have I been asleep?"

"You were not sleeping."

A midday light entered the room.

"Hell." I tried to jump up but my body ached and I fell back. "The boss is going to kill me. I should have been to work hours ago."

"You have missed two whole days already," Adamie said grinning. "I told the boss you would stay with me now. You work with me, stay here."

Adamie moved towards the table and picked up the pipe. He carried it gently as if it were a small sleeping child.

He turned to me.

"I accept your gift."

S. The time that Adamie put you into trance—was it like the deep phase of sleep?

J. No, I don't think so, it wasn't the same as sleeping.

S. Do you know the place where you're about to wake up but can't quite get into your body to activate it? Was it like that?

J. No, not quite, not really. There you still have will. But I had no will. I was just hanging there, nothing.

S. The part in you that makes you do things, intentional things, was gone.

J. I would say that's right. Whatever he had done, he had snatched me. I had no volition, I had no power of my own. I didn't eat and didn't sleep, I didn't think—I wasn't in my body any longer. Adamie had me, and for two days he had me. For two days he inspected me, looked at all the cracks in my soul, saw what he liked and what he didn't like.

S. How did you feel then, waking up?

J. Well, it was all over. The wise-ass disappeared at that point.

S. He went back to Brooklyn?

J. Right, he sure did, over the hill and gone. I was taking it all like it was happening to someone else, until that experience. I realized then that my power, as a civilized man, was nothing, almost not there; and this man had so much power.

S. Did you have any idea what Adamie wanted to do when he asked to "look at your soul?"

J. I had no notion at all. All I know is that things began to happen very quickly from then on.

Then Adamie proceeded to teach me. The initiation consisted of ordeals. It was a preparation for what was to come. If I had a structure, the idea was to break down that reality, to take away my structures until I had none.

I was bathed in ice water, I was whipped, badgered continuously both physically and psychologically, and all the time being taught

—being taught about the way of the spirits, about how the world was ordered in a different way than I had imagined.

It was a process of breaking down and reordering over and over again.

S. During the initiation, in the physical torture type of stuff, did you feel pushed to your limits?

J. I felt pushed past my limits. Kind of when you've been snow-shoeing too long and you've just really "had it." You can't stand it, but for some reason you keep on going through second winds and thirds.

S. Beatings and cold water?

J. Yes. It was a process of disintegration.

S. A bit like bioenergetic therapy?

J. Absolutely, like that, or Rolfing* . . . or more.

S. Did you get the shakes? Or rather, how bad were they?

J. Yes, all over, and exhaustion, hating it. Something in me saying "Why are you putting up with it?" But I didn't stop, a feeling like I had to go on. But after a while I wanted to go into my first seance, I think mainly to get away from the other ordeals.

FIRST MUSHROOM EXPERIENCE: DISMEMBERMENT

J. Adamie asked me if I was ready to meet the spirits. And I said "Yes." I ate mushrooms (*Amanita muscaria*) and there was drumming and a seance. It was a very frightening experience. The drug felt toxic and I didn't know how to deal with it.

S. Was it like that feeling that sometimes comes on peyote, like you're dying, or dead?

J. That's the feeling. It was like eating belladonna also. Like there's no way out now because those things with big teeth are coming. Everything was chaos and disorder. I wasn't ready, I didn't know enough, I couldn't put any pieces together.

I was physically ill, psychically terrified, close to death, no control, no direction. It was hell, an endless chaotic battle with no real point.

S. Was there any peak or resolution?

---

*"Rolfing," more formally, Structural Integration, is a technique of deep massage of the connective tissue, which, like the Bio-energetic therapy of Alexander Lowen, seems to involve simultaneous psychological release.

J. No, not really, I just gradually came out of it, still alive physically, but that's about it. It just stayed at one level of confrontation, and then it went away eventually.

S. How would you characterize your central affliction?

J. I thought I was going to die, terrified, violently slaughtered, and never come back.

Afterward Adamie asked me what had happened, and I explained to him what I'd experienced. He picked out each fear, each feeling, and he explained to me the spirit that controlled it. He told me spirit names, and what they did.

S. How long elapsed between that experience and the next one?

J. About two months. Before the first one I had thought. "They'll stop badgering me now." Before the second one I no longer wanted to stop it. Somehow the first time I found out that I was fucking up. The way I was, the thing I was holding on to was just not real. I had to stop holding on to that identity. That had to be chopped away. It wasn't very central, it wasn't strong.

S. And unless you let go on that level nothing would happen?

J. Right, I didn't want the vision, the dream to take me, to take me out of what I was. That had to be beaten out of me, psyched out of me. And then there was a moment . . .

And after that moment, it was time to start to learn. What are these forces that are tearing you apart. Let's give them a name and see what to do with them.

THE SECOND SEANCE: MEETING WITH THE SPIRIT

J. The next seance started with dancing and drumming. And this time I participated. I started to dance wildly and more wildly, getting more ecstatic. And then I felt this wave going up my spine, exploding in my head, and then I hit trance.

In trance I had a vision, I saw a bear. And the bear motioned for me to follow it. This was the spirit, the force I was to follow, to take my journey with. As I was following the bear it turned into a woman. And then there was a whole series of sexual imagery, buttocks, thighs, breasts, a whole swirl of sexuality, of flesh.

I was swirling and whirling, and I felt like I was falling to the center of the earth. And as I was going down, there were creatures on all sides of me. And they would rip and tear, take pieces from me as I went down. And when I hit bottom they all descended on me and tore me up: a falcon on my eyes, a many-toothed dog gnawing my backbone.

I was torn and torn. But somehow this time I was not afraid in the same way. I accepted it all. I obeyed the fear and went with it. I was torn until some spirit—some force—cried *Stop!* . . . And then I began to be put back together again. And as I was coming together again I didn't recognize what I saw coming together as me. It wasn't exactly right. Something was there that wasn't there before, but as it put itself, molded itself, back together I began to understand that something had been added. Instead of being structured 1—2—3, I was structured 1—2—3 and 4. That 4 was very important, it made the whole thing more than it had been.

My feelings were of high ecstasy, shock waves of energy traveling through me. I felt I could see through things, hearts, bones, souls. There was a sound, and it was coming up from within me. I was singing a song, the song of my experience, and I felt the song gave me new strength and power. I knew I must remember that song. It is my medicine song.

S. The second experience you went all the way?

J. Yes, there was terror, but there wasn't doubt.

S. Did you have any notion then of the shamanistic symbolism of dismemberment?

J. No. I was not well read in that literature at all. I only found out considerably later about that pattern. At the time it just happened, no expectations on my part.

S. How did you feel physically after the second trip?

J. Refreshed, no word but refreshed. Body felt integrated.

S. Could you say more about that dismemberment experience?

J. Yes, I had to meet with these energies, whatever they were, I had to be taught about meeting them. I had to isolate the energy patterns, find out what part of the body they came through, etc.

S. Were they recognizable parts of you that you had seen in your life before?

J. No, they weren't exactly history. They were archetypal.

S. They were given Adamie's cultural names, right? Could you tell me some of those?

J. There was the Sedna complex, he called her Beama, the lady who lives under the water.

S. The Mother of the Sea Creatures.

J. Yes, she was very important, she lives in the lakes too, the Great Slave, Great Bear Lake.

S. Did the energies come up in your life in between the sessions, or visions, could you feel them then?

J. Yes. They were there, in the psyche, in the body. There is a creature, an energy force in Adamie's world, who corresponds culturally to the abandoning father; the men go off to trade and trap. I guess there is a projection on the mythology. He played an important part in my initiation.

S. Does this correspond to anything in your personal history?

J. Yes, it does.

S. Did Adamie know that?

J. I don't know, he worked his way into it. I guess it was part of his cultural assumption too.

S. What techniques did they use?

J. One was massage. They feel when spirits come through, they use a certain part of your body: through your leg, your groin, your ass, your shoulders, your spine, any part. Each part would also have a particular group of negative energy forces to deal with. You have to deal with these things through the body, and when I hear accounts of Rolfing, it's incredibly similar.

S. It sounds like some LSD experiences, where certain experiences seem to originate in certain parts of the body.

*R.** It sounds also like medieval cases of spirit possession, and also like Swedenborg, who talked to spirits in specific parts of his body.

S. To what extent were you aware of ancestral elements present in your experience?

J. It was kind of muddled, but it was like "there is more here than simply me," not just being in my own personal history, but beyond only personal.

S. Did you feel it extended even further back, lets say into evolutionary history?

J. Most definitely.

S. How did it make you feel, that it wasn't just you?

J. Wonderful, just great.

(Mutual laughter.)

---

* Robin, my wife, was present during this part of the interview.

EPILOGUE

S. Have your tensions come back since (ten years later)?

J. Have they ever! It seems that there has to be a continual healing process.

S. When did you start thinking you would return to your regular social environment?

J. Not long after that second trip. I realized this was going to take a long, long time. I was twenty-one years old and not ready to give up the world.

S. Were you divided?

J. Very. One part said you are going to become an old man in the woods, you can't get an Indian woman, and everyone is going to be afraid of you. But no one is going to love you. Adamie is more respected than loved. But the other forces were calling me to continue the journey.

S. Adamie is a lonely old man, and I'm sure you gave him nice vibes, love and respect. Perhaps this is what Carlos gave to old Juan Matus. Remember the scene where don Juan goes to talk to all the young Yaqui bucks? He comes on like some kind of senile old Indian evangelist with his way of knowledge. And they don't want to hear it. They just want to get drunk and have a good time.

J. Most of the young men up there are like that, they're interested in going to the lodge and making a lot of bread off the white people.

S. There's an analogy to the priest of a dying religion who gets a disciple in troubled times.

J. The keeper of a dying culture. The tradition lives in Adamie. It has to be passed on to someone else.

S. Black Elk gives out his vision too, to white men. Maybe he felt the youth in his culture being already sucked into the white man's trip . . .

S. How does Adamie feel about those rich white men he guides on fishing trips?

J. Usually he's amused by them, but sometimes he gets angry. His culture is in a decline, you can see it. The people he trains are fewer. The familiar ground is being devastated.

S. Where do you feel you would be if you stayed there?

J. I would be a second-rate shaman if I stayed . . . A sort of crazy man who hung out in the woods and went down to Edmonton in midwinter, because I wasn't Indian and couldn't stand the barrenness. That's pretty much where I'd be. I would have been between two cultures.

S. You feel there are elements tying you to this culture?

J. Yes, I am definitely not of that culture.

S. Do you feel any kind of spiritual affinity for the culture?

J. No, not exactly, but I feel that the very flows of this culture can be used. It keeps making me sort through my values and doesn't provide any set package so that I have to keep sorting through till I say, "Aha, this is real for me."

S. Do you feel there's any sort of spiritual trip for you in this culture that would be an analogy of the one you almost went on?

J. It's coming back into the world with a song after having a vision—but then there aren't many people to share it with, not like a primitive tribe where you can come back and say, "Here are my bear's teeth or my vision, this is what my name is, this is the spirit who guides me." I can't really do that here.

S. Did you feel then for a while like a visionary who has come down out of the mountains?

J. When I came back I didn't feel like telling anyone much. In fact that was when I went to the lower East Side of New York and started living hard and ugly. I changed, became mean, like a shark, went through this awful stuff. I thought I would make a lot of money and get very cool. It took me a while to see the fantasy wasn't working out the way I wanted it to. I was becoming the evil shaman and dissipating my power to that evil.

S. Can you say some more about what it would have been like if you stayed with Adamie?

J. It would have been red suspenders and flannel shirts and taking our rich white men fishing. And going trapping in the winter . . . but that wasn't who I was, I wasn't a north woods Indian, and much as I could relate to the worlds of realities in their mythology, I couldn't adapt to their life style, make it mine, and stay there the rest of my life—let my hair grow down to my knees, wear an iron shaman's costume.

I felt I had to go back to my own culture, to work things out. I had to somehow take the little I'd mastered back to my own culture, and make it work there. There's no grounding mythology for

me here, no strong physical presence of a human guide, but the
song remains. The song is always there.

COMMENTARY

In the essentials, J. B.—possessed of a modern psyche, in-
cubated in Brooklyn, not the Arctic—goes through the selfsame archetypal process as a Siberian shaman or one of the
Australian Aranda: death, dismemberment, reconstitution, the
gaining of power through vision. But the visions obtained (as
we have seen to be true of all visions), require the stabilizing
anchor of enactment. The shaman must solve problems of
his culture, cure the sick and rescue souls. And it is to this
dimension of shamanism that J. B. finds himself unable to give
his commitment. He is not unwilling to become a shaman, but
unable to become an Indian.

Guided LSD experiences using high doses (200-400 micro-
grams), eyeshades, and earphones also hurl one out of ordinary
consciousness into what might be called the "living landscape"
within. And archetypal dramas—death, dismemberment, and
rebirth—are frequently encountered. The essentials of some
of these experiences (the deepest and most transforming ones)
are very similar to what J. B. went through. The archetypes
are blueprints, as it were, though the actual architecture of the
vision may be cultural or personal in appearance.

I find it impressive that Adamie was able to do an "extraction of soul" on a rationally indoctrinated white man. If we
are to believe most anthropologists, primitive people are much
more susceptible to this type of thing than we are, since their
belief systems include this kind of possibility and ours do not.
The "soul inspection," though, is an old technique of shamanistic initiation. Rasmussen says of Eskimo shamans that "the
old *angakok* (shaman) extracts the disciple's 'soul' from his
eyes, brain, and intestines, so that the spirits may know what
is best in him."[28] And J. B.'s account shows us that this is not
"mere mythology" but rather a profound and unmistakable
experience. We must conclude both that he, unlike the white

men Adamie takes hunting, was psychologically ready for such a depth experience and that Adamie is indeed, as we are told, "a man of power."

I find myself grateful to J. B. for going through this ecstatic, terrifying, sacred ordeal and sharing it with us. I have at times had an almost irresistible attraction to shamanistic experience and have thought seriously of going to find one to ask for initiation. But from my talks with J. B. I have come to feel, as he does, that we must find our own equivalents for shamanism, not seek initiation in a primitive culture. We must encounter and live our visions right here in the matrix of our own culture, barren womb for the gestation of the sacred as it may seem. When J. B. returns to his own culture he lacks a framework for validating his visionary experiences. He falls quickly into one of our indigenous cultural traps. And yet my feeling about this man, from my personal contact with him, is that he has been transformed, reborn in some basic life-affirming way.

I have questioned a number of times whether the term *shaman* is appropriate for the *brujo* don Juan, as some have suggested. Don Juan does not really seem to function as visionary or healer on the cultural level. Nor does he put Carlos through this immemorial ritual that J. B. undergoes. Carlos navigates through the labyrinth of wonders exposed to him with his ego still maddeningly intact. He does not undergo the ineluctably transforming experience of annihilation and ego dismemberment. Don Juan usually prefers to confound him by incomprehensible physical or perceptual illusions. He does not dismantle his self-structure.

The quest for psychospiritual learning, for apprenticeship to a "man of knowledge," is one of our enduring mythogems, reactivated once again in the face of our current predicament. Is it not a sign that despite our apparent mastery of physical reality we still cannot accept knowledge without the simultaneous presence of the mystery dimension?

A few months ago, a very interesting book showed up at my office in the mail. The way these things happen sometimes, it turned out to provide some very relevant material to the theme of this chapter. It is unassumingly entitled *Crossings: A Transpersonal Approach*, by Carl Levett.

The book opened with an autobiographical account of Levett's experiences over a period of two years. He was a professional psychotherapist in mid-life with a fairly successful private practice. One day at a gathering led by an East Indian Master, he locked eyes with the Master in a moment of spiritual rapport. He says,

After a few moments my eyes fused with his and all my self-consciousness slipped away. I surrendered completely to the two powerful beams of light which flowed from his eyes and flooded my being with effulgence. Suddenly, a series of uncontrollable vibrations or electrical charges broke loose with a powerful force within me. It was as if a boulder had been flung into the center of a tranquil pond. It seemed as if this energy was trying to break free of my body. Unexpectedly, the Master's attention shifted away, breaking off the rapturous flow of energy between us. He smiled and silently acknowledged that our contact—which had seemed timeless—was now over. Although at the time the sensations that I felt had seemed to signal the beginning of a greater inner freedom for me, what followed was quite the opposite. A painful muscular contraction began to form in my abdomen.[29]

Having expected ecstasy from his spiritual encounter, Levett instead got agony. Asking for a private interview with the Master, he was told "Don't concern yourself with that; just let the energy go."

But try as he might, he could not follow this well-meant advice. The pain in his abdomen began to grow worse. Summoning all his professional skills, he tried to work on the problem.

For the next month I became both patient and therapist, drawing on such special approaches as bio-energetic, gestalt and primal therapy—disciplines considered by many people to be advanced in the treatment of body spasm. Although these same procedures had proven quite beneficial to many of my patients, they brought surprisingly little relief to me.[30]

He tried medical doctors, pored over psychiatric and psychological journals, all to no avail. The pain persisted for close to two years. Dr. Levett found himself with the perennial *koan* which has never been an easy one for any therapist: "Physician, heal thyself." He faced in fact the selfsame dilemma the shaman does during the anguishing onset of his vocation. But Levett was apparently not at all acquainted with the shamanistic pattern.

However, conscious knowledge in dealing with archetypal dynamics, while it may be helpful, is not always necessary. Guidance may come from unexpected sources. Acting, it seemed, on pure whimsy, Levett one day found himself attracted to a set of bongo drums in a music shop. Now if you will look for a moment once again at the cover of this book, you will remember that the drum is the shaman's perennial, primary appliance. It is the doorway to the other realm, the vehicle of ecstasy that his spirit rides upon. Knowing nothing consciously about the role of the drum in shamanism, Levett began to play, at first quite aimlessly, in his idle hours. Then one day while practicing with his drum he encountered a peculiarly personal rhythm unlike anything he had done before. As he gradually worked with this pattern, turning himself over to the drumming,

. . . I was shocked by the sudden realization that the drumming was coming not from me, but from somewhere else. I doublechecked in disbelief, but it was a fact. The drumming continued in perfect rhythm, yet completely out of my control. Immediately my body began to convulse and energy surged from deep within me, becoming a liquid radiance which saturated every cell of my body. All conceptions I had of myself vanished as I dissolved into this flow. Suddenly I realized that the spasm had disappeared. A voice inside me was yelling *no more pain*! *It's gone*! *You've licked it!*[31]

And so it was for just a few moments. By surrendering himself to the force within him that was drumming, he momentarily freed himself from the spasm. But it returned, inexorably. He had caught a glimpse of the dynamism that was working in his guts, but only a glimpse. The pain persisted.

A few weeks later a dream came to him with shocking clarity and violence:

In an overgrown, serpentine jungle, a fire was blazing under a huge pumpkin. Daimonic aboriginals danced orgiastically around the flames wielding knobby clubs. Through the smoke I caught a glimpse of a body impaled on a spear. I realized with a shock that it was me.[32]

The theme of dismemberment seems to be a brutal but indispensable part of the shaman's transformation. Like the shaman, Levett here has been projected onto a vital plane of life and death in which there is no difference between primitive and civilized. He has been shocked, but brought still closer to the seriousness of what is happening to him.

Finally, through his praxis, his *sādhana* of drumming, he is led to the core of his experience with a *mantram*.

The syllables fell into perfect cadence with the drum's rhythm:

My life
My life
My life is in your hands

When I practiced drumming and chanting the phrase, an unusual merging of mind and feeling took place, drawing me downward to a beginning of something. As I trusted its vertical pull, it took me to the fundamental elements of life.

I became one with water—a glacier, the tides and waves; the rain, quenching thirst, nourishing life. I was the sun—a molten fireball, warming the solar system; the light of day; the moon's glow. I was air—the breath of life, sustaining flight; the wind off the ocean. And then I was earth—minerals, rocks, sand; the soil for flora; miniscule in an infinite universe.[33]

Surely this is a cosmic initiation through which Carl Levett is passing. Like the shaman's initiation, it involves a confrontation with the fundamental data of experience, and a merging

with the universe. And this includes the inevitable confrontation with death and birth. As he enters his inner silence,

An icy chill ricocheted through me; I suspected death was hover-
ing in the background. I lost all sense of dimension. Then I heard
a vague sound which very slowly became more audible, becoming
separate sounds and then forming into words:

ee, ell, ey, ee
pee, bell, bey, bee
pre- belly baby!

I was at the origin of life, a fetus spinning in a whirlpool.[34]

We are reminded of the way J. B. feels his medicine song
coming from within out of the fire of ecstasy; or as Isaac Tens
says, *A chant was coming out of me without my being able to
stop it. . . . Such visions happen when a man is about to become a shaman; they occur of their own accord.*

Even after this core experience, though, the knot in Carl
Levett's stomach remains. But something inside him seems to
have relaxed, given in to the fate that is gripping him.

Then one day, as he is sitting in his easy chair after an intense session of drumming, a numinous vision unfolds itself to
him.

As I opened my eyes I saw, seated in the chair opposite me, a
female figure—a kind of universal mother, enveloped in a pulsat-
ing aura. She gestured for me to approach, and as I did I became
the cosmic pre-belly baby.

The archetypal mother is replaced by a father figure, and then
the two merge into one.

The universal parent beckoned for me to enter an opening in the
lower part of its abdomen, and as I did, an enormous magnetic
force sucked the spasm from my gut. My surrender to that transpersonal figure produced within me a limitless sense of freedom.
Fresh energies poured through me, leading to a softening of
breath, feeding my being with an exquisite calm, and moving gently
within me.

My body released a tremendous sigh as I realized the spasm was completely gone. After two years of pain and struggle, I had made my first crossing to transpersonal consciousness.[35]

In this remarkable chronicle we see a recapitulation of the essential dynamics we have been studying throughout this book. And they may emerge, in someone willing to engage them fully and consciously, without the support of cultural framework or tradition. Carl Levett is a solitary shaman. But like any shaman, his own cure is only the preliminary for his further healing work with others. The subsequent sections of his book describe in depth the entirely new transpersonal psychotherapy he begins to practice—or really, that he finds happening through him.

He finds himself, like most shamans, the vehicle of spiritual powers originating from a place beyond his conscious control. As he says, "I was being converted into a conduit for the expression of that power which now moved like a river through the trunk of my body." And this power, he finds, is what may bring genuine healing to his patients, much more than his previous well-intended efforts.

We see here that initiation into spiritual and magical power need not take place at the hands of a human master; it may also take place spontaneously, as it has since time immemorial. What is necessary is attunement, patience, and relationship to the within.

4. *The Myth of the Crippled Tyrant*

The mythogenic themes we have explored so far have been forward-looking for the most part, pointing in positive directions of growth and self-discovery. Yet such themes might seem rather bland and optimistic without the addition of the shadow element, the dark regressive form that personifies inertia, the very essence of what resists transformation.

The following section touches this problematical dynamism very briefly and tentatively, perhaps just enough to set off the magnitude of the task of human growth that awaits our species, which must be undertaken not only by ourselves but by every generation to come if we are collectively to survive.

Few among us as yet are attuned, as were many of our ancestors, to the presence of the mythic in the everyday. A perception developed among abstract values and a linear sense of causality is unlikely to look for omens in the flight of birds or the entrails of beasts. Yet our ancestors seemed to know full well that if they did not "read" the portents in these pre-liminary, anticipatory ways they might emerge into events of national scale, producing perhaps irreversible disasters. There was a full recognition that the mythic permeated the ordinary, if not consciously, then unconsciously. The wise ruler con-sulted the oracles, read the portents, and suited his doings to the symbolic characteristics of the times—to the fates that might so easily eclipse the best-laid plans of men.

In a secularized society we have no state oracles, nor do our political leaders consult wise men before making major decisions. Yet this aspect of "progress" may be to our detri-ment rather than our gain, for our public life seems, often as not, to be a grand stage for mythological spectacles rather than the secular sociopolitical-economic ones we have been trained to expect. The disastrous events precipitated by Ger-man National Socialism represent one such drama, the myth-ological elements of which are impossible to overlook. The doings of Adolph Hitler and his associates were pervaded by occultism, mediumship, and mythic imagery.[36] And Jung had begun to pick up images of Wotan, the deity traditionally associated with German military nationalism, in the dreams of his German patients years before Hitler's meteoric rise to power.

The tragic events surrounding the Kennedy family seemed to many of us a nightmare, emerging with astonishing sudden-ness into the light of day. The assassination of John was the slaying of the youthful sun king by the powers of darkness, beloved Baldur undone by the twisted plots of Loki. And the events befalling his brothers complete a trilogy of tragedies:

the unexpected hand of fate, a veritable *deus ex machina* intervening in ordinary doings when least expected: the fall of the
House of Atreus.

Rollo May has written on the mythic quality of the slaugh-
ter of the innocents in the Kent State massacre and the life-
devouring cult of our foreign military involvements. Like the
Aztec sacrificial rituals or the legendary community besieged
by ogre or dragon, our old men send the youth of the country
to feed the monster of projected aggression. He writes,

> Let no one think for an instant that we in our vaunted civiliza-
> tion have gone beyond the primitive human sacrifice. We sacrifice
> our youths not by the dozens, but by the thousands. The name of
> the god whom we appease is Moloch. We have sacrificed 50,000
> of our youths in Vietnam, and when we add up the Vietnamese,
> the sacrifice goes up to several millions. Our Moloch's taste fits
> the age-old form: it is for virginal youths. Our Moloch is greedy
> —which means we have much inner aggression and violence to
> project.[37]

This mythical vision of horror is staged paradoxically
against the background of a culture which passionately wor-
ships youth; a sign, suggests May, of the jealousy of the elders
who declare the wars which destroy the envied innocents.

And our youth have in turn responded by rebellion and
passive resistance, by fleeing the country, by escaping into
altered states of consciousness. William Irwin Thompson
captures the myth cogently: ". . . our advanced technologies
of child rearing and police control seem to have brought us
back to the mythic situation in which Cronus tries to devour
his children and the children think if they castrate their father
they will be free."[38]

This enmity between the old man who resists giving up the
power he has struggled so long to gain and maintain and the
youthful aspirant to the seat of power is one of our grand,
mythological themes. It is the eternal war of the generations
in symbolic form.

Not only the myths of all lands, but also the fairy tales

describe the same theme in countless variations: The country is ruled by an aging king. Slowly, things begin to go wrong. Sometimes it is noticed, and sometimes not, that the infirmities in the land correspond to a deficiency in the king. His malady is most often rigidity, combined with a tyrannical or authoritarian enforcement of his petrifying will. Final disaster must come unless the old king is slain, transformed or redeemed, usually by a youthful protagonist.

We remember the rigidities of Creon or the aging Roman tyrant Tarquin. We think of Nebuchadnezzar going on all fours, or Oedipus in his afflicted kingdom. In the Grail legend it is the mysterious wounded Fisher-King who suffers in the midst of his wasteland-kingdom and must be redeemed by the young Grail knights, Parsifal or Galahad.

The crippled tyrant or old king must be seen as the symbol of the power urge that has outlived its usefulness, become anachronistic. Psychologically he represents the ego, which, having gained the ruling position in the psyche, petrifies and clings to the security of fixed values rather than yielding to the inevitable change that accompanies the flow of life.

Marie-Louise von Franz, a Jungian analyst, in a series of excellent studies on this achetype, calls this unredeemed old man the *senex*. She writes: "His deficiency consists mainly in an exaggerated egocentricity and hardening of the heart. . . ." His antagonist, the symbol of the spirit of life, is the eternal child, the *puer aeternus*.[39] The *puer* represents everything the *senex* has become cut off from: youth, beauty, feeling, sexuality, change. And the *senex* in turn represents what to the youth seems unattainable—or repugnant: stability, power, responsibility, and worldly wisdom. As in any archetypal dynamism, these pairs of opposites are forever in conflict yet inextricably bound together, the presence of one evoking the other.*

*The images of the old man and youthful antagonist, interestingly enough, also appear in the *Aquarian Age* symbolism. The two planetary rulers of the astrological sign Aquarius are Saturn and Uranus. Saturn is Father Time, the old man, limitation, tradition; in short the very *senex*. Uranus, on the other hand, is the planet associated with unorthodoxy, revolutions, technology, communication of new and radical kinds. It does not seem, really, as

Now switch again quickly from the mythscape to our current sociopolitical landscape and you may retain the image, blurred but unmistakable. We see the demonstrations of the sixties, marches on the Pentagon, the hardened old men in Congress and the courtrooms passing sentence on the young in the streets; Mayor Daley and Abbie Hoffman. And just recently, it seems to me, we have seen a remarkable mythic event in public life which displays not only this same theme but a variety of other mythopolitical elements as well: the rise and fall of Richard Nixon. If we can free our eyes for a moment from the sole focus of politics and open them partly to myth, there are powerful lessons of living to be learned from what otherwise might seem to be a purely political debacle.

It should be easy for us to understand why someone should covet the most powerful political office in a large and powerful nation. Ambition and power are very close to our national heart. These are the principles of our competitive economy and the mark of the successful man. We do become slightly uneasy, though, when someone courts that prestigious office inexorably, year after year through many failures and setbacks.

Politically we call this office the presidency. Mythologically (i.e., on the unconscious level of motivation), its holder seems equivalent to king. And this confusion indeed showed up in the behavior and actions of our recent president. He confused political service with a mythic mandate, perhaps resembling divine right.* It was quite evident at times that there was some confusion between his personal identity as a man who sought and was elected to an office, and the office itself— the role, or mask, any number of individuals might be asked

---

if there were room for the two of them in the same sign, but here again the unifying symbol of dialogue ($\approx\approx$) may provide the key. If the two polar modes stay open to each other, a kind of dialogue may emerge between innocence and experience, change and limitation, creativity and discipline.

*The rather royal conscious or unconscious assumptions made by Richard Nixon have been amply mentioned; of such works as *Tyrannus Nix? They Could Not Trust the King* and so on.[40]

to wear for a time in the service of the public. Public funds were used to create summer and winter palaces, the royal chariot (Air Force One) was used for private outings, and the man himself kept making Freudian slips confusing his personal ego and his political position. Even at the very end, when there was nothing more to hide, he continued to proclaim that by saving himself he was protecting a political institution: the presidency.

Now really, none of this should have come as much of a surprise to us. Richard Nixon was an ordinary man, and very few of us are immune to power, success, and glory. To hold such public office, to seem to be the very center that holds together an enormous nation, is bound to produce some inflation of the personal ego. It is so much more glorious to bask in the refulgence temporarily conferred by the role than to face up to the limitations of one's ordinary self. Bruce Mazlish, a psychohistorian noted in 1972, ". . . Richard Nixon thinks unusually well of himself. Does this intense narcissism border on megalomania, or is it absolutely normal behavior for all politicians?"[41]

Recognizing precisely this danger of mythic inflation, many of the earliest kingdoms of which we have any complete knowledge put an added little safety clause into their contract: During his reign the king might enjoy absolute sovereignty and complete power over his subjects; but there was a very definite term to his office. Although the kingship (part of the divinely ordained mythological order) was to go on, the king (the man filling the office) must die. "The fundamental concept of this whole archaic world . . . was that the reality, the true being of the king—as of any individual—is not in his character as individual, but as archetype."[42]

In the ritual regicide the focus of energy in the community was removed from the human field to the mythological order.*

---

*The theme of ritual regicide is one of the central elements in Sir James Frazer's *Golden Bough*. He focused particularly on the "year king" who belonged to the Sacred Grove at Nemi, but this practice was widespread throughout the entire ancient world.

The king was to serve as sacrifice to the transpersonal powers; to renew relationship with them. If things were going well the regicide would take place at regular intervals, often determined (in the Middle-Eastern hieratic city-states) by planetary conjunctions. If things were not going well, i.e., with drought, crops failing, and so forth, regicide as sacrifice might take place at any time, as remedy. The king, symbolic offering of the kingdom, must be sacrificed so that rebirth and a new beginning might take place for the community at large.

Such a ceremony could be very grisly indeed. Campbell describes one originally observed by Duarte Barbarossa in the sixteenth century in southern India.

When his time came the king had a wooden scaffolding constructed and spread over with hangings of silk. And when he had ritually bathed in a tank with great ceremonies and to the sound of music, he proceeded to the temple, where he paid worship to the divinity. Then he mounted the scaffolding and, before the people, took some very sharp knives and began to cut off parts of his body—nose, ears, lips, and all his members and as much of his flesh as he was able—throwing them away and round about until so much of his blood was spilled that he began to faint, whereupon he slit his throat.[43]

You will agree that the expectation of such an end to one's term might discourage one from coveting the office for purely personal reasons. It is an earlier, rather more rigorous enforcement of the same political wisdom that limits a president of the United States to no more than two terms.

The man is not to confuse himself personally with the office, which is of a transpersonal nature. Now the contemporary message brought home to us in 1974 is that if you get the two confused—if you mistake personal ego for transpersonal office and are caught at it redhanded, but will not mount the scaffold yourself—then the press and the public will execute the dismemberment. That this must have been an excruciating experience for the man is unmistakable. But that it clarifies the real nature of the office he occupied is also evident.

What was terrifying to any psychologist about the last days of Richard Nixon's administration was that it (collectively) evidenced all the classic psychoanalytic ego defense mechanisms: *projection, reaction formation, displacement, denial.* And it was indeed an ego that was being defended. With the passing of time the mechanisms grew increasingly solipsistic, as they do in any regressive disorder: *I don't care whether I'm hiding from you any more as long as I can hide from me.* What was doubly terrifying was that this classic neurotic surrounded by other neurotics was also obliged to make monumental daily decisions that could affect the well-being of us all—including the ultimate one of pushing certain buttons that could eliminate the anxiety-provoking situation for good for everyone.

"I get stronger under pressure," he told the press, and we flinched collectively as he held up the two-fingered victory salute. What a lesson for us all! In February of 1974 I began to write an article—to send to anybody, who would publish it —called "The Myth of the Crippled Tyrant," which spelled out the mythic-psychological dynamism I felt was being unfolded before us. Owing to pressures of other work the piece was never completed. But here indeed was the *senex*, eternal opponent of youth and regeneration: the crippled ego principle that holds to power long after the obvious answer is submission. It was only several months later that the first signs of phlebitis showed up—the physical world caught up with the myth in the most literal way.

The main deficiency of the *senex* is that he has cut himself off from the flow of life. He has retreated into a rigid posture in which all definitions and values have become finally established. Anything that does not correspond with these definitions is excluded. There is no give and take, no flow. How appropriate then that the physical symptom which showed that, despite his denials, the would-be tyrant was unmistakably crippled should be a disorder of the circulatory system. The flow of the vital fluid in the legs, the parts that support one and connect one to the ground, had been interrupted.

What was enacted there upon the public stage for us all to see was a lesson which may speak to each of us in a different way. The philosophy—both political and personal—that led up to the Watergate events was to know and control everything possible, to leave nothing up to chance. Even, as many astonished Nixon supporters averred, when there was little doubt that he would emerge victorious in the 1972 election. (Why then should he have authorized any of those risky and silly things?) Nixon also may have been telling the truth when he said he did not authorize the Watergate burglary. It was simply one, perhaps minor, facet of an overall program he had set in motion, which was already proceeding quite automatically. The program, as we now know, included espionage, political sabotage, lists of "public enemies," and other unsavory details which are still being unearthed.

These mechanisms of control and defense only emerge out of intense states of anxiety. As such a state was unwarranted by outer circumstances, we have to assume this was neurotic anxiety, a lack of the confidence and conviction of self-worth that come from within. What is evidently underlying these manifestations is a basic mistrust of the workings of fate, a refusal to dare that element of chance which all of us must face up to in the midst of an uncertain existence. It is noteworthy in this regard that what brought about the wholesale downfall of this administration was not the unpredictable "slings and arrows of outrageous fortune" but public revelation of the precise and deliberate defense mechanisms which had been instituted to ward off the unforseen. This is the identical case with personal neurosis: *the defense mechanisms themselves become the symptoms.*

But what we have seen here, while enacted through the lives of Richard Nixon and his aides, seems to me like a grand staging of our collective neurosis. When a problem that has arisen is not confronted on the individual, personal level by enough people, it emerges in a drama on the public stage, as metaphor, symbol, and myth for all to behold.

The drama does not need interpretation, but empathy,

experiential understanding. One might try indwelling some of
the key characters, or Nixon himself, and see what it feels
like. Probably it feels awful, but what, particularly? Which
characters or roles seem to evoke a resonance? Relate them
to your personal character, or a part of yourself. Pay most
attention to what arouses your particular loathing or envy.
Tune in, but don't drop out. Dig it.

In this way one might establish relationship to or dialogue
with political events beyond mere voting privilege. If I have
met my own crippled tyrant I am less likely to be amazed,
outraged, or repelled when I see the same character strutting
or limping across the public stage. I can meet with the actor
and know him, and perhaps by such a conscious relationship
forestall the often terrifying events that ensue when the drama
takes over and gets out of control.

When it was found that Senator Eagleton (McGovern's
selection for vice president in the 1972 electoral race) had at
one time in his career sought psychotherapy for a personal
problem, this seemed to disqualify him in the public eye for
political office. Well, we have lived to see in office the ironic
alternative to such a shortsighted way of judging human
worth. The man who won't admit anything could be wrong.
This is the deepest and most devastating flaw of the crippled
tyrant. The land is in waste. He is limping—suffering—shut
off from pleasure, spontaneity, life, and still he will not admit
there's a problem.

Like the kings of the Middle Empire of Egypt, Richard
Nixon seemed quite unwilling to submit to the sacrificial ritual.
He proffered in his stead, as did many a wily pharoah, his entire household of political servants, dressing them up in turn
as offerings to the implacable priests of dismemberment.* But

*See Joseph Campbell's excellent analysis of this ritual of substitution in
Oriental Mythology, pp. 58–95. He writes,

And so we are now to recognize in the history of our subject a secondary
stage of mythic seizure: not *mythic identification*, ego absorbed and lost
in God, but its opposite *mythic inflation*, the god lost and absorbed in ego.
The first, I would suggest, characterized the actual holiness of the sacrificial
kings of the early hieratic city states; and the second, the mock holiness

the mythic *geis* would not be satisfied in this case; everyone seemed to know *the king must die*. And when he did ever so reluctantly submit to the inevitable, it was like the suttee rites of the ancient kingdoms where the whole household, wives and servants, must be buried alive with the king.

The image of God is a *senex* in our dominant Western religious system: male, elderly, judgmental, opposed to spontaneity, down on human sexuality. Two great religious revisionings have sought to mediate such an awesome and unapproachable figure: one through the death of a young man, his son, to appease his judgmental wrath. The other the intercession of his earthly wife who was pictured as ascending to bring a feminine touch and a little more human compassion to his remote astral abode. But the awesome figure still persists for most of us. Men as they grow older in our culture are likely to sink into an *imitatio Dei*, i.e., to petrify into a judgmental, austere role. This lends to one's persona a certain dignity and the ability to make felt an awesome aura of righteousness: In the presence of someone projecting the *senex* archetype it is hard to feel oneself as anything but a child— as both children and wives of such men have testified.

Again the mythic pattern points the way to resolution. The complementary redeeming figures are the eternal youth and the feminine. Both represent, in different inflections, what the *senex* lacks: rejuvenation, love, creativity. If the *senex* is awake to his deficiency, even a little, he may be spared dismemberment. In fairy tales the wise old man is often accompanied by a beautiful young woman, his redemption and completion. Merlin, the immortal *senex* wizard, shows this one human weakness: the susceptibility to young women.

But our Congressmen read *Playboy* and sometimes sport in tidal basins with erotic young creatures. To enact the compulsion by itself is not enough; it must be accompanied by the

---

of the worshipped kings of the dynastic states. For these supposed that it was in their temporal character that they were god. That is to say, they were mad men.[44]

germ of consciousness, even the tiniest kernel of awareness that one is participating in an age-old drama of mythic import. In this way even our compulsions, our petty sins, can turn into rites of transformation.

5. *The Mythic Androgyne*

In perhaps no other place is there more need for dialogue than in the relationship between man and woman. Yet the problems are not only between people but also between those parts of ourselves we have traditionally called *masculine* and *feminine*. We must sort out our stereotypes and see whether, perhaps, they are archetypes as well. Whence come those subtle feeling-toned images we project on people of the opposite sex? They are often bright with allure and vivid with expectation. Yet it seems our mutual destiny to find that the projection almost never corresponds with the individual nature of this person we live with, lover or companion, familiar stranger.

At the present historical moment we are faced with a confrontation of the sexes both in person and in image. Women are discontented with the pneumatic, cosmeticized, inadequate images projected on them by men. And men are suffering as well under the big-chested image of the manly hero who never fails nor cries. We are questioning these mythic attributions now perhaps as never before.

I think it is important to distinguish between what we mean by *man* (male homo sapiens) and *woman* (female homo sapiens), and the archetypal or stereotypical qualities we project on them: *masculine* and *feminine*. Many of these qualities are obviously culture-bound. Others may be transcultural and perennial. It is these latter qualities that we might say are archetypal; as such they are not the exclusive possession of either sex. Like the Chinese *yang* and *yin*, they are qualities of a mythological order. The feminine is what is capable of passivity, gestation, nurturing; the masculine, what is capable of activity, fertilization, aggression. Men and women are biologically sexed creatures with varying and intermixed proportions of masculine and feminine qualities.

We are just emerging from a period in which we had the archetypal qualities rather rigidly attached to biological sex differentiation. In my psychotherapeutic practice I have encountered the fragmentation of many relationships—especially those in which the old boundaries were too rigidly kept. Most often these days it seems to be women who first become sensitive to the inequities in the relationship. Men, unconsciously enjoying their advantaged position, are shocked and bewildered to find their wives suddenly expressing discontent, walking out of what has become a nonrelationship for them.

At this precise moment in history, though, the symbolic figure of the mythic androgyne, the unisex a.c.–d.c. hipster, emerges onto the public stage, perhaps to remind us of the original indissociation between the sexes. At first only dimly visible in the pelvic movements of Elvis Presley, she/he has taken less than a decade to emerge more strikingly in Alice Cooper and Mick Jagger, in Tiny Tim, in gay liberation.*

The deity classically associated with androgyny, with orgiastic sexuality, and with the breaking of traditions and boundaries is Dionysus. And it seems to be Dionysus who is stealing the stage from our old aloof *Senex* God-image these days. He/she is visible to the attuned eye and ear in orgies and the music of wildness, in the flickering lights of the strobe, in day-glo-painted faces, and more explicitly in many of our dreams. Several Jungian analysts have reported catching unmistakable glimpses of the ancient form of the vine-garlanded Hermaphrodite, dancing once again amongst the tangled symbol-forms of their patients' dreams.†

Compare the two following sets of dreams presented to me

*William Irwin Thompson comments astutely in this regard that "in the contemporary counterculture we do not see the divine androgyne but the demonic hermaphrodite. . . . the profane always contains an exoteric mirror-image of a sacred, esoteric mystery. . . ."[45]
†See particularly the fascinating cases presented by Edward Whitmont in *The Symbolic Quest.*[46]

spontaneously a few weeks apart by clients, one male and one female, both in their early twenties. Neither had any conscious model of the mythogenic themes we are discussing.

R (male)

Dream 1   *I want to make love with C. (my girl friend) but also ask V., her (girl) cousin, to join us in bed. As we begin exploring each other, I find V. has a penis, but I don't mind at all. It is rather exciting.*

Dream 2   *I dream of having a woman's body, and it feels very voluptuous. I can get off by caressing and making love to myself.*

Dream 3   *G., who is effeminate, comes up to me in the high school auditorium. While a bunch of my old friends (male) look on mockingly, he makes homosexual advances to me. I am tremendously embarrassed and try to push him away. Then he turns into a woman, and finally, a man-eating tiger that chases me all over.*

In an escalating series of confrontations with his own androgyny, R. (who is on the conscious level heterosexual) is finally led into the real blockage which prevents his letting himself go in these unconsciously arising feelings: the chorus of jeering males (we all remember them from high school or the army) who enforce the manly ideal and the rigid boundaries of the sexes. The tiger, in the culminating dream, however, lets him know that there is a fierce and devouring power there behind the androgynous image, which if avoided becomes far more terrifying and destructive.

K. is a very bright, attractive woman in her early twenties. An earlier analysis was able successfully to help her establish contact with her own masculine side: self-assertiveness and intellectual aggression. Now a different task seems to await her. She presented the following dream in the first session of her work with me:

Dream

Part 1   *I am returning to my office in the late afternoon to complete some work I had begun. The office is rather empty. On my desk, with some file cards, is a huge cock, with balls. I am to dissect this, and take notes on the file cards. I am slightly unnerved by this, but everyone else expects me to do it, rather matter-of-factly. They might even help or offer advice.*

Part 2   *I am preparing a special meal. Present are my mother and cousin J. (female). Two men, S. and A., are there. Dinner is ready, and each person receives a serving of soup: penis in broth. I am the only one who is shocked, everyone else is chatting. Mother is checking to make sure the penis was "fresh enough." Everyone is talking matter-of-factly about S. having had his genitals removed.*

Freud might have had a little difficulty with this dream, as he was most used to looking for symbolic representation of the male genitalia in women's dreams as flagpoles, umbrellas, watering cans and the like. When he had identified such representations he might (trepidatiously or triumphantly) offer his interpretation, at the risk of offending the lady's sensibilities. But K. is a modern woman with far less effete sensibilities than her grandmother. What, then, does the undisguised instrument of male sexuality refer to?*

In the first part of the dream she is asked to dissect and analyze it—quite simply, to understand it. In the context of her daily life this seems to refer to her own newly found masculine traits of self-assertiveness, intellect, aggression. While it seems to be unavoidably necessary for most modern women

---

*During a psychoanalytic congress when Freud was enumerating the infinite disguises of phallic symbolism, Jung asked the obvious question that no one else had: "But Freud, what happens if the penis itself appears in the dream?" Freud had a hard time dealing with this, as the essence of the psychoanalytic method consists of confronting the patient with the inadmissible, the *repressed*.

to develop these traits if they are to hold their own in a male-dominated society, it also appeared that K. had overdone it a bit and had recently had more aggressive conflicts with both men and women than she would have liked. In addition she had acquired, intact and rather unconsciously, the male trait of hiding tears with aggression. The dream says (part 1): "You've got it, and it's a big one. Now take it apart, understand it."

In part 2, a totally different ritual must take place, resembling a sacrificial feast. Analysis by itself is not enough. Once you have understood it you must consciously reintegrate, incorporate it. The gathering to whom this strange phallic feast is to be served are, principally, beside the dreamer, two men and two women. These resemble an inner cast of characters, each representing a different part of the self. Particularly the two men are important. A. is intellectual but cold, aloof, devoid of human feeling. S. is intellectual too, but warm and human. He it was who had lost his genitals in the dream; i.e., the positive masculine part of K. had lost its potency, while a cold, aloof masculine image had taken over. It is S.'s genitals, his more human potency, that by implication reappear in the soup and ask for symbolic reintegration.

The two dreams show a counterpoint of imagery that seems highly relevant to our present psychosexual transition. It is of owning a sensuous woman's body that R., a man, dreams. Women have stayed in touch with the instinctual aspect of their bodies far better than men. They hold the archetypal key to physical being, to embodiment and the sensuality men have lost. And K., a woman, in turn dreams of how to integrate (not imitate) the power, energy, and aggressiveness of the male. This is an indispensable stage of growth for women if they are to find and accept themselves as people, with their own individual strength and value. They also must train themselves as adequate sparring partners for men, who with their unequal accretion of strength have knocked flat just about every other opponent on the planet.

Recently in psychotherapy I worked with a transvestite, a delightful and intelligent young man who much preferred heterosexuality to homosexuality but could not resist dressing up, every now and then, in women's clothing. As we explored his "problem," what emerged most clearly was his need to contact his own feminine nature, to explore his own ability for passive rather than conquering sexuality, his capacity for psychic receptivity, for feeling. Both of us felt the symptom not as something that needed to be cured, but related to, exfoliated, understood.

It is the lack of femininity, of receptivity, of patience that seems to be behind most of the one-sided excesses that men have perpetuated throughout history. The major themes have been conquest and aggression. Recently I reviewed about twenty LSD psychotherapy sessions among male professional volunteers: a variety of priests, professors, psychiatrists, and psychologists.* In each case, among those I judged to be deeply transforming—to have changed the personality in a positive, creative way—there was a meeting with an internal, feminine part of the self (the *anima* in Jung's description). Such a depth encounter was accompanied by a radical transformation of the subject's perception of women, his ability to understand motives and feelings. Several of these volunteers subsequently reported that their relationship with wives, mothers, daughters, and so forth had radically improved.

I quote below a few sections from one of the most interesting of these experiences, a professional psychotherapist in his forties who had a series of three guided LSD sessions. The imagery from these sessions, often shamanlike in its visionary character, takes up a number of related archetypal themes: death, rebirth, earthiness, and spirit, and finally a meeting with his own femininity. The following is from his second session; he has already done considerable work. While the first session and the beginning of the second are characterized by

*Conducted at Maryland Psychiatric Research Center, Baltimore.

struggle with himself and with physical matter, here a beautiful receptivity has come about.

I experienced myself as earth itself. Rain was falling on me and gently soaking down into my being. I produced life in various forms; it easily, quietly, gently and gracefully moved up through me to the sunlight. It was a magnificent feeling of fecundity. Then there was the almost explosive discovery that I was not frightened! Scriabin's music on my first trip had produced terror in me, and at the beginning of this session had made me very uncomfortable. But now I was floating with it and deeply enjoying the imagery it evoked. This led to another sudden discovery: I had died and been reborn! I was filled with sheer delight and joy. I took off my headphones and tried to explain to T. (his wife) that my fear was gone and that life was truly good. I tried to share some of this inexplicable, simple and hilariously obvious knowledge that life is good and that love really does drive out fear. I was weeping for joy and for tenderness for T. and felt totally inadequate to communicate what had really happened to me and what I wanted to share with her. At one point I was explaining my identification with the earth and had a sudden recalling of the book of Genesis: God took the earth and made man. I felt very much earth *and* man, and it was great. Echoes of Zorba and his earthiness pounded through my memory and I realized why I responded so deeply to this portrayal of man. While musing on this insight I reflected again on my struggle with Stan and had a sudden recalling of Jacob struggling with the angel of God at the River Jabbok.

His experience has led him to a greater acceptance of earthiness and physical being. When this has been accepted, his own potential for creativity—fecundity—is contacted as well. The rebirth imagery that showed up in earlier parts of the experience culminates in the experience of "being" the earth as it accepts the nourishing rain and begins to yield life out of itself. Many valuable insights for S. come out of this session, particularly that everything good is not born out of active struggle (as most of us have been indoctrinated) but that receptivity is what is really necessary to facilitate the creative. Physical matter here is experienced as feminine, a connection that has been made since time immemorial (*matter = mater*).

In his culminating LSD session two months later, S. is led to a peak experience, an intimate meeting with the feminine:

The next sequence came with Scriabin's Second Symphony. As the languorous and sensual opening strains poured out, my hands and bare feet explored the smooth satin of the sleeping bag, the nubby texture of the rug and the silky fuzz of the upholstering of a chair. Although I was partly aware of the physical referents of these sensations, I increasingly experienced them voluptuously as human flesh: the lining of the uterus, the birth canal, the vagina, the labia, thighs and belly. Pillows became hips and breasts. I began exploring my own body and felt both pride and pleasure in it. I caressed my head and face, chest, abdomen, thighs and genitals. I experienced deep satisfaction and approval and acceptance. My sexual feelings were as profound as any I'd ever felt, but rather than the probing, active, conquering sexuality that I feel as a male, it was soft, yielding and accepting sexuality that I had associated with femininity. I feel I've had an experience analogous to a feminine orgasm. Then, with no diminution of the sexual element I began to feel waves of birth pangs sweep over my abdomen. My body undulated and flopped about on the floor. At times I would be partly brought back to normal consciousness by my heels banging on the floor and causing some brief but startling pain.

Then I gave birth—to a bundle of blankets that had previously served as the placenta that restricted me. Celestial trumpets and choirs of angels proclaimed this wonderful birth; lightning flashed and comets arched through the heavens, giant sunrises and sunbursts pulsed through the entire universe. Music of indescribable sweetness and richness undulated through me and all the elements. I reached down and pulled my baby up to my face and glory of glories . . . it was me! But a transformed, almost spotless, perfected me. I remember no visual image, but I knew the baby was me and I smiled with ingenuous and boundless pride. I alternated between embracing my baby-self with hugs and kisses and offering him/me to the universe to see and acclaim. All the visual and aural splendors increased in magnificence. Their intensity would reach a peak that I felt I could not tolerate, and then a whole new range of glory would open up and unfold and swell to new heights. It was the opposite, and perhaps the undoing, of the deepening terror in my first experience when ever new depths of madness and nonexistence threatened to overcome me. It was a tremendous affirmation of me as a sensate, sensuous, begotten creature, who yet had powers of his own to beget and affect things. And who was acceptable!

S. has been guided through a complete cycle of transformation experiences to this marvelous culmination. The initial existential despair he felt is translated into struggle, and struggle into the birth of a sense of acceptance. His initial fear and disgust of matter is transformed into earthiness and finally into the feminine dimension of receptive creativity. He is permitted to experience a mystery usually only vouchsafed to women: giving birth.

Most contemporary therapists who work in depth with their patients know that behind the rigid, top-heavy posture of most contemporary men is a little child with years of stored up tears and fears. In such experiences as the one just described the hypertrophied male ego is compensated from within. And as I know from my own experiences of meeting with the feminine within, there is a softening of the physical body, an increased capacity for yielding to pleasure, and the dawn of a new, more accepting, less driven attitude toward life. The little boy within the man has found a mother; the man himself, a wife, a sister, his own soul.

These contemporary experiences offer a striking analogy to the symbolism of the transforming process as pictured in several older psychospiritual systems. Emanuel Swedenborg speaks of the mystical marriage that may take place within the soul of the *regenerating* personality. As the personality develops, the faculties of love (feminine) and wisdom (masculine) are to be balanced and conjoined. He pictures angels as androgynous beings, with a masculine and feminine aspect. And Carl Jung conceives the masterwork of the *individuation* process to be a relating of man to his inner woman (the *anima*) and the woman to her inner man (the *animus*).

Compare, too, the symbolism of the alchemical process shown below. Preliminary stages of the process involve the many levels of relationship between masculine and feminine. The culminating figure is the crowned androgyne, symbolic of a completed integration .

The divine androgyne offers the necessary compensation for the *Senex* image of God; he needs a Goddess to be complete. Even as the mischievous gods of Hindu mythology team up to engineer that marvelous cosmic love seduction in which voluptuous Śakti lures the meditating ascetic Śiva off his mountain, so the image of the feminine arises in our time to complement and ultimately to transform our image of the austere old celestial patriarch. Her softness, her *eros* is the only real antidote to his hardness, his *logos*. It is these mythic images, constellating our collective imagination, that shape our fantasies and feelings. Simultaneously our change in feeling, which is now arising irresistibly within us, needs new symbols to receive its bright projection.

Irene Claremont de Castillejo, in her lucid and loving book, *Knowing Woman*, offers an image of man to supplant that of

Preliminary Stage of the Alchemical Process of Relationship. Here is pictured a symbolic exchange of flowering wands between the Royal Couple, her left hand to his right and her right to his left, balancing the functions of unconscious and conscious for each. As a third element, the dove of Spirit descends to bless the union of masculine and feminine, solar and lunar. *(Rosarium Philosophorum, Frankfurt, 1550.)*

a.

b.

The Alchemical Union. In *a.* "Immersion in the Bath," a psychological, not biological process is being depicted. The solar qualities (of will, self assertiveness), are being joined with the lunar qualities (of feeling, receptivity) in the alchemical bath, the transformation of the self. The outcome of this process is not an earthly child but the *filius macrocosmos,* the child of the universe. This figure is depicted in *b.* as "The Crowned Hermaphrodite" incorporating both masculine and feminine qualities. *(Drawings by Robin Larsen adapted from the woodcuts of the Rosarium Philosophorum, 1550.)*

The Crowned Hermaphrodite. The integrated personality is depicted standing on the dragon of unawakened instinct, with wings newly unfurled for the flight of the spirit. *(From the manuscript "De Alchimia" attributed to St. Thomas Aquinas. Rijksuniversiteit Bibliotheek Leiden, Holland.)*

c.

the patriarch, the masculine authority figure, the doer. She calls him the Rainmaker. As she tells the old Chinese story:

> In a remote village in China a long drought had parched the fields, the harvest was in danger of being lost and the people were facing starvation in the months to come. The villagers did everything they could. They prayed to their ancestors; their priests took the images from the temples and marched them round the stricken fields. But no ritual and no prayers brought rain.
>
> In despair they sent for a "Rainmaker." When the little old man arrived, they asked him what he needed to effect his magic and he replied, "Nothing, only a quiet place where I can be alone." They gave him a little house and there he lived quietly doing the things one has to do in life, and on the third day the rain came.[47]

The little man speaks to us both as shaman and as Taoist. His task is to resolve a collective problem through attunement to the hidden causality of the universe. But he doesn't really *do* anything, he accomplishes what is needed in a most inconspicuous way. Ms. Castillejo says,

> If only we could be rainmakers! . . . I am thinking of those people (and I have met one or two) who go about their ordinary business with no fuss, not ostensibly helping others, not giving advice, not continuously and self-consciously praying for guidance or striving for mystical union with God, not even being especially noticeable, yet around whom things happen.
>
> Others seem to live more fully for their presence: possibilities of work appear unexpectedly or people offer their services unsought, houses fall vacant for the homeless, lovers meet. Life blossoms all around them without their lifting a finger and, as likely as not, without anyone attributing to them any credit for the happenings, least of all themselves. Rainmakers are inconspicuous. . . . The Rainmaker does not cause, he *allows* the rain to fall.[48]

Ms. Castillejo has captured here the essence of a feminine as opposed to masculine creativity. It is less goal-directed, less pushy, less artificial. Its essence is in allowing rather than making things to happen. Because it does not plan awfully far ahead, it is hard to disappoint. Because it is willing to work with what *is* there rather than what *ought* to be there, it is content. It is precisely the point of view that has been lacking in all our masculine enterprises of aggression and conquest. If we had a little more of it right now, we would not be raping the planet so savagely, or killing each other off so wickedly.

The process of coming to terms with one's inner masculine or feminine counterpart has profound consequences in the outer world. If my relationship with my inner mistress is well, so too with those outer women on whom I project her: friends, wife, mother. If the inner relationship is poor the outer is sure to follow suit. Marriage, as well as being the easiest to knock over of contemporary straw dogs, may also be one of the most complicated, fascinating, rewarding games of the age. As each realizes that he/she is two and the twosome is, in fact, a foursome, the possibilities grow richer, yet more demanding. The inner and the outer mirror each other in a magical series of reflections. But both sides must be willing to play. If either cuts off, plays some all-too-secret game, or interrupts dialogue, the game is over and considerable stakes are lost on the part of both.

I am personally very glad, in fact, to have given up the ascetic *sādhana* I once contemplated, the sterile mysticism of *brahmacharya*. My present *sādhana* of relationship to a living feminine counterplayer is far more interesting and rewarding. The outer game, the game of life we play together, is a running analogue to the life of the spirit that plays within each of us. It is not necessary to choke out the life of the body for the spirit to grow. It can grow also through the nurturing of symbols that touch meaning on both levels.

I like allowing the changes I find happening to me, to clients I work with, and to friends, changing us into Rainmaker-Shamans.

. . . The Rainmaker walks in the middle of the road, neither held back by the past nor hurrying toward the future, neither lured to the right nor to the left, but allowing the past and future, the outer world of the right and the inner images of the left all to play upon him while he attends, no more than attends, to the living moment in which these forces meet.

In those rare moments when all the opposites meet within a man, good and also evil, light and also darkness, spirit and also body, brain and also heart, masculine focused consciousness and at the same time feminine diffuse awareness, wisdom of maturity and childlike wonder; when all are allowed and none displaces any other in the mind of a man, then that man, though he may utter no word is in an attitude of prayer. Whether he knows it or not his own receptive allowing will affect those around him; rain will fall on the parched fields, and tears will turn bitter grief to flowering sorrow, while stricken children dry their eyes and laugh.[49]

Epilogue

A science fiction story has lingered in my mind, perhaps a bit dimly, from the late nineteen-fifties. I shall try to summarize the essentials for you, since I believe they reflect the same change in consciousness of which this book, too, is a reflection.

A kind of missionary expedition is sent out by a highly developed planetary, technological culture. This culture has already mastered deep-space interstellar travel. Their mission, it seems, is a galactic version of the white man's burden: to combat the insidious forces of entropy and cultural degeneration in the universe.

In a minor solar system they find what they are looking for, a planet that has fallen from a once-great civilization. The vast cities stand like deserted monuments with vegetation cracking the sidewalks while the degenerated inhabitants live in thatched cottages in the surrounding countryside. The chief missionary do-gooder engages the attentions of one of the seemingly peasantlike humans. "See how far you've fallen," he says, showing him the bygone splendor of the city from his airship.

As the story unfolds, though, we see the scientist-evangelist go through something like a recognition of *hubris*. It gradually begins to penetrate his opaque perceptions and attitudes that these people are more than they seem. They slowly allow him to see that they have psi powers: telepathy, telekinesis, and an inner wisdom that suddenly makes him begin to feel very young and foolish by comparison. They are, in fact, a race that has evolved far beyond the technological stage. They are advanced yogic shamans, masters of the physical universe as well as of their own minds and bodies. They have outgrown the need for the instruments of conquest and control, for they have gained an intimate mastery of matter along with wisdom.

In the conclusion of this beautifully tuned-in story we are shown that the little planet on which these shaman masters dwell is the third planet from a yellowish sun. It is, in fact, our own humble earth.

It seems to me this same image has arisen within many of us as a kind of countermythology to the overwhelming onslaught of technological revolution. Even as our present stage was indispensable to shake us out of the sleep of mythic identity, an almost immediate reflex has taken place within many of us: *Wake up, but don't forget the dream.* Myth is magic, it is power, it is "the lure of becoming," as Jean Houston calls it. Subsumed in myth we are dreaming, but having lost touch with the dream we have lost our own souls.

As Joseph Campbell says, in his own characteristically elegant but wise words:

Since mythology is born of fantasy any life or civilization brought to form as a result of a literal mythic identification . . . will necessarily bear the features of a nightmare, a dream game too seriously played—in other words, madness; whereas when the same mythological imagery is properly read as fantasy, and allowed to play into life as art, not as nature—with irony and grace, not fierce daemonic compulsion—the same psychological energies that were formerly in the capture of the compelling images take the images in capture, and can be deployed with optional spontaneity for life's enrichment. Moreover since life itself is indeed such stuff as dreams are made on, such a transfer of accent may conduce, in time, to a life lived in noble consciousness of its own nature.[1]

I conclude this book by reevoking a scene which has perhaps lingered in the reader's imagination from Chapter 2. Young Black Elk is being cured of his nervous illness by a marvelous ritual enactment in which the entire tribe helps him to perform the vision that came to him, years earlier, unbidden. As they sing their song and perform the dance, the horses on which they are riding and those grazing out on the plain, all begin to neigh, collaborating in the drama. "Then suddenly," as Black Elk recounts it,

as I sat there looking at the cloud, I saw my vision yonder once again—the tepee built of cloud and sewed with lightning, the flaming rainbow door and, underneath, the six Grandfathers sitting, and all the horses thronging in their quarters; and also there was I myself upon my bay before the tepee.

As the enactment once again evokes the vision, it comes shining into Black Elk's consciousness; and there for a moment the two are side by side: the mythic world aglow within the cloud, and the living pageant of men and women, horses and tepees, that embody the myth. This is a truly sacred and essential moment, a moment like those throughout history when men's eyes have opened to the insubstantiality of our solid-seeming world, and they have found reality—and themselves—transformed. Here for a transfixed instant the two dimensions are in a special relationship: the bright supernatural realm, in sympathy with the doings of men, is reaching "through the cracks in the visible universe" into time and space; and the human community has simultaneously opened itself to wonder, perfectly attuned to the mystery beyond and within the ordinary.

Reaching for this moment ourselves, as the vision-seekers in this chapter have shown we may, we might say with Black Elk,

I looked about me and could see that what we then were doing was like a shadow cast upon the earth from yonder vision in the heavens, so bright it was and clear. I knew the real was yonder and the darkened dream of it was here.

Source Notes

Introduction

1. Joseph Campbell, *The Masks of God: Primitive Mythology* (New York: Viking Press, 1959), p. 4.

2. Bertolt Brecht, "Galileo" in *Seven Plays* (New York: Grove Press, 1961), p. 358.

3. John Lilly, *The Center of the Cyclone* (New York: Julian Press, 1972).

4. Campbell, *Primitive Mythology.*

5. Mircea Eliade, *Images and Symbols* (New York: Sheed & Ward, 1961), p. 18.

6. Andrew Weil, *The Natural Mind: A New Way of Looking at Drugs and the Higher Consciousness* (Boston: Houghton Mifflin Co., 1972).

7. Jerome Bruner, "Myth and Identity," in Henry A. Murray, *Myth and Mythmaking* (Boston: Beacon Press, 1969).

Chapter 1: The Mythic Imagination

1. Sir James Frazer, *The Belief in Immortality*, vol. 1 (London: Dawsons of Pall Mall, 1968).

2. Sir James Frazer, quoted in Herbert Weisinger, "Some Meanings of Myth," *Comparative Literature*, Proceedings of the ICLA Congress in Chapel Hill, N.C. (Chapel Hill: University of North Carolina Press, 1959), p. 6.

3. Roland Barthes, *Mythologies* (New York: Hill & Wang, 1972).

4. Sigmund Freud, *The Future of an Illusion* (New York: Doubleday Anchor Books, 1957), p. 51.

5. Quoted from Richard Chase, *Quest for Myth* (Baton Rouge La.: Louisiana State University Press, 1949), p. 4.

6. C. Kerenyi and C. G. Jung, *Essays on a Science of Mythology*, Bollingen Series No. xxii also (New York: Harper Torchbooks, 1963), p. 1.

7. Joseph Campbell, *Myths to Live By* (New York: Viking Press, 1972), pp. 214, 215.

8. Jerome Bruner, "Myth and Identity," in Henry A. Murray, *Myth and Mythmaking* (Boston: Beacon Press, 1969), p. 286.

9. Lucien Levy-Bruhl, *The Soul of the Primitive*, trans. Lilian A. Clare (London: George Allen & Unwin, 1965).

10. Jean Piaget, *Language and Thought in the Child*, trans. M. Babain (London: Kegan Paul, Trench Trubner, 1932).

11. Sigmund Freud, *Collected Papers* (New York: Basic Books, 1959), 4:14.

12. C. G. Jung, *Symbols of Transformation*, Bollingen Series no. v (New York: Pantheon Books, 1956), p. 28.

13. Mark Schorer, "The Necessity of Myth," in Murray, *Myth and Mythmaking*, p. 355.

14. Eugene Gendlin, *Experiencing and the Creation of Meaning* (Glencoe, Ill.: The Free Press, 1962), p. 16.

15. Ibid., p. 3.

16. W. H. Auden, in *The Dyer's Hand and Other Essays* (New York: Randon House, 1962).

17. W. B. Yeats, "The Celtic Element in Literature" in *Essays and Introductions* (New York: The Macmillan Co., 1961), p. 174.

18. Rudolf Otto, *The Idea of the Holy*, trans. John W. Aarvey (New York: Oxford University Press, 1958).

19. Quoted in Marghanita Laski, *Ecstasy, A Study of Some Secular and Religious Experiences* (New York: Greenword Press, 1968) p. 119.

20. Ibid, p. 120.

21. Jerome Rothenberg, *Technicians of the Sacred* (New York: Doubleday Anchor Books, 1968), p. 81.

22. Quoted in Joseph Campbell, "The Historical Development of Mythology," in Murray, *Myth and Mythmaking*, p. 40.

23. Ibid, p. 33.

24. Ikid., p. 40.

25. C. G. Jung, *Archetypes and the Collective Unconscious* (New York: Pantheon Books, 1959), p. 9.

26. Ibid., p. 8.

27. Heinz Werner, *The Comparative Psychology of Mental Development* (New York: Science Editions, 1948).

28. George W. Kisker, *The Disorganized Personality*, Tape Series (New York: McGraw-Hill Publishing Co., 1963).

29. Joanne Greenberg, *I Never Promised You a Rose Garden*, pseudonym Hannah Green (New York: Holt, Rinehart and Winston, 1964).

30. Carmen Blacker, "Animal Witchcraft in Japan," in *The Witch Figure*, ed. Venetia Newall (London & Boston: Routledge & Kegan Paul, 1973), p. 2.

31. Maya Deren, *Divine Horsemen: The Voodoo Gods of Haiti* (New York: Dell Publishing Co., 1970).

32. Ibid., p. 29.

33. Ibid., p. 105.

34. Joseph Rock, "Sungmas, Living Oracles of the Tibetan Religion," *National Geographic*, Oct. 1929, pp. 476–78.

35. Ibid.

36. Ibid.

37. Mircea Eliade, *Shamanism: Archaic Techniques of Ecstasy*, Bollingen Series no. lxxvi (Princeton, N.J.: Princeton University Press, 1970). See also for further information on Shamanism by Knud Rasmussen *Across Arctic America* (N.Y. and London: G.P. Putnam's and Sons, 1927), and *The People of the Polar North* (London; Kegan Paul, 1908). Also S. M. Shirokogoroff *Psychomental Complex of the Tungus* (London: Kegan Paul 1965).

38. Ibid., Elaide, p. 13.

39. Ibid., p. 27.

40. This story is paraphrased from my notes of a lecture on "Shamanism" by Joseph Campbell, at Ulster County Community College, Stone Ridge, N. Y. 1973.

41. Andreas Lommel, *Shamanism: The Beginnings of Art* (New York: McGraw-Hill Book Co., 1967), p. 56.

42. Ibid., p. 57.

43. Eliade, *Shamanism*, p. 436.

44. Jung, *Symbols of Transformation*, p. 232.

45. Stanislav Grof, "Beyond Psychoanalysis," *Darshana International* 10, no. 3 (July 1970), p. 62.

46. Ibid., p. 65.

47. Mircea Eliade, *Myths, Dreams and Mysteries* trans. Philip Mariet (New York: Harper, 1961), p. 106.

48. Eliade, *Shamanism*, p. 131.

49. Joseph Campbell, *The Masks of God: Primitive Mythology* (New York: Viking Press, 1959), p. 255.

50. Eliade, *Shamanism*, pp. 127, 428.

51. Rothenberg, *Technicians*, p. 50.

52. Ibid., p. 52.

53. Quoted from Lommel, *Shamanism*, pp. 59–60.

54. Campbell, *Primitive Mythology*, pp. 253–54.

55. Timothy Leary, *High Priest* (New York: College Notes and Texts, 1968), p. 320.

Chapter 2: The Enactment of Vision

1. Knud Rasmussen's account, *Thulefahrt*, Frankfurt, 1925. Translated and quoted in Andreas Lommel, *Shamanism: The Beginnings of Art* (New York: McGraw-Hill Book Co., 1967), p. 78.

2. C. G. Jung, *Symbols of Transformation,* Bollingen Series v (New York: Pantheon Books, 1956), p. 327.

3. Erich Neumann, *The Origins and History of Consciousness*, Bollingen Series. XLII (New York: Pantheon Books, 1954), p. 87.

4. In Joseph Campbell, *Hero with a Thousand Faces* (Cleveland and New York: Meridian Books, 1956), pp. 116–17. Paperback.

5. See W. M. Fenton, "The Seneca Society of Faces," *Scientific American* XLIV (1937).

6. Ibid. See also, Fenton, "Masked Medicine Societies," *Annual Report of the Smithsonian Institution* (Washington, D.C., 1940); Arthur C. Parker, "Secret Medicine Societies of the Seneca," *American Anthropologist* (1909); and A.F.C. Wallace, "Dreams and Wishes of the Soul," *American Anthropologist* (1958).

7. Ibid., p. 224.

8. *Jesuit Relations*, (Thwaites edition). Quoted in A.F.C. Wallace "Dreams and Wishes of the Soul" a type of psychoanalytic theory among the 17th century Iroquois, *American Anthropologist* v. 60 (April, 1958) p. 236.

9. Ibid.

10. J.N.B. Hewitt, "The Iroquoian Concept of the Soul," *Journal of American Folklore* VIII 1895, p. 112.

11. Edward C. Whitmont, *The Symbolic Quest* (New York: G.P. Putnam's Sons, 1969), p. 216.

12. C. G. Jung, *Memories, Dreams, Reflections* (New York: Pantheon Books, 1963), pp. 348–49.

13. Hewitt, "Iroquoian Concepts," pp. 110–111.

14. Ibid., p. 115.

15. C. G. Jung, in his *Psychological Reflections*, Bollingen Series XXXI (Princeton, N.J.: Princeton University Press, 1970), p. 76.

16. See also Frank G. Speck, *Naskapi* (Norman, Okla.: University of Oklahoma, 1935).

17. C. G. Jung, *The Practice of Psychotherapy*, Bollingen Series XVI (Princeton, N.J.: Princeton University Press, 1954 and 1966), p. 86.

18. Kilton Stewart, *Dream Theory in Malaya*, by permission of Mrs. Kilton Stewart Published in Charles T. Tart, *Altered States of Consciousness* (New York: Doubleday & Co., 1969), pp. 164, 165.

19. Ibid, p. 162.

20. Ibid., p. 163.

21. Ibid, pp. 163, 164.

22. Ibid., p. 166.

23. Ibid., p. 168.

24. John G. Neihardt, *Black Elk Speaks* (Lincoln, Neb.: University of Nebraska Press, 1961), pp. 21–23.

25. Ibid., p. 25.

26. Ibid., p. 40.

27. Ibid., p. 43.

28. Ibid., p. 50.

29. Ibid., p. 163.

30. Ibid., p. 165.

31. Edward C. Whitmont, unpublished lecture, 1971.

32. C. G. Jung, *Psychology and Religion* (Bollingen Series No. 11, Princeton, N.J.: Princeton University Press, 1969) par. 534.

33. R. E. L. Masters and Jean Houston, *The Varieties of Psychedelic Experience* (New York: Delta Books, 1966), p. 247.

34. Neihardt, *Black Elk Speaks*, p. 48.

35. Joseph Campbell, *The Flight of the Wild Gander* (New York: Viking Press, 1951, 1969), p. 117.

36. Neihardt, *Black Elk Speaks*, p. 166.

37. Ibid., pp. 166–67.

38. Ibid., pp. 173–74.

39. Ibid.
40. Ibid., p. 179.
41. Ibid.

Chapter 3: Priests, Scientists, Yogis

1. Joseph Campbell, "The Historical Development of Mythology," in Henry A. Murray, *Myth and Mythmaking* (Boston: Beacon Press, 1969), p. 30.

2. Ibid.

3. Edward F. Heenan, ed., *Mystery, Magic and Miracle: Religion in a Post-Aquarian Age* (Englewood Cliffs, N.J.: Prentice-Hall, 1973), p. 141.

4. Ibid., p. 140.

5. Michael Polanyi, *Personal Knowledge; Towards a Post-Critical Philosophy* (New York: Harper Torchbooks, 1964), p. 8.

6. Pauwels and Bergier, *Morning of The Magicians* (New York: Avon Books, 1968).

7. Polanyi, *Personal Knowledge*, p. 27.

8. Ibid., p. 4.

9. C. G. Jung, *Memories, Dreams, Reflections* (New York: Pantheon Books 1963), p. 151.

10. Ibid., Appendix I, p. 363.

11. Ibid.

12. Robert Ornstein, *The Psychology of Consciousness* (San Francisco: W. H. Freeman & Co., 1972) p. 41. Paperback

13. Katha Upanishad II iii 2, in *The Upanishads*, Swami Nikhilananda, trans. (New York: Harper Torchbooks, 1964), p. 81.

14. Sir John Woodroffe, *Sákti and Sákta* (Madras: Ganesh & Co., 1965), p. 27.

15. Ibid.

16. W. Y. Evans-Wentz, *Tibetan Yoga* (New York: Oxford University Press, 1967), p. 163. Paperback.

17. C. G. Jung, in his Introduction to *The Tibetan Book of the Great Liberation*, W. Y. Evans-Wentz (New York: Oxford University Press, 1969), p. xxxvii. Paperback.

18. *The Yoga Sutras of Patanjali*, trans. and with an introduction by Charles Johnston (London: John M. Watkins, 1964).

19. John P. Zubek, ed., *Sensory Deprivation, Fifteen Years of Research* (New York: Appleton-Century-Crofts, 1969).

20. Jack Vernon, *Inside the Black Room* (New York: Clarkson Potter, 1963).

21. Zubek, *Sensory Deprivation.*

22. Mircea Eliade, *Yoga: Immortality and Freedom* tr. Willard R. Trask, Bollingen Series 56 (Princeton N.J.: Princeton University Press, 1969), p. 42.

23. Katha Upanishad, II iii.

24. Jung, Introduction, *Tibetan Book of Liberation*, p. xxxviiii.

25. Ibid., p. xxxvii.

26. Ibid., p. xxxvii.

27. Ibid., p. xlvi.

28. Ibid.

29. Ibid., xlvii.

30. Sam Keen, *To a Dancing God* (New York: Harper & Row, 1970), p. 51.

31. See p. 172 and footnote 78 in Joseph Campbell *The Flight of the Wild Gander* (New York: The Viking Press, 1951).

Chapter 4: Myths of Relationship and Integration

1. John G. Neihardt, *Black Elk Speaks* (Lincoln, Neb.: University of Nebraska Press, 1961), p. 37.

2. See Peter Tompkins and Christopher Bird, "Love among the Cabbages," *Harper's*, November 1972.

3. Joseph Campbell, *The Masks of God: Primitive Mythology* (New York: Viking Press, 1959).

4. "Epic of Creation" (tablet IV, vv. 39–104), Dhorme's translation, *New Larousse Encyclopedia of Mythology* (New York: Hamlyn Publishing Group, 1959), p. 53.

5. Henry Berne, "Patriarchal Propaganda in the Old Testament" (Ph.D. dissertation, The Union Graduate School, Yellow Springs, Ohio, 1974).

6. Erich Neumann, *The Origins and History of Consciousness*, Bollingen Series XLII, (New York: Pantheon Books, 1964).

7. Thomas Hanna, *Bodies in Revolt* (New York: Holt, Rinehart and Winston, 1970).

8. Eugen Herrigel, *Zen in the Art of Archery* (New York: Pantheon Books, 1963).

9. Michael Murphy, *Golf in the Kingdom*, Esalen Series (New York: Viking Press, 1972).

10. Erich Von Daniken, *Chariots of the Gods* (New York: Putnam Co., 1970).

11. C. G. Jung, Introduction to the *Tibetan Book of the Great Liberation*, ed. W. Y. Evans-Wentz (New York: Oxford University Press, 1969), p. xlix. Paperback.

12. Ibid p. xliv.

13. Webster's Third New World Dictionary, 1955.

14. William Irwin Thompson, interview in *East-West Journal* 111, no. 4 (April 1973).

15. Andrew Weil, *The Natural Mind* (Boston: Houghton Mifflin Co., 1972).

16. Wilson Van Dusen, *The Presence of Spirits in Madness* (New York: the Swedenborg Foundation, 1968), F. Note: The complete works of Swedenborg may also be obtained from the foundation at 139 E. 23rd St., New York, N.Y., 10010. Some of the thirty five volumes are available in paperback. I refer the interested reader particularly to *Heaven and Its Wonders and Hell* and *The Spiritual Diary*.

17. Ibid., p. 13.

18. Aldous Huxley, *The Devils of London* (New York: Harper & Row, 1974) and Traugott, Konstantin Oesterreich, *Possession, Demoniacal and Other, among Primitive Races in Antiquity, the Middle Ages, and Modern Times*, trans. D. Ibberson (New Hyde Park, N.Y.: University Books, 1966).

19. Oesterreich, Ibid., p. 112.

20. Carmen Blacker, "Animal Witchcraft in Japan" in *The Witch Figure*, ed. Venetia Newell (London and Boston: Routledge & Kegan Paul, 1973).

21. Robert Heinlein, *Stranger in a Strange Land* (Berkeley, Calif.: Medallion, 1968).

22. Piers Anthony, *Macroscope* (New York: Avon Books, 1969). Paperback.

23. Joel Bernstein, "Caves and Hunters," unpublished poems, 1974.

24. The "Sorcière" is a paleolithic painting from a wall of the cave of Les Trois Frères in Southern France and it appears to be a dancing shaman in animal skins and antlered headdress.

25. Carlos Castaneda, *The Teachings of Don Juan, a Yaqui Way of Knowledge* (Berkeley, Calif.: University of California

Press, 1968). See also by Castaneda *A Separate Reality* (New York: Simon and Schuster, 1971), *Journey to Ixtlan* (New York: Simon and Schuster, 1972), and *Tales of Power* (New York: Simon and Schuster, 1974).

26. Maya Deren, *Divine Horsemen: The Voodoo Gods of Haiti* (New York: Dell Publishing Co., 1970).

27. Ibid.

28. Mircea Eliade, *Shamanism: Archaic Techniques of Ecstasy*, Bollingen Series no. 76 (Princeton, N.J.: Princeton University Press, 1970).

29. Carl Levett, *Crossings: A Transpersonal Approach* (Ridgefield, Conn.: Quiet Song, Inc., 1974).

30. Ibid. Note: *Crossings* does not have pages numbered.

31. Ibid.

32. Ibid.

33. Ibid.

34. Ibid.

35. Ibid.

36. Trevor Ravenscroft, *The Spear of Destiny* (New York: G. P. Putnam's Sons, 1973).

37. Rollo May, "The Innocent Murderers" *Psychology Today*, December 1972.

38. William Irwin Thompson, *At the Edge of History* (New York: Harper & Row, Colophon Books, 1971), p. 76.

39. Marie Louis von Franz, The Puer Aeternus (New York: Spring Publications, 1970).

40. William V. Shannon, *They Could Not Trust the King* (New York: Collier Books, Macmillan Publishing Co., 1974). Lawrence Ferlinghetti, *Tyrannus Nix* (New York: New Directions Publishing Corp., 1969).

41. Bruce Mazlish, "Psychohistory and Richard M. Nixon" in *Psychology Today*, June 1972.

42. Campbell, *Primitive Mythology*, p. 412.

43. From Duarte Barbarossa's *Description of the Coasts of East Africa and Malabar in the Beginning of the Sixteenth Century*. Quoted in Campbell, *Primitive Mythology*, pp. 165–67.

44. Joseph Campbell, *Oriental Mythology* (New York: The Viking Press, Viking Compass Edition, 1962), p. 80.

45. William Irwin Thompson, *Passages about the Earth* (New

York: Harper & Row, 1973, 1974), pp. 110, 111.

46. Edward C. Whitmont, *The Symbolic Quest* (New York: G. P. Putnam's Sons, 1969).

47. Irene Claremont de Castillejo, *Knowing Woman* (New York: Harper & Row, Colophon Books, 1974), p. 132.

48. Ibid.

49. Ibid.

Epilogue

1. Joseph Campbell, *The Masks of God: Oriental Mythology* (New York, The Viking Press, Viking Compass Book 1962), p. 96.

Bibliography

Anthony, Piers. *Macroscope*. New York: Avon Books, 1969.

Auden, W. H. *The Dyer's Hand and Other Essays*. New York: Random House, 1962.

Barbarossa, Duarte. *Description of the Coasts of East Africa and Malabar in the Beginning of the Sixteenth Century*. Quoted in Campbell, Joseph. *The Masks of God: Primitive Mythology*. New York: The Viking Press, 1950.

Barthes, Roland. *Mythologies*. New York: Hill & Wang, 1972.

Belo, Jane. *Trance in Bali*. New York: Columbia University Press, 1960.

Berne, Henry. "Patriarchal Propaganda in the Old Testament." Ph.D. dissertation. The Union Graduate School, Yellow Springs, Ohio, 1974.

Bernstein, Joel. "Caves and Hunters." Unpublished poems, 1974.

Blacker, Carmen. "Animal Witchcraft in Japan." In *The Witch Figure*. Edited by Venetia Newall. London and Boston: Routledge & Kegan Paul, 1973.

————. *The Catalpa Bow*. London: George, Allen & Unwin, 1975.

Brecht, Bertolt. "Galileo." In *Seven Plays*. New York: Grove Press, 1961.

Brodsky, Ann, Editor. *Stones Bones and Skin*. Toronto: Arts Canada, 1977.

Brown, Joseph Epes. *The Sacred Pipe: Black Elk's Account of the Seven Rites of the Oglala Sioux*. Norman: University of Oklahoma Press, 1963.

Bruner, Jerome. "Myth and Identity." In Murray, Henry A. *Myth and Mythmaking*. Boston: Beacon Press, 1969.

Campbell, Joseph. *The Flight of the Wild Gander*. New York: The Viking Press, 1951, 1969.

_____. *Hero with Thousand Faces*. Cleveland and New York: Meridian Books, 1956.

_____. "The Historical Development of Mythology." In Murray, Henry A. *Myth and Mythmaking*. Boston: Beacon Press, 1969.

_____. *The Masks of God: Oriental Mythology*. New York: The Viking Press, Viking Compass Edition, 1962.

_____. *The Masks of God: Primitive Mythology*. New York: The Viking Press, 1959.

_____. *Myths To Live By*. New York: The Viking Press, 1972.

_____. *The Way of The Animal Powers*. New York: Alfred van Der Marck, 1983.

Castaneda, Carlos. *The Teachings of Don Juan, a Yaqui Way of Knowledge*. Berkeley: University of California Press, 1968.

_____. *A Separate Reality*. New York: Simon and Schuster, 1971.

_____. *Journey to Ixtlan*. New York: Simon and Schuster, 1972.

_____. *Tales of Power*. New York: Simon and Schuster, 1974.

de Castillejo, Irene Claremont. *Knowing Woman*. New York: Harper & Row, Colophon Books, 1974.

Chase, Richard. *Quest for Myth*. Baton Rouge: Louisiana State University Press, 1949.

Chung, K. C. *Art, Myth and Ritual*. Cambridge: Harvard University Press, 1973.

De Mallie, J. Raymond. *The Sixth Grandfather: Black Elk's Teachings Given to John G. Neihardt*. Lincoln: University of Nebraska Press, 1984.

Deren, Maya. *Divine Horsemen: The Voodoo Gods of Haiti*. New Paltz, New York: McPherson and Co., 1985.

Dole, George F., Editor and Translator. *Emanuel Swedenborg The Universal Human and Soul-Body Interaction*. Introduction by Stephen Larsen. Preface by Robert H. Kirven. Ramsey, NJ: Paulist Press, 1984.

Doore, Gary, Editor. *Shaman's Path Healing Personal Growth and*

Empowerment. Boston: Shambhala, 1987.

Duerr, Hans Peter. *Dreamtime: Concerning the Boundary between Wilderness and Civilization*. Translated by Felicitas Goodman. New York and London: Basel Blackwell, 1985.

Eliade, Mircea. *From Primitives to Zen: A Thematic Sourcebook of the History of Religions*. New York: Harper & Row, 1967.

————. *Images and Symbols*. New York: Sheed & Ward, 1961.

————. *Myths, Dreams and Mysteries*. Translated by Philip Mariet. New York: Harper & Row, 1961.

————. *Shamanism: Archaic Techniques of Ecstasy*. Princeton: Princeton University Press, Bollingen Series No. LXXVI, 1970.

————. *Yoga: Immortality and Freedom*. Translated by Willard R. Trask. Princeton: Princeton University Press, Bollingen Series 56, 1969.

Evans-Wentz, W. Y. *The Fairy-Faith in Celtic Countries*. New York: University Books, 1966.

————. *Tibetan Yoga and Secret Doctrines*. New York: Oxford University Press, 1967.

Fenton, W. M. "The Seneca Society of Faces." In *Scientific American XLIV*, 1937.

————. "Masked Medicine Societies." In *Annual Report of the Smithsonian Institution*, Washington, D.C., 1940.

Ferlinghetti, Lawrence. *Tyrannus Nix*. New York: New Directions Publishing Corp., 1969.

von Franz, Marie Louis. *The Puer Aeternus*. New York: Spring Publications, 1970.

Frazer, Sir James. *The Belief in Immortality*, Vol. I. London: Dawsons of Pall Mall, 1968.

————. In Weisinger, Herbert. "Some Meanings in Myth," *Comparative Literature*, Proceedings of the ICLA Congress in Chapel Hill, N.C. Chapel Hill: University of North Carolina Press, 1959.

Freud, Sigmund. *Collected Papers*. New York: Basic Books, 1959.

————. *The Future of an Illusion*. New York: Doubleday Anchor Books, 1957.

Furst, Peter. Editor, *Flesh of the Gods* The Ritual Use of Hallucinogens. New York and Washington: Praeger Publishers, 1972.

Furst, Peter. *Hallucinogens and Shamanism.*

Gallejos, Elijio Stephen. *The Personal Totem Pole: Animal Imagery, the Chakras, and Psychotherapy.* Santa Fe: Moon Bear Press, 1987.

Garfield, Patricia. *Creative Dreaming.* New York: Simon & Schuster, 1974.

Gendlin, Eugene. *Experiencing and the Creation of Meaning.* Glencoe: The Free Press, 1962.

Goldstein, K. "Concerning the Concept of Primitivity," in *Primitive Views of the World.* Edited by S. Diamond. New York: Columbia University Press, 1960, 64.

Greenberg, Joanne. *I Never Promised You a Rose Garden*, pseudonym Hannah Green. New York: Holt, Rinehart and Winston, 1964.

Grof, Stanislav. "Beyond Psychoanalysis." In *Darshana International 10, No. 3*, July 1970.

_____. *Beyond the Brain: Birth, Death and Transformation in Psychotherapy.* Albany: State University of New York, 1985.

_____. *LSD Psychotherapy.* Pomona: Hunter House, Inc. Publishers, 1980.

_____. *Realms of the Human Unconscious.* New York: Dutton, 1976.

Halifax, Joan. *Shaman: The Wounded Healer.* New York: Crossroads, 1982.

_____. *Shamanic Voices: A Survey of Visionary Narratives.* New York: E. P. Dulton, 1979.

Hanna, Thomas. *Bodies in Revolt.* New York: Holt, Rinehart and Winston, 1970.

Harner, Michael. *The Jivaro.* New York: Doubleday, 1972.

_____. *The Way of the Shaman: A Guide to Power and Healing.* New York: Bantam Books, 1982.

Heenan, Edward F., Editor. *Mystery, Magic and Miracle: Religion in a Post-Aquarian Age.* Englewood Cliffs: Prentice-Hall, 1973.

Heinlein, Robert. *Stranger in a Strange Land.* Berkeley: Medallion, 1968.

Heinze, Dr. Ruth Inge. *Proceedings of the International Conference on the Study of Shamanism 1984-88*. Berkeley: Center for South and Southeast Asian Studies, University of California

————. *Trance and Healing in Southeast Asia Today*. Berkeley: Independent Scholars of Asia, 1984.

Herrigel, Eugen. *Zen in the Art of Archery*. London: Routledge and Kegan Paul, 1953.

Hewitt, J. N. B. "The Iroquoian Concept of the Soul." in *Journal of American Folklore VIII*, 1895.

Hillman, James. *Dreams and The Underworld*. New York: Harper & Row, 1979.

Huxley, Aldous. *The Devils of London*. New York: Harper & Row, 1974.

————. *The Doors of Perception*. New York: Perennial Library, Harper & Row, 1954.

Johnston, Charles. Introduction to and translation of *The Yoga Sutras of Patanjali*. London: John M. Watkins, 1964.

Jung. C. G. *Archetypes and the Collective Unconscious*. New York: Pantheon Books, 1959.

————. *Memories, Dreams, Reflections*. New York: Pantheon Books, 1963.

————. *The Practice of Psychotherapy*. Princeton: Princeton University Press, Bollingen Series XVI, 1954 and 1966.

————. *Psychological Reflections*. Princeton: Princeton University Press, Bollingen Series XXXI, 1970.

————. *Psychology and Religion*. Princeton: Princeton University Press, Bollingen Series No. 11, 1969.

————. Introduction to Evans-Wentz, W. Y. *The Tibetan Book of the Great Liberation*. New York: Oxford University Press, 1969.

————. *Symbols of Transformation*. New York: Pantheon Books, Bollingen Series No. V, 1956.

Kalweit, Holger. *Dreamtime and Inner Space*. The World of the Shaman. Boston: Boston: Shambhala, 1987.

Keen, Sam. *To a Dancing God*. New York: Harper & Row, 1970.

Kerenyi, C. and Jung, C. G. *Essays on a Science of Mythology*. New York: Harper Torchbooks, 1963. Also Bollingen Series No. XXII.

Kisker, George W. *The Disorganized Personality*. Tape Series. New York: McGraw-Hill Publishing Co., 1963.

Krippner, Stanley and Vulloldo, Alberto. *The Realms of Healing*. Millbrae: Celestial Arts, 1976.

Kuhn, T. *The Structure of Scientific Revolution*. Chicago: University of Chicago Press, 1962.

Larsen, Stephen. "The Healing Mask" in *Parabola*, Summer 1980.

_____. Notes of a lecture on "Shamanism" by Joseph Campbell, at Ulster County Community College, Stone Ridge, New York, 1973.

_____. "Swedenborg and the Visionary Tradition" in *Studio Swedenborgiana*, Vol. 3, No. 4, June 1980.

_____. *Swedenborg's Spritual Psychology*. Edited by Stephen Larsen. New York: the Swedenborg Foundation, 1988.

Laski, Marghanita. *Ecstasy, A Study of Some Secular and Religious Experiences*. New York: Greenword Press, 1968.

Leacock, Seth and Ruth. *Spirit of the Deep: A Study of an Afro-Brazilian Cult*. New York: Doubleday Natural History Press, 1972.

Leary, Timothy. *High Priest*. New York: College Notes and Texts, 1968.

Levett, Carl. *Crossings: A Transpersonal Approach*. Ridgefield: Quiet Song, Inc., 1974.

Levy-Bruhl, Lucien. *The Soul of the Primitive*. Translated by Lillian A. Clare. London: George Allen & Unwin, 1965.

Lewis, I. *Ecstatic Religion*. Harmondworth, Middlesex: Penguin Books, 1971.

Lilly, John. *The Center of the Cyclone*. New York: Julian Press, 1972.

Lommel, Andreas. *Shamanism: The Beginning of Art*. New York: McGraw Hill, 1967.

Markides, Kyriacos. *The Magus of Strovolus: The Extraordinary World of a Spiritual Healer*. Boston and London: Routledge & Kegan Paul, 1985.

Masters, R. E. L. and Houston, Jean. *The Varieties of Psychedelic Experience*. New York: Delta Books, 1966.

May, Rollo. "The Innocent Murderers." In *Psychology Today*, December, 1972.

Mazlish. "Psychohistory and Richard M. Nixon." In *Psychology Today*, June 1972.

Murphy, Michael. *Golf in the Kingdom*. New York: The Viking Press, Esalen Series, 1972.

Naranjo, Claudio. *The Healing Journey*. New York: Pantheon Books (1974, copyright 1973)

_____. *The One Quest*. New York: Ballantine Walden Edition, 1972.

Neihardt, John G. *Black Elk Speaks*. Lincoln, NA: University of Nebraska Press, 1961.

_____. *When the Tree Flowered: An Authentic Tale of the Old Sioux World*. New York: Macmillan, 1951.

Neumann, Erich. *The Origins and History of Consciousness*. New York: Pantheon Books, Bollingen Series No. XLII, 1954.

New Larousse Encyclopedia of Mythology. New York: Hamlyn Publishing Group, 1959.

Nikhilananda, Swami. Translated Katha Upanishad II iii 2, in *The Upanishads*. New York: Harper Torchbooks, 1964.

Oesterreich, Traugott Konstantin. *Possession and Exorcism*. New York: Causeway, 1974 (1921).

_____. *Possession, Demoniacal and Other, among Primitive Races in Antiquity, the Middle Ages and Modern Times*. Translated by D. Ibberson. New Hyde Park: University Books, 1966.

Ornstein, Robert. *The Psychology of Consciousness*. San Francisco: W. H. Freeman & Co., 1972.

Otto, Rudolf. *The Idea of the Holy*. Translated by John W. Aarvey. New York: Oxford University Press, 1958.

Parker, Arthur C. "Secret Medicine Societies of the Seneca." In *American Anthropologist*, 1909

Pauwels and Berger. *Morning of the Magicians*. New York: Avon Books, 1968.

Perry, J. W. *The Far Side of Madness*. Englewood Cliffs: Prentice-Hall, 1974.

_____. *The Roots of Renewal in Myth and Madness*. San Francisco: Jossey-Bass, 1976.

Piaget, Jean. *Language and Thought in the Child*. Translated by M. Babain. London: Kegan Paul, Trench Trubner, 1932.

Polanyi, Michael. *Personal Knowledge; Towards a Post-Critical Philosophy*. New York: Harper Torchbooks, 1964.

Radin, P. *Primitive Man as Philosopher*. New York: Dover, 1927, 1957.

Rasmusen, Kund. *Across Arctic America*. New York and London: G. P. Putnam's and Sons, 1927.

_____. *The People of the Polar North*. London: Kegan Paul, 1908.

_____. *Thulefahrt*. Frankfurt, 1925. Translated and quoted in Lommel, Andreas. *Shamanism: The Beginnings of Art*. New York: McGraw-Hill Book Co., 1967.

Ravenscroft, Trevor. *The Spear of Destiny*. New York: G. P. Putnam's Sons, 1973.

Reichel-Dolmatoff, G. *The Shaman and the Jaguar Temple*. Philadelphia: Temple University Press, 1975.

Rock, Joseph. "Sungmas, Living Oracles of the Tibetan Religion." In *National Geographic*, October, 1929.

Rokeach, Milton. *Three Christs of Ypsilanti*. New York: Vintage Books, a division of Random House, 1964.

Rothenberg, Jerome. *Technicians of the Sacred*. New York: Doubleday Anchor Books, 1968.

Schorer, Mark. "The Necessity of Myth." In Murray, *Myth and Mythmaking*.

Shannon, William V. *They Could Not Trust the King*. New York: Collier Books, Macmillan Publishing Co., 1974.

Sharon, Douglas. *The Wizard of the Four Winds*. New York: The Free Press, 1978.

Shirokogoroff, S. M. *Psychomental Complex of the Tungus*. London: Kegan Paul, 1965.

Speck, Frank G. *Midwinter Rites of the Cayuga Longhouse*. Philadelphia: University of Pennsylvania Press, 1949.

_____. *Naskapi*. Norman, OK: University of Oklahoma, 1935.

Stewart, Kilton. *Dream Theory in Malaya*. By permission of Mrs. Kilton Stewart. Published in Tart, Charles T. *Altered States of Consciousness*. New York: Doubleday & Co., 1969.

Swedenborg, Emanuel. *Heavenly Secrets (Arcana Coelestia)* 12 Volumes. New York: the Swedenborg Foundation, Inc., 1949.

Thompson, William Irwin. *At the Edge of History*. New York: Harper & Row, Colophon Books, 1971.

_____. *Passages about the Earth*. New York: Harper & Row, 1973.

_____. Interview in *East-West Journal* 111, No. 4, April 1973.

Tompkins, Peter and Bird, Christopher. "Love among the Cabbages." In *Harper's*, November, 1972.

Vernon, Jack. *Inside the Black Room*. New York: Clarkson Potter, 1963.

Van Dusen, Wilson. *The Presence of Other Worlds*. New York: the Swedenborg Foundation, 1981.

Van Dusen, Wilson. *The Presence of Spirits in Madness*. New York: the Swedenborg Foundation, 1968.

Von Daniken. *Chariots of the Gods*. New York: Putnam Co., 1970.

Waley, A. *The Nine Songs: A Study of Shamanism in Ancient China*. London: George Allen & Unwin, Ltd., 1955.

Wallace, A. F. C. "Dreams and Wishes of the Soul." In *American Anthropologist*, 1958.

Jesuit Relations. Thwaites edition. In Wallace, A. F. C. "Dreams and Wishes of the Soul." In *American Anthropologist*, 1958.

Weil, Andrew. *The Natural Mind: A New Way of Looking at Drugs and the Higher Consciousness*. Boston: Houghton Mifflin Co., 1972.

———. *The Marriage of the Sun and Moon: A Quest for the Unity in Consciousness*. Boston: Houghton Mifflin Company, 1980.

Werner, Heinz. *The Comparative Psychology of Mental Development*. New York: Science Editions, 1948.

Whitmont, Edward C. *The Symbolic Quest*. New York: G. P. Putnam's Sons, 1969.

———. Unpublished lecture, 1971.

Woodroffe, Sir John. *Sakti and Sakta*. Madras: Ganesh & Co., 1965.

Woolger, Roger J. *Other Lives, Other Selves: A Jungian Psychotherapist Discovers Past Lives*. New York: Doubleday, 1987.

Yeats, W. B. "The Celtic Element in Literature." In *Essays and Introductions*. New York: The Macmillan Co., 1961.

Zimmer, Heinrich. *The King and the Corpse*. Tales of the Soul's Conquest of Evil. Edited by Joseph Campbell. Princeton: Princeton University Press, Series XI, 1957.

Zubek, John P., Editor. *Sensory Deprivation, Fifteen Years of Research*. New York: Appleton-Century-Crofts, 1969.

Journals

Phoenix: The Journal of Transpersonal Anthropology. Edited by Shirley Lee. 2001 Tibbets Avenue, Troy, New York 12180.

The Shaman's Drum. The Cross Cultural Shamanism Network, P.O. Box 2636, Berkeley, California 94702.

Parabola. 150 Fifth Avenue, New York, New York.

Index

Adamantine body, 69
Adamie, shaman, 188, 189, 190, 199
Alpert, Richard, footnote 48
Amurakh (Eskimo concept, shaman sickness), 61
Androgyne, mythic, 216-229
Angakok (Eskimo shaman), 199
Anima (Jungian concept), 221, 224
Animal mother, 69
Animus, 224
Aquarian Age, theme of, 171
Aquinas, St. Thomas, 125
Archetypes (concept, Carl Jung), 48, 64
Aua (Eskimo helping spirit), 77-79

Barthes, Roland, 18
Black Elk (Oglala Sioux shaman), 103-116, footnote 159
Brecht, Bertolt, 5
Brimures (snakes in Australian shamanism), 69
Bruner, Jerome, 13

Campbell, Joseph, 31, footnote 66, 80, 86, 163
Castaneda, Carlos, 8, 166, 183, 186, quote 197

Checin (Tibetan deity), 56-58
Children of God, 124, 125
Christian Sacrament, 63
Clare, Saint, 125
Claremont de Castillejo, Irene, 225
Colas, Huichol shaman, illustration 74
Crippled tyrant, myth of, 205-216

Death and rebirth, 63-65, 72, 211
Deganawidah (Iroquois statesman), footnote 90
Deren, Maya (filmmaker, writer), 55, 187-188
Devil, 49
Dismemberment, 63-65, 72, 211
Disorganized personality, the film series re. schizophrenia, 49-52

Eliade, Mircea, 27
Eliot, T. S., 13
Eochaid, five sons of, 86
Euhemerism, 17
Euhemerus the Messenian, 17
Exorcism, 53-54, 178-179
Extraction of soul. *See* inspection of soul Eysenck, Hans, 61

False-face masks, 90, illustration
    91
Francis, Saint, 125
Frazer, Sir James, 17, 19
Freud, Sigmund, 8, 18, 24-25,
    101

Galileo, Galilei, 5
Gendlin, Eugene, 27
Golem, the, 165
Golden Bough, 17
Gorgons, 86
Graves, Robert, 17
Green, Hannah, footnote 52
Grof, Stanislav, 64-65
Guidance concept, 20-22

Hecate underworld goddess, 85
Hewitt, J. N. B., anthropologist,
    94
Hokkai (Japanese concept of
    universe) ri and ji, 94
Houngan (voodoo priest), 55
Hitler, Adolph, 206

Inspection of soul, 191-192, 199
Iroquois. See Chapter 2, 88-97,
    Nations footnote 90

Janet, Pierre, 179
Japanese fox spirits, 53-54
J. B. (poet and shamanic
    adventurer), 188-200
Jesuit missionaries among
    Iroquois, 90
Jesus, 63
Jung, Carl, 24-25, 33-34, 64,
    85, 96-97, 172-173, 221, 224

Kerenyi, Carl, 19

Laing, R. D., 61
Lamas, Tibetan, 56-57
Lascaux, Paleolithic art, 66,
    illustration 67
Leary, Timothy, 81
Levett, Carl, 201-205
Levy-Bruhl, Lucien, 23
Loa (Voudon deity), 55
Lon-gompas (Tibetan long
    distance trance runners), 141
Lowen, Alexander, Bioenergetic
    analysis, 181
LSD, 64, 81, 199, 221

Marduk (Babylonian god),
    164-165
Mask, False-Face, 90
May, Rollo, 207
Meaning, primary, secondary,
    27-28
Medina-Silva, Ramon Huichol
    shaman, illustration 73
Moloch, God, 207
Mother of Sea Creatures, the,
    82-88

Naskapi Indians, 96
National Geographic Team, 56
Neihardt, John, 103, footnote
    159
Nicholas of Flue (Brother Klaus),
    33
Nixon, Richard, 208-216
Numinors (concept of), 30

Orientation, definition, 21

Otto, Rudolf, 30

Participation mystique concept, 23
Perls, Fritz, 97
Piaget, Jean, 23

Quartz crystals, 69

Ragueneau, Father, Jesuit priest, 93
Rainbow-serpent, 69
Rainbow symbolism, 69
Rainmaker (Chinese concept), 227
Ram Dass, Baba, 48. *See* also R. Alpert.
Ramakrishna (Indian saint), 30
Rangda (Balinese goddess), 85
Rasmussen, Knud (Danish Arctic explorer), 77, 82, 199
Rope climbing, shamanic, 69

Sadhana, 142-143, 228
Sakti (psychic power sanskrit), *maya* and *cit*, 94
Schizophrenia, 45-81, especially 59-61
Schorer, Mark, 27
Science, 126-141, also 35-45
Self (from Carl Jung), 95
Senex, Jungian concept, 208, 224
Senoi, Chapter 2, 96-103
Siberian shamanism, 69, costumes illustrations 70-71
Social emanation theory, 18
Sorciere of Les Trois Freres,

illustration 9, 196
Stages of mythic engagement, 33-45, diagram 42
Stewart, Kilton (re. "Dream Theory in Malaya"), 97-102
Sullivan, H. S., 27
Sungma (Tibetan oracle), 56-58
Swedenborg, Emanuel, 177-178, 196
Szasz, Thomas, 61

Tamerlane, 162
Temiar (Malay tribe, also *Senoi*), footnote 97
Tens, Isaac (Gitksan Indian), 72, 79, 204
Tha-ro-hya-wa-ku, Iroquois Sky-God, 95
Tibetan Tantrism, 63
Transcendent function, 173
Tummo or *Gtummo*, Tibetan practice of psychic heat, 141
Tungus (Siberian tribe), 60, 62
Turkish shaman, illustration 75

Umkes (personal mythology), 47-48

Vajra (sanskrit diamond or thunderbolt body, "adamantine"), 69
Van Dusen, Wilson, 177-179
Vocation, shamanic, 59
Von Daniken, Erich, 169
von Franz, Marie-Louise, 208
Voudon (voodoo), Haitian religion, 54-56, 187

Weil, Andrew, 176
Werner, Heinz, 49
Whitmont, E. C., footnote 171
Witchcraft, 187
Wotan (German deity), 206

Yakut (Siberian tribe), 62
Yeats, W. B., 29
Yoga, 40, 139-158. Hatha, 181

Zen, 43, 172. and Archery, 166